BY MOSHE KASHER

Subculture Vulture
Kasher in the Rye

SUBCULTURE VULTURE

SUBCULTURE
VULTURE
MOSHE KASHER

RANDOM HOUSE NEW YORK

A Memoir

in Six Scenes

Published in the United States by Random House, an imprint
and division of Penguin Random House LLC, New York.

RANDOM HOUSE and the HOUSE colophon are registered
trademarks of Penguin Random House LLC.

LIBRARY OF CONGRESS CATALOGING-IN-PUBLICATION DATA
Names: Kasher, Moshe, author.
Title: Subculture vulture: a memoir in six scenes / Moshe Kasher.
Description: New York: Random House, [2024]
Identifiers: LCCN 2023015659 (print) | LCCN 2023015660 (ebook) |
ISBN 9780593231371 (hardcover) | ISBN 9780593231395 (ebook)
Subjects: LCSH: Kasher, Moshe. | Comedians—United States—Biography. |
Subculture—United States.
Classification: LCC PN2287.K26 A3 2024 (print) | LCC PN2287.K26 (ebook) |
DDC 792.7/6028092 [B]—dc23/eng/20230803
LC record available at https://lccn.loc.gov/2023015659
LC ebook record available at https://lccn.loc.gov/2023015660

Printed in the United States of America on acid-free paper

randomhousebooks.com

9 8 7 6 5 4 3 2 1

FIRST EDITION

Book design by Simon M. Sullivan

To FCK—this is all for you

Contents

Introduction

Part of growing up is realizing that you haven't been walking a straight road to where you are now, that it's been a labyrinth the whole time. It's only in hindsight that you see how twisted the path has been.

I wrote my first memoir in 2009. A chronicle of addiction and ridiculousness that ended when I was fifteen and left rehab for the last time. I was a kid.

That was almost thirty years ago and now I'm a grown-up, I guess, despite the fact that my generation was the first to stop growing up altogether. Since that book came out, I've thought a lot about what happened next. How did I escape the chaos that was my life? How did I go from there to here? This is my attempt to turn that chaos into a story.

But it's not one story. It's six.

I've lived a lot of lives and yes, I do wonder if it's possible to write "I've lived a lot of lives" without you rolling your eyes and dismissing me as a pretentious fuck. I sure hope so, because . . . I've lived a lot of lives. I have spent my life being seduced by the charms of groups, of subcultures, of tiny communities.

I have at times been a professional raver/DJ/ecstasy dealer; a boy-king of Alcoholics Anonymous surrounded by throngs of other confused young people getting sober; a Burning Man attendee and then employee stuffing the psychedelic sausage; a conflicted but proud Jew attempting to make sense of the ultra-Hasidic world I'd been raised in; an American Sign Language interpreter who was at once both insider and outsider in the deaf community; and what I am today, a stand-up comedian, which is the thing that eventually became my living and the reason I have enough cultural cachet to be writing a book at all.

Each segment contains a ramshackle history of the worlds I have inhabited, starting at the beginning and examining how they came to be. I actually did a lot of research to tell these histories, but I am not a historian so don't expect any groundbreaking discoveries about the author of the Bible or the guy who invented trance music. At a certain point in each of these histories, I intersect with the world I'm describing and tell the story of how these communities became a part of my DNA.

Laid on top of one another, these six stories become one: They become my story. The history of me.

Laid on top of one another, they become, once again, a labyrinth. So let's start in the center of the maze, where the way out seemed the most opaque. Where the path forward seemed the most twisted. Where I despaired of ever finding my way again. Let's start where my last book ended. The day I got sober. Freshly broken, fully lost, and sure my life was over. It had just begun.

SUBCULTURE VULTURE

1 | *AA, or 10,000 Days at a Time*

On December 25, 1994, I took my last drink. I was fifteen years old.

Getting sober at fifteen sucks.

Getting sober at fifteen on Christmas sucks more.

Getting sober on Christmas as a Jew is more or less neutral. It neither sucks nor does it not suck.

I didn't have to worry about how to make it through a Christmas family gathering sober, staring wistfully at the bowl of eggnog, wishing it was spiked.

But I did have to worry about New Year's Eve.

Getting sober on Christmas sucks because, by virtue of the unchangeable nature of the calendar, you will be, should you make it, six days sober on the most important drinking night of the year: New Year's Eve. Amateur night. I knew that even if I made it to December 31, I wouldn't make it any further. I was doomed before I started.

Of course, I was getting ahead of myself. As I am now. I should start at the beginning. The day I quit. Day One.

Actually, no, I should start before the beginning. The days I tried and failed to get sober. When I'd quit and then immediately un-quit the second I felt a craving. The second I felt anything at all. I should start there, before I stopped. That's the real beginning.

Actually, no, I should start before then, at the *real* real beginning. June 10, 1935. That's the day Dr. Robert Smith, an Akron-based proctologist and lead singer of the Cure, took his last drink and got sober with the help of Bill Wilson, a failed New York stockbroker. The birthdate of Alcoholics Anonymous.

Or I guess we should start before that. How's April 2, 1840? That's when six alcoholics founded a mutual aid society, the Washingtonians, and found a way to stop drinking by helping one another.

Shoot, I don't know where to start. Let's go back to the beginning of human history, when one caveman looked at another caveman as he wiped fermented saber-toothed tiger piss off his beard and said, "Ogg, you think you might have drinking problem?"

Seemingly from the time humankind learned the counterintuitive process of rotting a beverage to make *it* taste worse and *you* feel better, there have been those who lost control.

The drunks. The addicts.* The lushes. Your dad. Me.

Until the 1940s, alcoholics were thought of as lost causes, not worth the time or energy it took to try to help them. Because they never took that help. They never stopped. They always, every time, broke your heart and never got better. If you had the bad luck of marrying a drunk, you had few choices:

Pray for a miracle of healing.

Kill your spouse.

Pray for the miracle of your spouse spontaneously dying.

The dead-spouse option was by far the most likely to occur.

Alcoholics were doomed.

Then came Sigmund Freud, who said, "Alcoholics aren't doomed, they're gay!"

Not kidding. I'm barely even paraphrasing.

Freud postulated that "problem drinkers" were merely latent homosexuals drinking to cover that up and that all the drunk needed was to submit to a full battery of Freudian analysis, integrate the self and he would emerge sober, thirsty only for vagina.

If you can believe it, Freud's theories did not make a huge impact on recovery rates for alcoholism.

---

* Throughout this section I will be using the terms *alcoholic* and *addict, drugs* and *alcohol,* and *high* and *drunk* interchangeably.

By and large, heading into the 1930s, hospitals straight up wouldn't treat alcoholics. Refused at the door. Alcoholism was seen as a moral failure, a weakness of the will. Medicine couldn't treat that any more than it could treat a chronic thief. If a drunk was particularly bad off, they might get thrown into the "loony bin" for a night and tossed out on their asses in the morning but that was about it.

There were some exceptions. In New York City, an alcoholic could get dedicated inpatient help at a comedically dangerous clinic called the "Towns Hospital."

Charles B. Towns was a former life insurance salesman with zero medical training who just opened a fucking hospital because I guess you could do that back then? The Towns Hospital was a high-priced clinic for well-to-do drunkards and junkies who could afford to pay the up-front fee for a cushy five-day stay, which included a round of Mr. Towns's notorious belladonna treatment, the recipe to which, and I'm not making this up, was given to him by a "mysterious stranger" who said he'd discovered a compound that would cure alcoholism. It was a noxious cocktail of, and I'm not making *this* up, equal doses of "deadly nightshade" and "insane root." You'd hallucinate, puke and purge, and when you started taking, and I'm once again not making this up, big watery shits, they figured you were ready for discharge (physical, not rectal). Towns Hospital self-reported a cure rate of 90 percent based on, and I swear I'm not even making *this* up, assuming patients who never returned to the hospital had been cured. I guess it never occurred to Mr. Towns that perhaps dying of alcoholism was preferable to riding the snake of the insane-root-and-diarrhea treatment.

It was about this time that a new idea began to formulate around the "Just what is wrong with alcoholics?" conundrum. What if they were not constitutionally weak reprobates? What if they were sick?

The head physician of Towns Hospital, William D. Silkworth, a man whose name sounds like a stoned caterpillar in a psychedelic 1970s animated film, began to describe alcoholism as a disease rather than a moral failing. This idea eventually took ahold of the American understanding of what it meant to be an alcoholic and addict. These were not bad people struggling to be good; they were sick people trying to get well. By the time I hit my first AA meeting in 1993, barely fourteen years old and fresh out of my first rehab, this idea was well integrated into the American cultural understanding of substance abuse. It was a foregone conclusion.

But back then, no one agreed with Silkworth. His contemporaries scoffed at the idea of disease as anything more than a useful metaphor, and it took a national movement and the full, sustained lobbying force of the National Council on Alcoholism to get the psychological community to submit to the disease model.

The truth is, it's hard to know what addiction really is.

It's a kind of limbo problem: neither psychological disorder nor not, neither physical malady nor not, neither moral failing nor not. It's easier to describe what it isn't than what it actually is.

It's a mystery why some people drink like pigs and some people find it easy to drink enough to enjoy themselves. And it's not just drinking a lot that makes you an alcoholic. Even Silkworth admitted that some non-alcoholics actually consume more alcohol than people who develop alcoholism.

We all know those people. They drink constantly but it doesn't seem to affect their lives. They are jolly, hardworking, and productive despite drinking enough each night to kill a Shetland pony. We even came up with a word for people like this: "Irish."

So what *is* an alcoholic, exactly? What differentiates them from the rest of the world? I guess it's twofold and within each of those folds is an MC Escher painting-worth of nooks and crannies of pathological complexity. But to simplify:

1. Your life begins to deteriorate due to your drinking and drug use.
2. Despite the deterioration, you are unable to stop or regulate it.

In other words, drinking fucks up your life and you can't stop. That's a waterslide to rock bottom. My slide was short.

By the time December 25, 1994, rolled around, I'd been in and out of four rehabs, locked in a mental hospital, arrested more times than I remember, assailed with a battery of psychological diagnoses such as Conduct Disorder, Oppositional Defiant Disorder, Clinical Depression, ADHD, and White Kid Who Thinks He's Black Disorder.

I was on an array of psychological medications, including Zoloft and Desipramine, which never made me feel less crazy, never seemed to help at all. I'd dropped out of school in the eighth grade, got sucked into the special-education-school-to-prison pipeline, mandated to schools for the severely emotionally disturbed (those are actual kinds of schools!), picked myself up by my Fila straps, got into a high school, flunked ninth grade, got kicked out, went to another school for the mentally disturbed, dropped out, went back, flunked again, started home study, didn't do the study part, flunked again. That was quite a run-on sentence but what do you expect from a writer who flunked ninth grade three times?

But none of that made me an alcoholic. Plenty of people have chaotic lives and make a mess of their school careers. Many people flunk and have psychological problems.

What marked me as alcoholic was the realization that all these widgets of chaos were a direct result of my drinking and drug use. It was a realization that resonated in my bones like a tuning fork that had found its right frequency. With this realization came another. I knew what to do. I would steel myself to stop for long enough to get my life together. But I always drank the next day. I was fifteen years old and I'd totally lost control of my drinking and drug use. I couldn't stop.

Back in 1933, Bill Wilson was having a similar experience. Fresh out of his third trip through Towns Hospital, Bill was approaching his rock bottom. All the treatment he'd tried had failed. Even the good old reliable insane root.

At his lowest point, he was approached by an old friend, Ebby Thatcher, who was then a member of the Oxford Group, which was an American Protestant back-to-basics Christian religious order whose mission was to spread the gospel through acts of service. Ebby had become sober with the help of the group and was convinced that helping another person to stop drinking was the only way he'd be able to stay stopped. Bill rejected the help because, let's be honest, Shakespeare couldn't create a character more annoying than "Guy who stopped drinking seven weeks ago, found Jesus, and is back to make sure you get sober and find him, too." But that night, after Ebby left, Bill had a white-light religious experience that convinced him Ebby was right. Bill stopped drinking and never started again.

Five months later, Bill was on his way to America's bustling rubber capital—Akron, Ohio—for a stockholders meeting and, if you can believe it, they were not thrilled with the performance of the fresh-out-of-diarrhea-rehab broker in charge of their account. The meeting went poorly. Humiliated, Bill slunk back to his hotel to sleep off the shame. The only problem? In the lobby, precariously placed between the hotel entrance and the elevators, was a cocktail bar, alive with the kind of bustling nightlife energy you picture instantly when you think "Hotel bar in Akron, Ohio."

Bill began to sweat.

Bar. Elevator.

Bar. Elevator

Bar. Elevator.

He wasn't going to make it. Five months sober, and he'd been bested by a bad day and a taproom. This moment, the moment where willpower crumbles under the weight of a craving, was a moment he'd lived through before. It's one every addict has experienced. Sometimes it's only an hour after your proclamation to stop; sometimes it's five months later. But it always seems to come. It's the moment when you realize willpower is not enough to get you past the bar and into the elevator. The bar wins. Every time.

But then Bill happened to look between the bar and the elevator. Sliced into the wall, like a life ring bobbing in a churning sea, was a pay phone. Next to the pay phone was a contact sheet for local houses of worship. Bill remembered Ebby's visit, how Ebby had just reached out to Bill in order to save his own skin. Ebby was sure the only way to stay sober was to talk to someone who was still drinking and try to convince him to stop. Bill reached into his pocket and pulled out a handful of change. He knew he couldn't make it past the bar all the way to the elevator. But he could make it to the phone. He could make it halfway. He just hoped someone would be there waiting for him.

Sitting down at the pay phone at the Mayflower Hotel in Akron that night, Bill started calling local churches at random. When someone picked up, he'd explain that he was an alcoholic and he needed to talk to another alcoholic. Unsurprisingly, again and again, they hung up. I mean, imagine you're a rabbi and you get a phone call from a man with the sounds of an orgy in the background, asking you to connect him to another sex addict. You probably wouldn't assume the best. On his last nickel, Bill got a sympathetic pastor with some experience dealing with problem drinkers. "I know someone. Sit there and I'll have them call you back." That someone was Dr. Bob. And that call would save not only Bill's and Bob's lives but mine too, sixty-five years later.

With just that tiny action, the mere attempt to help someone, Bill had relieved the pressure of the craving enough to drag himself the rest of the way to the elevator and go to sleep, sober one more day.

A quick note: In the above paragraph, I suggested that the pastor put Bill in touch with Dr. Bob directly, but that was a lie, told for stylistic reasons. It worked best in the sentence I wrote and, as a non-historian, I'm allowed to do whatever I want and no review board will ever come for my tenure or call me out for academic censure. Watch: Dr. Bob had a famously long and elastic flaccid penis and would wrap entire flasks of brandy up in its ribbon-like form in order to hide bottles from his wife. See? Silence. Just you and me here, pal.

But speaking of Dr. Bob's wife, *that's* who Bill got connected with on the phone that night in Akron. Dr. Bob was passed out, drunk, unable to give consent to meeting with some weird newly religious ex-drunk stranger, but Bob's wife, Anne Ripley Smith, assured Bill he'd be up for it.

The next day Bob woke up hungover and grumpy when Anne revealed the news: "You have a date tonight with a guy I've never met." Bob was furious and refused. Anne then did some Ohio doctor's wife version of "You're never getting this booty again if you don't," and Bob relented. Resentfully, Dr. Bob agreed to meet with Bill Wilson for fifteen minutes, if only to appease his wife.

Bill came over, passionately kissed Anne while making deep eye contact with Dr. Bob and whispering in Bob's ear "Are you willing to go to any length to stay sober?" Yes, OK, I made that up too. And while it isn't "historically accurate," they're all dead now and can't prove it didn't happen.

What definitely did happen is Bob and Bill awkwardly greeted each other and retired into a room, just the two of them, for this fifteen-minute meeting. Bob didn't come back out for hours. Something happened in that room that would bend the arc of history, change the destiny of millions of people, and provide a spark of hope to otherwise hopeless alcoholics and addicts from that point on. Something that at the time felt insignificant, a chance meeting between two random people, one sick, one sicker, that in hindsight was a pebble in the pool whose ripple effect would cascade through time, growing wider and wider. It was a demarcation point in the timeline. And someday that line would wind its way to me.

Bob sat down expecting what he'd always gotten, a lecture on his drinking and a finger-wagging admonishment that he needed to stop. But Bill didn't even mention Bob's drinking. He talked only about his own. Bill didn't arrive there to get Bob sober; he came that day to keep sober himself. This inversion of traditional approaches to sober outreach seemed to strike a chord with Bob—something was different about hearing a man who'd suffered in the drink himself instead of a highly educated insane-root salesman. Bob could hear him, could relate, could say, "Yes, this man drank like me and look at him now. He's gotten sober; perhaps I can, too." With that inversion, AA began.

Bob didn't get sober instantly after that meeting. It took a few weeks and a few drinks to taper the good doctor off the sauce. His last drink came immediately prior to an anal surgery he was performing on a patient and for which he took a drink to calm his nerves. That last part I am *not* making up, and it's one of the most delightfully disturbing parts of early AA history. Ahh, the thirties, when men were men, and a proctologist, shaking with withdrawals, would, rather than simply bowing out of a surgery, sip a little gin, steel himself, and stick a scalpel in your butthole.

So now there were two people sober in AA—which did not yet exist as it was really just two old dudes not drinking. But even this early, they realized that the only hope the two of them had of staying sober themselves was to find new blood. Think of it like a spiritual Ponzi scheme: The pyramid didn't work unless the base kept growing.

Enter AA member number three. Bill and Bob went to a local hospital together and talked to a man there about the miracle they'd found: each other. Now they encountered the hard part at the beginning of a religious order—the sheer lack of numbers makes it hard to stake a claim on any discovered truth. "If this information was so valuable, why aren't more people on board?!" "If you'd get on board, we'd have more people!" Luckily for Bill and Bob, the alcoholic dilemma was dire, and people were desperately seeking solutions. Bill Dotson, the man in the hospital, took to the message delivered to him, and upon discharge from the Akron hospital never drank again. AA was now a group of three.

Bill, other Bill, and Dr. Bob spent the summer tracking down alcoholics and convincing them that sobriety was possible through the tenets of the Oxford Group. It began to work.

Satisfied that his job in Akron was done, Original Bill went back to New York invigorated and determined to start a group there.

Bill started the first New York AA group in his home. I keep calling this AA but the truth is that it wasn't until years later when the organization would look back and realize that's what it was. At the time, everyone in Akron and New York thought they were simply members of the Oxford Group: the bad-boy club of ex-drinkers within the religious order. But there was tension. The Oxford Group's specifically Protestant Christianity would agitate against the grain of sand that was to be AA until it finally cut ties with the Oxford Group and emerged as its own little pearl.

As this proto-AA continued to grow, it attracted more and more people who didn't fit into a Protestant mold. Catholics and agnostics and Jews and Hindus and Muslims all drink too much. All needed an answer. The early members saw this need, this primary purpose: to carry its message to the suffering alcoholic—whoever that alcoholic might be or pray to. So they began a painful extraction from Oxford. This breakup was tough but was made easier the way most messy breakups are made easier: Someone starts praising Hitler.

Frank Buchman, the founder of the Oxford Group, went on record thanking heaven for Hitler because at least he fought off the bloody commies and, thank heaven for Hitler, AA had its official cause to leave.

AA, now entirely off on its own, needed a way to introduce itself to the world, a way to show people what AA was all about. They decided to write a book. In this book, they outline their program, their ideas of what alcoholism is and how to get better from it. Many of the ideas in this book were borrowed directly from the Oxford Group's list of spiritual principles, but AA left Christ out and thus offered everyone salvation.

With the publication of its book, *Alcoholics Anonymous*, AA was truly born. And somehow, against all odds or logic, six decades later, fifteen-year-old juvenile delinquent me would find in that book all of the wisdom and inspiration I needed to leap off, once and for all, the hedonic treadmill on which I had been running. This chance meeting between senior citizens of the 1930s, this book written by and for losers, was all I needed to recover. At least for a while.

When I finally, for real for real, totally, this time I mean it, decided to get sober, I was already in AA. I got sent to rehab for the *first time* when I was thirteen, only a year into drinking and doing drugs. But, man, was I good at it! I stuffed a lot of dysfunction into just that first year. By the time I got to whatever it was I considered rock bottom and decided to join AA, I had already been attending meetings on and off for two years. Since that first rehab, I'd been sent to and kicked out of three more, always for behavioral issues. I really hated rehab. There was something truly pointless and inane about the system of juvenile rehab programs. Out of all four of the rehabs I consider alma maters, I know of only two people who actually got sober.

So why did it seem everyone I knew got sent to rehab?

The answer is Nancy Reagan for some reason.

As early AA expanded, it became clear that infrastructure would be needed to handle the influx of people trying to get sober. Now that there was a solution that did not include insane root or lashing yourself to a tree to wait for the cravings to leave you, there was a surge of addicts trying to stop. With the increase in demand came an increase in the need for places people could go to dry out in an environment that was safe and medically sound. Enter the idea of rehab.

Rehabs vary in scope and severity, from Betty Ford clinic–style mansions overlooking the Pacific, to sprawling medical complexes with state-of-the-art facilities, to basically an apartment building run by a pair of shady ex-cons who have spray-painted the word REHAB on the front of the building. There was something about the lay expertise of AA's recovery platform that ported easily over to the world of rehabilitation. AA was by and for alcoholics, and therefore *being* an alcoholic was seen as qualification enough to run a rehab. As a result of this lack of oversight, the system had massive potential for abuse. The first rehab to fall victim to the potential for abuse was . . . the first rehab. Well, it was one of the first anyway. It was founded by a charismatic AA member named Chuck Dederich, who took acid, had a breakthrough, quit AA, got other AA members and people fresh out of prison to follow him, and set up shop at a storefront in Venice Beach in 1958. For a while, Chuck called it the Tender Loving Care Group before ultimately settling on the name Synanon. Its innovation was twofold: 1. The advent of the reformed addict as professional drug counselor, and 2. The invention of "attack therapy."

In Synanon, they played "the Game," which was essentially a group therapy session where the members of Synanon, newly sober or struggling to be so, would sit around and attack one another. They'd call one another out for lying, for hypocrisy, for bad hygiene. No rules, no limits. This attack group was fundamental to the functioning of Synanon. Even the leadership was fair play, as they would jot down the attacks and use them to make policy adjustments. The Game was a new and exciting way to do therapy. No one had ever thought of the therapeutic benefits of being called a stupid fucking piece of absolute shit by a two-day-sober heroin addict. Synanon seemed to keep people sober. Treatment was long-term, two or three years. Then they made a, let's just say, rather extreme adjustment to their treatment plan. They became Hotel California. Chuck decided addicts were not really ever capable of recovery and therefore should stay at Synanon for a bit longer: their entire lives. And somehow this did not dampen the enthusiasm for the program?? By the time Synanon fell apart as an organization, it had swelled to include 1,300 full-time clients/patients/heads shaved. It somehow grew and grew in popularity while getting weirder and weirder, like Michael Jackson, Elon Musk, and the United States of America.

Was Synanon a cult? Let's see.

Everyone must shave their heads? CHECK.

Couples must ask permission to get married? CHECK.

Mass divorce, couple swapping, and forced abortions? CHECK.

Attempted murder by dropping a rattlesnake in someone's mailbox? CHECK! CHECK! CHECK!

After the attempt at snake murder, Synanon fell apart. And yet, against what would seem to be obvious logic, the tactics and techniques forged by Synanon lived on. The idea of a rehab you can never leave was more or less abandoned, but inexplicably, the other brainchild of an alcoholic's acid revelation became a standard technique in rehabs for years to come: attack therapy. This "therapeutic" "modality," straight out of the mouth of the drill sergeant from *Full Metal Jacket,* became commonplace. In rehab after rehab, this method was employed with nothing but anecdotal proof that it did anything therapeutic. Abuse-as-therapy provided a smoke screen for all sorts of other abuses to come. Anything that looked suspect or abusive could easily be excused away as a mysterious and nonintuitive tactic sprung out of the deep wisdom of a practitioner who was almost always just some random guy whose only qualification was that he nearly drank himself to death. Try googling it yourself and you'll see that just about every result of "attack therapy" will start with the word *controversial* and end with the words *shut down due to allegations of abuse.*

You would think that this kind of sadistic therapy through torture would have lived a short life, but then came the crack panic of the 1980s, tough love, and Just Say No. And that's when the throat goat herself, Nancy Reagan, took it upon herself to stamp out drugs, and a generation of kids had to sit through elementary school lectures on the scourge of drugs co-presented by a cop and an ex-gangbanger who would pop and lock and rap about how he caught hepatitis from a needle. For most kids, that was as far as it went. But for those of us who got addicted to drugs young or, just as likely, those who simply dabbled in drugs but had panicked parents, we were sent to rehab, flooding the system throughout the late 1980s and early '90s. How much abuse you faced at these rehabs was largely luck of the draw. Terrified parents trying to keep their kids alive weren't the best vetters of a program's therapeutic modalities and as a result, a lot of kids were put through "scared straight" carnage sessions.

But no amount of abuse scandals made the rehab fever break. I never felt particularly abused in rehab, more like bemused. To me the counselors were just another group of adults telling me what to do. They might as well have been telling a dog to speak mandarin.

I hated adults. It was sort of a defining characteristic. To me, adults meant authority, and authority meant someone telling me what to do. I viewed my job at that age as telling anyone who was telling me what to do to go fuck themselves. But it was more than that. I'd been swatted around from adult to adult, authority figure to authority figure, for my whole life, each of them playing a new tune in what felt like a psychic symphony meant to tie me up in a web of control. From therapists, guidance counselors, teachers, and principals to police, rehab counselors, and psychiatric diagnostic technicians, every adult I knew or met seemed to be telling me what to do, informing me of what was best for me, demanding I walk a path laid out by them. I seethed with resentment. I vibrated with hatred for anyone who was an adult.

Then I got to AA, and it was all adults. I was totally screwed. Never gonna work. It was filled with people who looked like my mom, the cops, the teachers, and, since it was AA, some reformed prison Nazis, too. Adults. They'll just tell me what to do, I'll tell them to fuck off, and they'll hate me.

Then they started to talk.

And they didn't much mention what I should do; they talked mostly about what *they* did. Talked about how they hated everyone around them. Hated authority. Hated the cops. Drank to deal with the hatred of others and the consequences that living with that kind of hate had on their own lives. They drank like me. They talked like me. They couldn't stop drinking like me. They were just like me. Except they didn't drink. Maybe I could stop like them.

But I was fifteen. One day sober. I didn't know how to stop. I didn't even know if I wanted to. I just knew I couldn't keep living like that, bouncing from institution to institution while trying my best to get fucked up on the way to each. And so, for the first time in my whole chaotic run at life, I asked for help.

In this post–Nancy Reagan rehab world, most big cities had established "Young People in AA" groups to cater to the massive influx of younger members. I was young even by these standards. I was, by at least five years, the youngest person in any meeting I stepped into. At my age now, five years is nothing. A forty-three-year-old and a forty-eight-year-old are the same. But when you're a young teenager, five years is a giant chasm. On one end is a kid trading Pokémon cards and on the other is a dude lighting a cigarette after fucking his girlfriend. Or in my case, lying about having a girlfriend.

I raised my hand at the Monday Night Young People's meeting at 2910 Telegraph Avenue in Oakland and said the words that seem to be a requisite for the kind of medicine offered by AA: "I am an alcoholic. I need help."

And then I got up and left.

Classic alcoholic cry for help. "I will do whatever it takes. Now, see you later, I'm off to see if that help is out in the hallway!"

But a little piece of AA magic happened when I left. One of the residual grains of AA stardust left over from that phone call Bill W. made to Dr. Bob from the Mayflower Hotel that night so many decades ago: The way to stay sober yourself is to help someone else find their way to sobriety. That ethic, ingrained in the mind of every sober member of AA, is so pronounced that, though I didn't know it then, someone was bound to follow me outside and offer me the help I asked for.

Someone did.

His name was Pidgeon, now a divinity school professor, but back then a recently sober guy trying to get his shit together. He walked out into the hallway, threw his arms around me, and told me, "It's going to be okay."

Somehow, that hug was enough to stabilize me, get me back into the meeting, and really synthesize the first piece of wisdom AA has to offer. A slogan so ever-present it has become a joke, the main thing you hear an AA guy say on "The One Where Chandler Gets Cirrhosis" episode of *Friends* or whatever: "One day at a time."

On its face this idea is laughably simplistic, the kind of advice I hate most because it's so obvious it feels like an insult. Like, yeah I get that you're saying "One day at a time," but it's pretty obvious you mean "One day at a time, for the *rest* of time, say goodbye to having a *good* time."

But there's deep wisdom in the concept. When you've found drugs and alcohol to be the only thing that's ever made your life feel okay, the problem is never about staying sober for a day. Anyone could do that if they had to. The problem is *being* sober from now on. Living without your medicine, living in that pain, living like this from now on. *That's* the terror.

The power is in the hyper-focus on the twenty-four hours in front of you. Just stay sober *today*. Don't worry about staying sober for the rest of your life; that's impossible. Worry about not drinking until you go to bed tonight. Worry about tomorrow when it comes, and if you have to, fuck it, just get high then. But stay sober *today*. Then of course, you wake up tomorrow, ready to snort a line, and realize, to your horror, that it's not tomorrow, that it's become today again. NOOOOOO! Tomorrow never comes. You start the process over. Just for today.

A day at a time you start cobbling days together. One day becomes two. Two becomes three. Three becomes six. Then it's New Year's Eve. Or, it was for me.

So back to where we started: six days sober and it was New Year's Eve. Bad timing. Then to make matters worse, I got invited to a party. I'm not sure I can overstate how exciting a party invitation is to a fifteen-year-old, and it was even more so for me because my friends and I *never* got invited to parties anymore. We were the types to crash your party, throw the keg through a window, call you a bitch, and then leave. Word got out quickly and our social engagement calendar had dried up. But somehow, someone in the suburbs outside of Oakland made the foolish decision to extend an invite for a New Year's rager to my crew.

Now I was faced with a dilemma. I was six days sober and absolutely *aching* to get high. I knew in the marrow of my still-forming bones that to attend the party meant to drink again. Who cares, right? It's just six days. Not much to rebuild. But here's the thing: I'd never gone six days before. This was the longest streak of sobriety I'd put together since the first time I got high. Six days takes way more work than six years. Anybody can cobble together years once you get past the hump of days, but how do you get from zero to six days? That's the miracle. So I had a choice to make. Go to the party, celebrate the new year and throw those half-dozen days into the fire, or stay sober one more day. And I did have options for the night. A super fun teenage party or an AA dance.

The AA dance is hard to describe to the uninitiated. Imagine a disco, pumping with the energy and vibration of *Saturday Night Fever*. Imagine the electronic music tent at Coachella, thousands of festivalgoers gathering for a final exuberant celebration of their night, the headliner's stage empty, the tent filled with only those who want to squeeze as much party out of their night as possible, the energy electric and filled with possibility. Imagine that.

Got the image? The AA dance is the exact opposite of that.

Now imagine a Vietnam vet on oxygen for his emphysema shaking his tail feather in a wheelchair to "It's Raining Men" with a former (?) prostitute on a small dance floor in an old church with the lights on. That's the vibe.

So, fun party at the risk of losing everything, or a night of torture at a Rotary Club?

I chose the AA dance.

And it was awful.

Boring. Torture. Rotary Club.

I found the only other person in the room under sixty, a girl named Rose, and we sat outside smoking cigarettes and talking about how thoroughly our lives sucked. At 12:01 my mommy picked me up and drove me home. The worst New Year's ever. At least at the time. In hindsight, I can see how monumental that night was. What a tectonic shift that choice was to go suffer and *stay* rather than party and *go*. I've had many cool New Year's Eve experiences. Packed comedy clubs where I was the star of the show. Vacations where I watched fireworks on the beaches of Mexico. Raves where I DJ'd and danced in the new year surrounded by thousands of the most beautiful people imaginable. But that night, sitting under a sad floodlight with Rose smoking Newports, both of us wondering what was going to happen to our lives next, that night was the best New Year's of my life. It was the New Year's when I chose my life. This was who I was. This was what I wanted. I wanted to live. The next day I woke up, and New Year's was yesterday.

Today was, once again, today. I was a full week sober.

A week becomes a month. A month becomes three months. Your brain clears. Now you're sober. Most people think that getting sober is the start and finish of the process. The problem is the drinking; the solution is arresting it. But of course, that's not true at all.

The *symptom* is the drinking, but for most people, by the time they arrive in AA, that symptom is so pronounced, so loud, that it seems to be the entire disease. The process of simply not drinking clears the way to figuring out what the actual problem is. Once you get sober, you start the painful work of figuring out *why* you drank like that in the first place; why you're the type of person who, once it began to affect your life, didn't immediately stop, or curtail it. Or why you tried and failed countless times. Why you swore you were done and then watched yourself drink again. No one likes getting high more than having a good life, not even the alcoholic, so why are so many willing to drink their lives away? Well, some people just can't help it. And mostly because we can't seem to figure out what "it" is.

I've heard the analogy of an alcoholic being something like a car with a mechanical issue. The first thing you need to do is get off the road and bring it to a mechanic. That's getting sober and going to a meeting or a rehab or a therapist. Most people who drink too much are like the guy who, hearing an awful noise in the engine, just keeps driving in the hopes that their car has an immune system and will figure out a way to self-repair. The noise gets worse. The problems spread. What was a noise is now a clunk. The clunk becomes a grinding. The grinding becomes smoke. Finally, you surrender. You have to take the car in and ask for help.

Once at the mechanic, *you find out what the problem is.* Busted transmission, engine failure, acute cirrhosis. That knowledge is VITAL. Without it you cannot move forward. But that knowledge doesn't fix the car. It only makes the fixing of the car possible.

That knowledge is the famous first step in AA's twelve-step program of recovery:

1. We admitted we were powerless over alcohol—that our lives had become unmanageable.

The unmanageable part, that's the loud part. Figuring that out is pretty easy from the outside. It manifests itself in a litany of consequences, from constantly being late to work all the way to killing a family in a drunk-driving accident. Those are the consequences that come with a life of drugs and drinking untempered by moderation. The alcoholic creates a wake of wreckage behind them. And the consequences get slowly worse over time. As you descend into the pit, all you're focused on is the pendulum swing of day-to-day living, which starts mild: I'm stressed, my wife doesn't understand me, I got too drunk and offended the bartender. Then it gets a bit worse: Do I have drugs? Am I dope sick? Maybe I'll steal some money from my kids. Then it approaches the gutter: My liver's failing. My family left me. I died.

But it's harder to see it from the inside. The problem with the hyper-focus on the immediate ups and downs of the life spent in a bottle is that you don't notice the descent. You slide down slowly, so slowly you don't realize you're sliding. Until one day, like the frog in the pot, you're cooked before you notice. And sometimes it's not even about noticing. Sometimes you literally can't remember what happened.

Blackouts are the scariest and most potentially hilarious facet of dysfunctional alcoholic drinking. Here are the top four greatest blackout stories I heard in AA:

1. A person started drinking in San Francisco and woke up in Jerusalem.
2. A person started drinking, woke up in the middle of beating someone up, had no idea why, processed it, figured the guy must have done something to deserve it, and kept going.
3. A person started drinking and woke up in a toddler's bedroom. No toddler present, thank God. With no idea why he was there, he opened up the window and slipped out into the backyard.
4. A person started drinking and woke up in a threesome with his monogamous girlfriend and his best friend. He stayed present long enough to understand what he was seeing, screamed "Fuck yeah!," and slipped back into a blackout.

From the outside, of course, it's clear. It's unmanageable. If your life is like this, the answer is obvious. Stop drinking. Entire problem literally solved. If only most problems had solutions that clear.

But no addict stops. Because they can't. They just keep focused on that daily up and down, and keep cracking the bottle to deal with it. That's being powerless. That's the real problem. Powerlessness and unmanageability.

Or to put it another way: I had two problems. Strawberries and mindfuck.

The problem with the alcoholic/addict is a lot like having an allergy to, say, strawberries. Whenever I ate strawberries, bad things would occur. Rash, itchy throat, random swelling. I could not eat strawberries without some kind of unpredictable allergic reaction. The solution should be obvious and easy to implement. Avoid the strawberry at all costs. Just don't eat strawberries! It's not that complicated. Lots of people have allergies and you don't see them dancing on a knife's edge, nibbling at a peanut, hoping they can eat just enough to stave off anaphylactic shock.

But I also have mindfuck! Mindfuck works like this: Despite knowing full well that I cannot eat the strawberry and be okay, every time I see a strawberry, all I can think is: *Strawberries!*

The sweet juicy bliss of nature's red bulb of nectar. The thin outer skin breaking apart under the slightest pressure from my teeth, the delicate crunch of that perfect grid of seeds, the rapture of sinking into the meat of the thing. Tart, refreshing, perfection.

Oh the strawberry!

Strawberry pie! Strawberry ice cream! Strawberry soup!

I. Must. Have. Strawberries.

You grab a strawberry, take a bite, and the allergic reaction hits you immediately. How did this happen again?

That's how mindfuck works. The AA book describes this mental process as "*being unable to recall with sufficient force the memory of the suffering of even a week or a month ago*" and "*strange mental blank spots.*" Walking through the world, you are fully aware of how you react to drinking and drugs. You know how bad they are for you. You know the consequences. But the moment you see or think of the bottle, all you can remember is the good feelings waiting for you in there, the party contained in the aquarium. To put it simply, I get really hazy thinking when I stare at a bottle of gin. That's unmanageability and powerlessness. That's strawberries and mindfuck.

So if you can't control your drinking using your own mind because it can't seem to remember why you weren't drinking in the first place, if you've lost all power over the bottle, what do you need? Having no power means you need . . . like a Tim Allen catchphrase . . . *more power*. And is that power located inside the mind of the very person who just admitted it was powerless? I don't think so, Tim. It's time for some Home Improvement. But where do you find it? UNNNGH?!

This brings us to steps two and three of AA's twelve steps:

2. Came to believe that a Power greater than ourselves could restore us to sanity.

And:

3. Made a decision to turn our will and our lives over to the care of God as we understood Him.

Uh-oh. The God dilemma. There's a lot of song and dance around this sticking point, where AA members insist that they aren't a religion and that that power greater than yourself can be anything you want, anything at all, including purposefully absurd suggestions such as adopting a doorknob as a god.

This is a cute trick meant to either a) clear the way for people with an aversion to religion so as many people as possible can get help, or b) try to distract from an inconvenient truth: AA *is* a religion.

It's a sticky reality that most AA members choose to ignore. AA is a mystical, deity-driven solution to a public health crisis, and if you are an atheist, at best you must engage in some willful cognitive dissonance in order to take advantage of what it has to offer.

AA wants to have it both ways—to be a medically sound solution to alcoholism, which it frames as a physical allergy and a disease, and to be a soul-enriching solution to alcoholism, which it frames as a spiritual malady. And it may be both, but imagine going to the doctor for a yeast infection and having him suggest "Have you tried sacrificing a vulture to Zoroaster? If that doesn't work for you, how about a doorknob?"

I'm not an atheist, never had religious anxieties, and didn't personally find this to be a sticking point, but the longer I stayed in AA, the more I thought about the person who arrived as a true non-believer and who would invariably be treated as though their belief system was a manifestation of ego or an unwillingness to get better rather than a fundamental problem with a program that purports to be for all but cannot work without conformity of belief on at least some level. People in AA will say "AA isn't religious, it's spiritual" like that's a knowledge bomb drop, ignoring the fact that the dictionary definition of spiritual is "relating to religion."

That said, despite the fact that, to me, it is clearly a religion, AA *as* a religion has a remarkably lax policy on what you need to believe in. If more religions resembled AA, the world would be a much more peaceful place. AA ascribes to God no attributes but love and power. The two things most lacking in an alcoholic's life.

Some AA members are fantastically religious in their faith of origin, some are tree-worshipping deists, some are true agnostics who simply believe in the power of the collective consciousness of AA, the goodwill and mutual aid a sufficient power to effect change. I have not, so far, ever met a person who actually believes in a doorknob.

Of course, there's another explanation of how and why AA plays so fast and loose with the God dilemma: It knows (as much as a leaderless organization can "know" anything) that it's a contradiction in terms, and embraces the incongruity. Since AA has no leadership, since it has no clergy or governing body, it can make its own rules. Ground into the sausage of AA are the inconsistencies. These are not evidence of bullshit, but rather useful idiocies, paradoxes that don't make too much sense, but do make healing possible. God therefore is not a door*knob* but a door*stop,* a small wedge keeping open the entrance into newfound freedom, a dogma of non-dogma, a way in.

I think I believe in all of these explanations. That all of these ideas exist in AA at once, that AA contains multitudes. I appreciate the low bar AA sets to get you to the power you need.

And look, it shouldn't be that hard to admit you need a power greater than yourself. If you are on step two then it seems safe to assume you just did step one. Literally *one step ago* you admitted you were powerless over alcohol. A beverage. A fucking beverage, for sale right now at a 7-Eleven, has beaten you to such a pulp that you need to change your entire life. So yeah, if you're powerless over a beverage, it shouldn't stretch you to your breaking point to say, "I need a power greater than myself if I want to regain my sanity."

There's a saying that I think sums up the concept of step two quite nicely and explains, I think, the spirit behind the doorknob: "It doesn't matter *what* your higher power is, as long as it isn't you."

Because the problem is you and, as they say in AA, "A broken window can't fix a broken window."

The idea with steps one through three is to realize what's happening, diagnose what's wrong, and then get out of the way so that it can be fixed. How do we do that? We do it like Michelangelo. Not the Teenage Mutant Ninja Turtle. Don't try to solve an addiction problem by eating a sewer pizza and trying to fuck an intrepid human reporter. I was talking about the other Michelangelo. Someone once asked the Italian Renaissance master how he was able to make a thing as perfect as the sculpture of David. Michelangelo said, "It was easy, I just got a block of marble and chipped away all the parts that weren't David." Okay, did Michelangelo really say this? Unlikely, unless in addition to being one of the great artists in history, he also spoke in perfect parable. But it's precisely what AA is asking you to do, to take away all the parts that aren't you until you return to form. Your true self, unencumbered and free. A masterpiece. Just get out of the way and let the artist do his work. All you have to do in steps one through three is admit, understand, and allow. And how do you actually chip away the "not David" parts of you? By working the rest of the steps!

Steps four and five are the heavy-lifting steps. "The work" as they'd call it if AA was filled with vapid Hollywood actors, which it is, so they do.

4. Made a searching and fearless moral inventory of ourselves.
5. Admitted to God, to ourselves, and to another human being the exact nature of our wrongs.

This is the scary part and definitely where most people stop, realize what's being asked of them, and bail back into a bottle. The hell I know is better than the hell I imagine.

Taking a true and honest hard look at ourselves was exactly what most alcoholics were drinking to avoid. But without this deep look at the self, one has little hope of recovery or sobriety in the long term. Most alcoholics and, as I've gotten older I've started to believe, most humans, live on the propulsion of trauma. At some point in our lives, something happens that hurts us, scares us, causes us pain. It's inevitable, it's life. When a trauma happens that is too big to face, process, and recover from, we retreat from the trauma, guard from the pain, build a wall around our distress. From that point on, a sliver of our brain power is spent on avoiding what's behind that wall. If we get too close to the wall, to the pain, we get scared and recoil, bouncing hard away, retreating to where the pain isn't, to where it's safe. What was once a straight path in our brains is now a safer detour around the tender part.

Depending on the severity of the trauma, most of us can handle one of these. But when they start to build up, when you have to wall off multiple traumas and find yourself propelled in multiple directions by multiple indelible instances of pain, it's quite easy to get lost in the maze that your mind has become and to find yourself living a life that isn't really under your control. There are so many forces pushing you forward in so many different directions in order to avoid ever having to look at your pain that what should and could have been a straight walk forward now looks more like a pinball's travel history, bouncing from wall to wall, slamming around, unsure of which direction you were headed in the first place. You have lost the thread of yourself, you have lost control. You are now a passenger in your own life, traveling only the convoluted paths you've paved by walling off other ones. You are now just trying to hold on. This is why you'll sometimes meet a person with a dysfunction so glaring and a solution so apparent that you feel like shaking them and screaming at them, "It's so obvious what you need to do to get better! Why won't you just fucking do it?!" And you're right! It is obvious. It would be easy to change. For you. But for them it's impossible; they can't see what you can. They can't see over the wall.

The fourth and fifth steps are an archaeological dig. Wall discovery. An analysis of the self and a walk backward through the strata, deeper and deeper, to find and dismantle, to get back to the self, to set the trajectory right again. To open the roads.

It's a simple but terrifying process, trauma by trauma, fear by fear, resentment by resentment, you put them down on paper until it's all there in black-and-white. A life of frenzied propulsion now static in a notebook. Then you open that notebook and read it to someone else.

I did this. Somehow I made it through the two steps that tend to stymie most people. I wrote it all down and sat with my sponsor, ready to confess.

Which reminds me that I should have mentioned sponsors earlier. The "sponsor" is an organic outcropping of the connection between Ebby and Bill, then Bill and Bob. One-to-one connection was the way the program began and has become as close to a "must" as AA has. When you get sober you are expected to ask someone, nervously, like a pubescent boy at a school dance, if they will sponsor you. This does not mean they provide a logo for your race car; it means that they become your confidant and guide through the AA program and its twelve steps. Over time it has also come to take on a general mentor-like role as well, a lay therapist walking you through all of life's decisions. Some sponsors are laid-back, never-prescriptive spiritual guru types who happily feed you enough rope to hang yourself with, dispensing small bits of fun wisdom, often in the form of light mockery.* Some are really heavy-handed militaristic types who demand you not make a single decision without running it by them. I had one of these once.

Right after my father died and my life felt totally unmoored, I thought maybe a Big AA Daddy could help me make the decisions I was feeling incapable of making alone. Part of his regimen was that every day I had to call him and tell him *something* that I could use his help with. This made for some awkward conversations on the days when nothing was bothering me. One day, excruciatingly searching my brain for something to bring up, I made a tactical mistake. "Uh, well, I guess this girl did ask me out but she seems a bit off and I'm not into her at all, so I said I didn't think it was a good idea."

Like a shark smelling chum in the water, my sponsor pounced: "Oh! And tell me, just HOW is *your way* going when it comes to finding a partner?!"

Confused, I told him what he wanted to hear: "I guess, like, badly?"

He smiled. "YES! VERY badly! You need to call that woman and tell her you'd LOVE to take her out!"

This didn't sound right to me and I said, "But I'm extremely unattracted to her."

He cocked his eyebrow, daring me to continue.

I sighed, "Okay, fine, I guess I'll go out with her."

She and I spent a very awkward hour with each other over coffee.

---

* I was once with a friend who sat next to me talking to his sponsor on the phone, complaining about an upcoming court date he had the following week and how unfairly he was sure the judge would treat him. He explained his dilemma and then instantly had to start over at the beginning, louder this time. When he was done, he did it again, now screaming into the phone what he was sure was going to happen in that hearing. Then suddenly he frowned and put the phone down. "What was that?" I asked. My friend sighed and said, "He kept saying he couldn't hear me. Then he said, 'Sorry, it seems like you're calling in from a week in the future, the connection isn't good.' And he hung up on me."

She kept offering to convert to Judaism in order to marry me. I came home that same night to a $300 arrangement of roses in a cartoon M&M vase she'd had delivered with a note that read "Think about my offer!" I called my sponsor and told him all of that, and he gulped, "Yeah, maybe that was a bad idea."

We stopped working together shortly thereafter.

Getting sober so young was a particular challenge when it came to sponsorship. I didn't want to get mentored by some old loser. Some of these people were seriously old. Like, twenty-seven! My first sponsor was a guy named Ron who was barely nine months sober himself but had fallen in with a traditionalist faction of AA in the Bay Area and was pretty fired up about his recovery. I was in puppy love with a girl from my rehab and was whining about it to him one night when he stopped me and recited advice that he was clearly repeating verbatim from someone further up the sponsorship food chain: "You just need to tell her that you're interested in a relationship that's spiritual, emotional, and physical with the goal of marriage in mind." Why was everyone in AA obsessed with me getting married!?

I shook my head. "Dude, I'm fifteen."

So a traditionalist wouldn't work. I decided I'd go to a meeting, scan the room for the coolest-dressed person, and ask one of them. I ended up finding a guy named Eddie whose message of recovery to me was: "Someday, you'll look around the room at all the women in the meetings and be able to tell yourself, 'I fucked her, I fucked her, I fucked her. . . .'"

With this kind of motivation, I began making my way through the twelve steps hoping to someday squirm in my seat as a dozen middle-aged alcoholic women stared daggers at me. Eventually I limped through enough steps to arrive at the grand confessional.

The fifth step is simple, you just sit there, open up the pages of your resentments, fears, and the harms you have done to others and read them out loud to a barely interested sponsor.

It's an ancient ritual, the confession. There seems to be power in saying things you already know out loud to someone else. You start to see patterns of behavior, strands of fear running through your life that have been your primary operating system. You see how you react, again and again, in exactly the same way, to the things that make you uncomfortable. You see how your actions have created the world you inhabit and how your perception of the world has been shaped by these actions. You peer over the walls you have built and what's held back there is never quite as scary again. That's the primary power of confession, at least in AA: Once you read your darkest secrets to another person and see that that person is largely unimpressed, that it's just kind of standard operating procedure to them, it's hard to stay ashamed of those secrets.

When I completed my fifth step, my first sponsor looked at me and with great gravity asked, "Is there anything you left off of this that you haven't told me? Anything you said you'd never admit to *anyone*? Have you taken human life or had sex with an animal?"

Over the years I repeated a version of this question (without the specifics) to all of the people whose fifth steps I heard. One guy looked at me and said, with a casualness I can't forget, "Well, me and my mom made out a couple of times, but we were both adults."

There was something about the breezy use of the term *made out* that really struck me. I tried not to betray any surprise and just said in support, "Thank you for admitting to Frenching your mom. You don't need to be ashamed of this anymore."

He shook his head, no. "Oh, I'm not ashamed of it, I just don't talk about it much."

Yeah. I get that.

Having read my fifth step out loud, I felt freer and more buoyant in the world. I'd begun to tear down the walls in my mind, and it was feeling like an easier place to get around in. I had a chance. Here's the nasty truth: Most people in AA drink again before they get past the fifth step. For many, the ugliness of who they think they are is just too much to face. People can waltz through the first three steps but when the time comes to truly face the life they've made, many alcoholics freeze. For them, the unexamined life is worth dying over.

Having made my confession, it was time to start attempting to live a better life. This is the meat of steps six and seven:

6. Were entirely ready to have God remove all these defects of character.
7. Humbly asked God to remove our shortcomings.

It basically comes down to this: Having made a list of all your problems and shared them out loud with someone takes away the shame and makes it possible to adjust your way of living, but, just like stopping drinking, it does not *fix* you. The fix comes through diligence, willingness, and incremental change. Sure, praying to a deity is a nice gesture, but that's simply laying the groundwork of willingness for the real work that lies ahead. And the worst part of that work follows steps six and seven immediately. It's the part we all know from movies and TV: making amends.

8. Made a list of all persons we had harmed, and became willing to make amends to them all.
9. Made direct amends to such people wherever possible, except when to do so would injure them or others.

There's no way around it; it fucking sucks. As I said, most people don't get past step five, but the survivors aren't safe yet. Like a rake at a casino, a big ol' claw comes and removes a huge chunk here, too.

I mean, it makes sense. It's one thing to admit to yourself and one other guy what you are and what you've done. It's entirely another to call up your aunt and admit to stealing her anxiety medication. The amends steps are daunting, made more so by the length of time you spent drinking and hurting people. The longer you were out there, the more people you have to apologize to. One of the biggest problems with the ninth step is that addicts are profuse apologizers before they enter recovery. Living in a manner that alienates everyone you love, constantly decimating their trust in you, one has to develop a hair trigger on saying sorry. Sorry, I stole your money! Sorry, I rented out the spare room in our house to a crack buddy who paid rent in rocks! Sorry, I said sorry and then almost immediately did the thing I said I was sorry for again! Sorry, I lied to you, I promise it will never happen again! Sorry, that also was a lie!

It gets to be so that the people who love you stop buying it, but you just keep trying to sell the apology anyway since that's all you have to offer. And you *are* sorry. You just lack any ability to translate that "sorry" energy into "not doing it again" energy. By the time an alcoholic gets sober she or he has generally exhausted their friends' and families' ability to give a fuck about an apology. The trust bucket fills up a drop at a time, but it only takes one kick to knock it over. So, once in recovery and arriving at the ninth step, the apologies stop and the amends begin. To amend behavior is to make better, to change. Sometimes this change begins with a formal mea culpa, but rarely does it end there. It's common for an attempt at an amends to be spurned, rejected entirely, but that doesn't stop the change. There's a caveat in the ninth step that some people in AA take advantage of to justify not apologizing directly: *except when to do so would injure them or others.*

That single line has been manipulated in the recovery community as much as "a well regulated Militia" has in the school shooter community.

One of the funniest passages in the AA book is the segment where they explain why telling your wife you used to cheat on her while you were drinking is not always necessary. I mean, look, I have no clue what the most ethical answer is for fessing up to an affair, but the idea of a bunch of old men, newly sober, sitting around having a symposium on how to tackle their alcoholism and deciding, "You know what, it might actually be *better* if we didn't tell our wives about the prostitutes! Better, you know, for them!" is such perfect comedy, I salute them for the ability to write it with a straight face.

The principle behind "except when to do so would injure them or others" is sound, however. It sometimes makes more sense to start living like you're sorry than to simply say you're sorry. If living well is the best revenge, it might also be the best amends. Change your life and you'll often find people more receptive to your apologies. Because, of course, the problem was never the apology; it was the person making it. Once you demonstrate you have changed into a person whose word you can trust, an apology becomes more possible to accept. So how do you become that person?

The change comes in what AA calls the "maintenance steps," steps ten, eleven, and twelve:

10. Continued to take personal inventory and when we were wrong promptly admitted it.
11. Sought through prayer and meditation to improve our conscious contact with God as we understood Him, praying only for knowledge of His will for us and the power to carry that out.
12. Having had a spiritual awakening as the result of these steps, we tried to carry this message to alcoholics, and to practice these principles in all our affairs.

These are the "take these tools and apply them to your life" steps. Step ten is about changing your attitudinal perspective on yourself. Becoming disciplined about your decency. I started learning, very slowly, about the process of becoming a good person. It was difficult work made easier by the fact that since I was fifteen, my patterns of behavior hadn't been entirely fused into my nervous system. I was malleable and ready to be re-formed. Someone once described the process of getting better like this:

At first I would lie. Then I would lie and return a week later and say, "Last week I lied to you. Sorry." Then I would lie and immediately admit, "You know what, that was a lie. Sorry." Then I would stop the lie as I was about to tell it, beat it back, and tell the truth instead. And then, after a while, I found I no longer wanted to lie.

AA is like that. It's a bizarrely effective holistic cognitive behavior overhaul. Through the twelve steps and a culture of publicly re-inforced moralism, the alcoholic gets shocked out of their instinctual shadiness. The lies, the manipulation, the abuse and narcissism are attacked from multiple angles like a psychological chemotherapy until it goes into full remission. Until the instincts are changed. It rearranges your molecules. Is it brainwashing? Yes. But as a popu-

lar AA speaker once said, "Maybe you could use a good scrub-
bing!"

The eleventh step is the "spiritual journey" part of AA's twelve
steps and it's so fantastically vague, it can literally mean anything.
I gave it a shot. I read *Siddhartha* and was vibrating for a week,
tempted to hug a tree growing in front of a coffee shop I frequented.
That wore off. I thought about Transcendental Meditation, but de-
clined due to the signup fee. I did guided meditations and prayer
beads and morning readings and read *The Way of the Peaceful Warrior*. Nothing seemed to transform me in any powerful way.

Then, when I was sixteen and about a year sober, I was on my
way to an AA conference in Reno, Nevada, and stopped for gas.
The attendant, a striking fifty-year-old Polynesian man with long
black hair and bracelets covering his wrists, walked right up to me
with a quizzical look in his eye. "You're headed to the AA conference, aren't you?" he asked. My mind was blown. "How did you
know?!" I asked, forgetting the large AA medallion I wore around
my neck. He smiled gently. "I had a dream about you. I knew you'd
be coming. I'm Saul, I've been sober twenty years, and I'm going to
help you learn to meditate." This was the sign from above I'd been
waiting for. Truly amazed, I felt like I was walking on air. Saul attended the conference that weekend. I spent it under his wing. He
explained that he was a Hawaiian kahuna and that he'd had some
vision of me. I eagerly accepted the role of his spiritual charge. After
that weekend, I'd spend hours on the phone with him, learning to
meditate, a jade pig he'd sent me resting on my root chakra, breathing energy into its little form, feeling the spiritual power of what he
called "talisman meditation."

One day Saul simply fell out of my life, but he always dwelled in
my memory as a holy man who drifted into my life at exactly the
right moment, zapped me with spirit, and sent me on my path.

Years later, a sober guy who'd moved from Reno to Oakland
cocked an eyebrow when I mentioned I'd once had a kahuna from
Reno AA teach me how to meditate.

"Saul?" he asked, his voice dripping with skepticism.

"Yes! That was the guy!"

"Yeah, Saul tried to fuck me and every other young dude who got sober back then."

"Hmm," I said, thinking of the jade pig resting two inches from my cock, as Saul's breathy voice urged me to breathe deeper. "That *does* make more sense than a kahuna who works at a mini mart having a psychic vision of my arrival."

But since he never got as close to me as the pig did, I decided to keep him as a positive memory. So what if he was quietly masturbating during our meditation sessions? He too had a talisman to focus his energy toward: pubescent wannabe gangsters trying to find themselves.

Before he lost interest in me (which, now that I think about it, was right around when I started shaving), Saul sent me a book of Hawaiian spirituality, written, like many books of Polynesian wisdom, by a white woman. In it I read a passage that I'd never forget as it seemed to typify the entire journey through transformative spirituality that I had embarked upon. It read, "The world and the people in it are the cause of all of your problems. But obviously you cannot change the world and all the people in it. Change yourself and you will find that the world and the people in it have changed around you."

Slowly but surely, I started to change.

I got to the end of the steps and emerged a diametrically altered person. But like that book told me, the change was terraforming. At the end of the steps, I lifted my head up to find that the world had changed. Every adult who'd been my enemy had become just a person, their radioactivity muted under a thousand pounds of spiritual lead. I'd despaired of ever righting my course, and suddenly I felt like the world held promise for me. I wasn't angry anymore. Anger and rage had been my defining characteristics for much of my young life, and they now seemed stripped from me. My old self was like a chimera who'd taken control of me and had suddenly departed the organism. I didn't just feel different; I felt transformed. Totally and fundamentally. I'm really trying hard here not to say I was born again but there was little difference. As the AA book describes and my experience bore out, I was on "the broad highway, shot into the fourth dimension of existence."

The steps had worked on me.

I was sixteen years old.

Bizarrely, though the twelve steps are the AA program of recovery, countless people go to AA for years and simply never work through them. I don't mean the people who work them and get stuck on one, the difficult soul-wrenching work simply too much for them. That I can understand. It's terrifying to get deep down into the muck of your own psyche. It's too much for some to bear. I'm talking about the incredibly common phenomenon of people who come to AA, attend meetings, participate in the communal aspect of it, and simply never even attempt to do the work.

They're called twelve step groups! Because of the whole "twelve step" part! Not doing the steps when you've joined AA is a lot like this. . . .

Forget alcoholism. That's not your problem. Your problem is that you're broke. You need money and you need it bad. Everything you've tried to do to make money has failed you. You're powerless. Then suddenly, there's some hope. One night you're watching TV and you see an infomercial with a guy saying, "I made millions taking out real estate ads in newspapers around the country." This seems promising! Your problem is a lack of money; this guy seems to have money! Bingo bango.

At the end of the infomercial the guy says to attend a meeting to find out more. They meet at the conference room of the Courtyard by Marriott on Tuesdays! Even better! An in-person meeting. You're gonna attend the fuck out of that meeting and find out more. So Tuesday comes. It's a nice group of people. The speaker, this time a lady, says she, too, made millions selling real estate ads in newspapers around the country. "This is promising!" you think. "It worked for this lady, too! I'm gonna come back here next week and get even more info!" A week goes by, you go back to the Courtyard by Marriott, dip one of those stale Danish sugar cookies that the meeting provided into a nasty cup of coffee, and tuck in to hear this week's keynote speaker. This guy, a gay Black man in a wheelchair, says he *also* made millions selling real estate ads in newspapers around the country. At this point you're convinced: It worked for the guy on TV, it worked for the woman, it worked for the gay Black guy in the wheelchair, it seems like it will work for anyone! It could work for you, too. In fact, it will work for you. You're sure of it.

The next step is obvious. Attend next week's meeting.

This goes on for years. Every week you are in that meeting, every week someone else is talking about all the money they made selling real estate ads in newspapers around the country. You're now friends with most of them. You go to a local diner to eat after the meeting every Tuesday. They offer to pay. They all have money now. But you're as broke as ever. It's not working for you like it's working for all of them. In fact, you haven't made a fucking cent this whole time and, worse yet, you've wasted a year of Tuesday evenings in these fucking meetings when you could have been home watching the new season of *CSI: Bakersfield*.

Infuriated, you realize this stupid program is a lie; it doesn't work at all. They lied to you!

Do you see the problem here? The problem is that you forgot to actually do anything. You didn't call a single newspaper. You didn't take out a single ad. You didn't even take anyone's advice. You didn't take any action at all. So of course you're still broke. All you did was go to meetings and listen to other people talk about their money.

This is absurd, right? No one would do this. It doesn't even make sense. But people in AA do it all the time. The vast, vast majority of people in AA who I saw drink again did so without having completed the steps. I'm not saying it's easy to do them. It's not. But it, quite literally, *is* AA. Deciding AA doesn't work without doing the steps is like deciding a sandwich won't fill you up without eating it.

This isn't to say AA meetings themselves have no value. Without the meeting, I'm not sure what AA even is. Sure, the steps are the actual spiritual program of action, but the meeting is the house of worship. The in-person arm of AA is the meeting. Across the world, every night, in every city, there are groups of alcoholics having a meeting. They vary in size and structure, but the general experience is something like this:

In the basement of a local church or a meeting room in a hospital or Masonic lodge, an AA group has rented out the space and transformed it into a lighthouse for the chronically thirsty. You, a person who's trying to get sober, look up the nearest meeting online and you show up, not knowing what to expect. When you arrive, you will notice a smoking band of miscreants, not exactly looking like they fit in at the entrance of a church. More than that, they don't look like they fit together. Hipster Joe and Gangbanger Steve are hugging and sharing a laugh. Housewife Barb laughs at an off-color joke that Biker Nick made. As you approach, however, they all turn in notice of you. A hand is extended; it's Gangbanger Steve.

"Are you new?" he asks.

You have absolutely no clue what he means by this. "Yeah, I'm like super new. Or wait . . ." You pause, wondering what the right answer here is: "No. I'm old. I'm as old as the wind."

The miscreants laugh at what to them is a familiar confusion. "You're new!" shouts Barb. "Welcome! Go on in and grab a seat, the meeting starts soon." You smile and walk in. The conviviality out front is so unexpected, you can't even discern if it was mockery or earnestness. You're so brittle and scared, everything feels like an affront. It's incredibly embarrassing for you to be there, but for them, it's as cool as anything could be. They are people who, having gotten sober and fallen in love with AA, have absolutely zero self-consciousness about being alcoholics. You do not share this lack of shame.

A quick side note about shame before we come back to that meeting: To get sober now is to be incredibly lucky on a historical level. Almost everyone thinks being a recovering alcoholic is cool. The stigma is nearly completely wiped out. But in the early days it was acute and painful and was, I think, one of the main reasons for the second *A* in AA. The "Anonymous" was such an important ethic back then. To admit you were here, to admit you were an alcoholic, was to commit social and professional suicide. I didn't fully appreciate this until, years into AA, I hit bottom on sexual compulsivity. A girl I didn't want to sleep with had propositioned me and, at the time, I lacked even the slightest ability to say no when it came to sex. My policy was, if you were willing, I was game. No exceptions. This led to some *Dark Crystal, Fraggle Rock*–type nights that I'd sooner forget.

This was one.

She came over and I couldn't help noticing, postcoital, my partner for the evening was furiously scratching a bright red spot on her butt. "Oh great," I started to panic. "She's got Butt AIDS. Or Butt Crabs or butt something." I smiled politely and said good night, even though she was in my house. The second she was out the door I ran, fully melting down, into the cabinet under the sink to find something to kill the phantom infection. I grabbed a can of Lysol and stripped naked, spraying my body with disinfectant. I looked out the window and saw her walking by, truly hoping that she hadn't looked in the window and seen me, freshly fucked, delousing myself, though perhaps that might've been a wakeup call for her, too.

At that moment I realized I needed to make a change of some sort. I finally understood the saying "Part of a healthy sex life is never having to douse yourself in benzalkonium chloride." The next day I went to a Sex Addicts Anonymous meeting. I pulled up and was instantly filled with anxiety as I stared at the fifty-yard walk I'd have to make from the car to the entrance. For years I'd been attending AA meetings, and only right then did I finally understand how ashamed those early AA members must have been to attend meetings before the world had met cool sober people like Sam Malone and Eminem. Society does not think sex addicts are "cool." I didn't want anyone to see me slink into that meeting. My heart was pounding. I pulled my hat down and hustled into the meeting. The gathering itself was pretty much a relief. I almost instantly understood that whatever I had, it was different from what these people were struggling with. I was a slut. They were suffering from a malady way beyond their control. They talked about liquidating their savings accounts on prostitutes, about getting off work at 5:00 P.M., flipping on the computer to watch porn the second they got home, and before they knew it, the sun was coming up. I was more of a porn from 11:00–11:08 P.M. type.

I honored these people in their struggle and silently thanked them for helping me put my own sex life into perspective. There was one quirk of that program that left me less than magnanimously free of judgment, though. In Sex Addicts Anonymous, or at least at that meeting, everyone who shared started off by announcing how long they had been "sober." This isn't done in AA, at least not as an official custom. Maybe the fact that sex addiction, like food addiction and some others, is one of those incredibly rough forms of habituation where fully abstaining isn't an option. The challenge in these programs is finding a way to stay "sober" while still engaging in a healthy version of the thing that brought you to your knees, no pun intended. So perhaps smaller milestones of abstinence needed to be announced to affirm to the group that it was possible. Their definition of sobriety was the length of time it had been since they'd last engaged in some form of destructive sexual behavior. So again, every person who spoke would introduce themselves, "Hi I'm So-and-So, I'm a sex addict, and I've been sober X amount of time" and then begin sharing their thoughts.

A guy showed up close to the end of the meeting, sat down right next to me, and raised his hand to speak. They called on him and he said, "I'm Richard, I'm a sex addict, and I've been sober for thirty minutes." *Thirty. Minutes.* He kept talking, but I stopped listening. I panicked, knowing what was coming next. The meeting was about to end and, like every twelve step group, it would end the same way: We would stand, hold hands, and say the Serenity Prayer. I was sweating looking at those thirty-minute-sober hands, the fingers still moist from fingering a sex worker in the car in the parking lot of the meeting. I knew that momentarily those cum-drenched hands would be outstretched to me to join in a communal prayer of support. I love my fellow man but not that much. The second the meeting ended I beelined for the door, tipping my cap to the brave and horny men and women in that meeting. Nothing but respect to them, but that was one hand I could not hold. I'd forgotten my Lysol.

Anyway, back to our friend's first AA meeting.

The meeting starts. Inexplicably, Gangbanger Steve is the secretary of the meeting and, you assume, the president of all of AA? Calling the meeting to order, Steve instructs the group to begin in a prayer. "Oh shit," you think, "here comes the religion." But it's the Serenity Prayer: *"God, grant me the serenity to accept the things I cannot change, the courage to change the things I can, and the wisdom to know the difference."*

"Okay," you think, "that wasn't so bad. I wouldn't say group prayer is firmly in my comfort zone, but as prayers go that one was pretty inoffensive."

Steve continues reading the standard preamble to any AA meeting, and then gets to a terrifying part: *"Not to embarrass you but rather to give us a chance to get to know you better. Are there any newcomers? We define newcomers as people in their first thirty days of sobriety. Please introduce yourself by your first name only."*

You freeze, panicked. This was *not* what you'd had in mind. You were just here to check things out, to sit quietly and observe. But now all eyes are on you. Housewife Barb smiles big and nods: "That's you!" Hipster Joe looks in your direction: "What's your name, bro?" Fuck. You aren't going to be able to escape this. Okay, what did they say, "by your first name only"? Okay, you take a deep breath and say your name: "Bob." You think the worst has passed. It has not. Everyone looks at you in confusion, clearly you have said something wrong. "Uh. It's Bob. I'm Bob."

Silence.

You fumble for a new approach. "Er . . . uh . . . my name is Robert?"

Hipster Joe's eyes go soft in compassion, "And what *are* you?"

What? You do not have a clue. "Uh, Jewish? Libertarian?"

Joe smiles again, "Are you an alcoholic?"

You don't fucking know what you are! How would you? You're in minute four of your first AA meeting ever. Terrified of engaging further you relent, "Oh! Oh yeah. Yes, alcoholic here. Big-time." Everyone smiles and begins to applaud. Hipster Joe shakes your hand, with a hearty Stepford-feeling "Welcome!"

If this was "not to embarrass you" they somehow chose the most embarrassing format possible. You exhale. The meeting moves on. Steve introduces the evening's speaker; it's Biker Nick. He begins, "Hi, I'm Nick and I'm an alcoholic." Everyone answers back, "Hi, Nick!" So *that's* how you introduce yourself here.

Nick tells his "story." It's a classic formula you'll hear at pretty much any AA meeting. Depending on where you are in the country, it will be called "sharing," "giving your pitch," or your "qualification." And it is certainly all three, sharing who you are, a sales pitch on why the listener should stay in AA and a proof testimony that you actually qualify to call yourself an alcoholic. It's a short rundown of your drinking, a description account of the consequences it wrought, and then a description of the journey into recovery and the bounty it bestowed on the speaker. In short:

I drank and it was the only thing that made me feel okay. Eventually it destroyed me, I entered AA, got better, and then . . . I went to college.

By the time I finished the steps, I found myself a fairly transformed person. It was not subtle or progressive; it was dramatic and profound. I was sixteen years old, I'd struggled with my mental health and general emotional stability all of my life, and I suddenly found myself in control of those faculties. I'd flunked school so many grades in a row I'd given up on making it all the way through. But now I wanted to, and set out to take my GED. Somehow I was able to focus when it came to preparing for the test, and I passed. I still remember my hands shaking when the letter came from the state of California, trembling as I broke the seal in the envelope, crushing the letter in my hand that said I passed, jumping up and down with my mother and grandmother in celebration. Breathing this massive sigh of relief as I suddenly realized my struggle with school was over.

Never again would I be required to learn anything I didn't volunteer for. This might seem like a strange milestone, but you'd have to have had my life, had to have sat with me through all those special-ed classes, all the IEP meetings, all the aptitude tests, all the learning-disability diagnostic sessions. You'd have had to hear clinician after clinician tell you that your brain was broken and, even though you knew you were smart, find it basically impossible to prove them wrong. When they'd forget to hire a professional ASL interpreter, you'd have to have been the person relaying this awful news to a deaf mother about her son, which is you. Meeting after meeting, diagnosis after diagnosis, I took on the identity of a kid without hope.

That GED was a way out. Maybe my brain was broken but not as badly as they thought.

The moment I opened that envelope, my mother relaxed her grip on my life. She, who had made it her sacred duty to find me help even if it destroyed me in the process, had a seemingly instant transformation once my high school career came to an end. I assume she saw the commitment to sobriety and the high school equivalency as as good as it was going to get and decided to let go. To stop worrying.

Strangely, though I got held back so much, I was out of school early; though I had been chronically irresponsible and wildly out of control behaviorally, I suddenly no longer had any rules to abide by, no curfew to respect, no one to answer to. I was sixteen and emancipated. I was six months sober and free.

My grandmother, despite being a lifelong atheist, always said she thanked God for AA for saving her grandson's life. She thanked a God she did not believe in. That's how powerful the medicine in AA is. As a graduation present she sent me to the 1995 AA International Convention in San Diego.

Every five years, AA holds its mega-event, a gathering of AA members from all over the world. It's like the AA Olympics, and it's the closest you'll ever come to an assembly of the entire body of AA at once. There is a flag ceremony, meetings in baseball stadiums, huge block parties. It's quite an affair. My grandmother bought a hotel room and a plane ticket for me and my brother David, who would be attending as my chaperone. The second we checked into the hotel, David, who was not a natural chaperone, told me he was headed to Tijuana to go get drunk and high and that he'd see me at the end of the weekend.

I struck out to explore this mini-city of AA, and by the time I sat in the main meeting Saturday night, surrounded by sixty thousand other alcoholics and addicts, cheering as the flags from over a hundred nations were placed onstage by sober people from those countries, I had been fully converted. I was vibrating with spiritual energy. I was one among many. A sober alcoholic who could do anything with my life. I, who had felt doomed, who had grown up poor and been institutionalized more times than I remembered, who had been told I was worthless and would amount to nothing, had found my way out. I'd found my home. I'd found my people. This was my Saint Paul on the road to Damascus. This was my Buddha under the lotus. I was a member of AA, and I would do what it took to stay sober, in AA, for the rest of my life, one day at a time. I realized in that stadium that I'd been given a gift, a reprieve, a chance I *had* to take and use it to help others like me. The possibilities of my life were now endless. I was all potential. All life. All coiled up energy, all kinetic possibility.

I was free. I was free. I was free.

Now I needed to figure out what I was going to do.

One of the main things people who get sober are terrified of is, once they stop drinking and getting high, they will have nothing to do. It seems a reasonable fear, but if you look at it again, even for a second, you'll realize there's something very wrong with the worldview that manifests such a fear. If you worry that if you stop drinking and getting high you will have *nothing to do,* it stands to figure that *all you do* is drink and get high. Drugs are meant to be a supplement to life, not a substitute for one. This is the fear not of a party animal but of a drug addict. But again, it makes sense that if all you do is one thing, quitting that one thing will make you feel like you'll never do anything again. But actually the inverse is true. If all you do is get high, and you successfully stop, you will come to find that there is space to do literally every other thing.

I set about doing just that.

For the first few years I was basically the mascot at Oakland AA meetings. I was barely a teenager, the shiny new thing, the kid who inspired fawning seventy-year-olds to tell me how lucky I was to have gotten sober so young. How lucky. So lucky. It always felt like "Hmm, *this* is lucky? This is what you call lucky?"

"Hey, it's Saturday night, what's everybody up to?"

"RECOVERY BOWLING!" they'd scream.

And I'd wince, but once I got past that, it actually was fun.

Those adults, the ones I'd hated, didn't just stop being awful; they became dear to me. They became my friends. They taught me how to live. They taught me to grow up. I remember in my last high school, right after I got sober, I was talking to a kid about a conversation I'd had with a friend, "Old Man Bill," a sweet man who loved me from the second I started attending meetings. Every time I'd come to a meeting, he'd shake my hand and tell me, "I'm so proud of you. I'm so glad you're still here, Moshey." He literally never pronounced my name correctly despite the fact that AA is famous for being the place where people introduce themselves by shouting their own names out loud. I loved him for that.

The kid I was talking to stopped me. "Old Man Bill? How old is this guy?"

I thought about it. "Hmm, like maybe seventy-five?"

The kid was baffled. "You have a seventy-five-year-old friend?"

I smiled, proud. "Yeah. I guess I do."

Time went by, and I stopped being the youngest person in the room. As I grew, so did my fervency for the message of AA. I became a cheerleader, an evangelist for the cause. My life became consumed by AA. Other than a six-month hiatus I spent as a drug dealer (more on that later), I went to a meeting every single day for years. I loved it. I was absolutely convinced that I'd found the truth and was absolutely on fire to tell other people about it.

I was unique in the fact that I'd gotten sober so young. I was exceptional in the fact that I knew how to articulate my journey so well. I started to get asked to speak at AA meetings and conventions around the country. It was here that I first experienced what it was like to perform for a crowd. To make them laugh. To make them feel things with my words. People say that the best speakers in the world can be found at Toastmasters, an organization that teaches socially awkward people how to give compelling speeches about sales trends, and in AA. Sure, you've got your TED Talkers and your Brené Browns, but those people are experts. AA contains the largest talent pool for amateur public speakers in the world. It was easy to talk about AA.

The topics are compelling: alcoholism, venereal disease, bank robbery, and then hope! And God even! AA is like church but with premarital sex.

AA does a *way* better job of providing a "cool" version of spirituality than these weird hipster evangelical preachers with their oversized glasses frames, A.P.C. drop-crotch pants, and T-shirts that read "Dabbin' for Christ." AA is a homegrown, uniquely American pseudo-religious form that only appeals to a specific demographic: the naughty. Where else will you see men covered in tattoos who admit to taking human life and talk about meditation? Where else do you find movie stars talking with union steelworkers about the best way to remain humble and vulnerable? Where else do you find such sexy, broken people talking with such earnestness about self-improvement? One year, *The Village Voice* pseudo-jokingly declared a particularly sceney AA meeting in SoHo to be the "best place to see and be seen in New York." The next week the meeting quadrupled in size, a bunch of sudden alcoholics made manifest by *The Village Voice*'s "Best of" edition. Those interlopers came and went, but AA's veneer can be so seductive that once in a while, alcoholics actually are created out of thin air. I've seen it. A non-alcoholic will come to an open meeting to "support a friend" and be so enamored of what they find there that they will ask to attend another meeting. And another. And another. Suddenly, quite out of nowhere this person "realizes" they are actually an alcoholic. Are they? Or is AA just providing a form of spirituality and life improvement that doesn't really exist anywhere else? Invariably this person stays sober long enough to be asked to speak at a meeting and then the burden falls on everyone else to pretend to take this person seriously as they describe their "rock bottom" as a single night out drinking with the gals that ended with giving an anonymous hand job at a dance club.

"Sounds like fun," says one real alcoholic, listening quietly.

"I gave one of those dead sober last week," says another.

But no one tells them to leave. There's an internal taboo in AA about ever outwardly doubting someone's claims of legitimacy when it comes to their alcoholism.

And for very good reason. No one knows who is or is not an alcoholic.

The person you declare non-alcoholic might die of an overdose the night you tell them to leave. I'm certainly lucky that no one told me I was too young as a teenager getting sober. I might have *been* too young, but I was in AA long enough to watch people younger than me die upon relapse. Better to leave the doors wide open and welcome those who may not truly "belong" in AA than to make that door hard to walk through and shut out those who do. So people, in general, try to keep their mouths shut. But that doesn't mean no one rolls their eyes when hearing someone describe the consequences of their drinking by describing the look of disappointment they saw in their pet horse's eyes.

I wasn't like this. I was a fucking absolute mess of a kid. I know that for sure.

But I was still a kid.

Around fifteen years sober, at thirty years of age, as fundamentalist a believer in AA dogma as a person could be, I started to feel something I never thought would be possible: doubt.

I'd worked the steps into the core of my intellectual being. I was a firebrand AA speaker—an absolute and total believer. I made a pretty compelling case for AA as a funny guy with little orthodoxy in my general beliefs but plenty of it in my AA message. In other words, I was cool and open-minded about everything but AA. When it came to the program, my message was unique, but it was unambiguous: AA worked and it worked absolutely. It worked if you worked it. Always. I helped a lot of people with this version of AA. But I also found myself exasperated by the people who wouldn't work it or wouldn't work it right. Why wouldn't they save themselves? And didn't they know that by speaking about the wishy-washiness of their own program they were diluting the AA message? Didn't they know they were killing people?

Fundamentalism takes a toll on you and on the people around you. Knowing everything means that people who act or believe in another way are not different, but wrong. In some ways I can't be blamed for the fundamentalist I became. And compared to some factions in AA, I was certainly no traditionalist. AA had been in a "back to basics" creep since the 1980s. This kind of thing happens with a lot of old-fashioned movements when they begin to encounter modernism.

In the '80s, the "inner child" era of psychology became prevalent. People in AA were, for the first time, confronting their traumas and childhood wounds through means other than the steps. At first this was welcomed, as AA has no official opinion on getting outside help or supplemental assistance with issues not pertaining to drinking. In fact, AA has no official opinion on anything. But when people started bringing stuffed animals to meetings, cuddling with them to nurture their inner children, when people started to gender-neutralize the twelve steps by substituting "God as we understood Him" with "God as we understood God," when people started bringing the lessons they'd learned from the therapeutic couch into the halls of AA, the stalwarts in AA began to rebel.

This rebellion was the dominant strain of AA when I got sober: an angry AA fighting against the phantom villain of the watering-down of a formerly pure and perfect program. The past-perfect principle is not unique to AA, but in a younger spiritual path *like* AA, it is easier to see its effects. If you wanted to make people listen in AA, declaring it perfect in its principles but in danger of being destroyed was a shortcut for attention. Shouting at a drug addict for talking about drugs too much in an AA meeting was commonplace.[*]

---

[*] In AA there is perhaps no area of cognitive dissonance more pronounced than "old-fashioned AA's" relationship with drugs and drug addiction. Narcotics Anonymous has a much more coherent understanding of the relationship between alcoholism and addiction, which is that there is no "relationship" because they are one phenomenon. In AA, people bend over backward to convince themselves there is something unique or peculiar about alcoholism versus drug addic-

None of this sentiment has anything like the force of law behind it, by the way. There is no mechanism of control in AA other than pressure. No one is in charge. You can, quite literally, stand up at any AA meeting in the world and scream *"Fuck you and fuck AA! I've been drinking in the bathroom, and I'm here to fuck someone right now!"* and the *worst* that could happen to you is that you'll be asked to leave that meeting, that night. Come back the next week and you'll be welcomed.

Anyway, as a result of this desperate attempt to "save" AA, countless offshoots were created in an arms race to be the purest strain, the dankest version of AA.

The big-daddy of offshoot AA was the Pacific Group, which boasted of hosting the largest meeting in the world. It's still around. Every week, twelve hundred alcoholics gather in Los Angeles and adhere to an oddly rigid behavioral code that you'll find yourself wondering how it applies to not drinking. Pacific Group members are not to let their facial hair grow, not to swear, not to discuss drugs. They must wear a tie every time they speak, ladies must wear dresses (or, adjusting to progressive feminism, a sharp pantsuit). The Pacific Group became so influential that it spawned a number of clones throughout the country including the Atlantic Group in New York. Many of these clones, like a game of telephone, slightly altered the strictures imposed on their members, and over time some became disturbingly extreme.

There were the Pod People, a particularly amusing subgroup in AA, so nicknamed due to their eerie similarity to the villains in *Invasion of the Body Snatchers*. Their leader, a shoe shiner in San Francisco, figured out an incredibly specific system of working all twelve steps in about ten minutes, on a single sheet of paper. They all, for fear of being kicked out of the group, did the steps like this, twice daily, after which they spent twenty minutes in Transcendental

---

tion. None of it adheres to much logic. Don't get me wrong, most people in AA don't care at all, but there's always some guy grumbling about how you shouldn't talk about drugs in an AA meeting because it's an "outside issue." Tell that same person you're sober five years but smoked meth last night, and he'll tell you you're no longer sober.

Meditation. Should you have desired, say, Zen meditation instead, you would have been booted and told, "We can't help *you*."

They all shared an oddly similar inflection, a manic, mile-a-minute cadence with the words *fuckin'* and *used to want to fucking kill myself* sprinkled in literally every sentence. It was strange the fixation on suicide they had. It was almost as if working the twelve steps in this abbreviated way gave them an abbreviated reprieve. It gave them ten minutes' worth of recovery. To this day, with a blindfold on, I could still tell you if I'm listening to a pod person speaking.

There was the Midtown Group in Washington D.C., a bizarre offshoot of the Pacific Group where mostly suburban white people in Abercrombie outfits would encourage their mostly young members to not only *stop* dating people from outside the group, but *to begin* dating people within it. It devolved into a weird sex and sobriety group for teens before *Newsweek* did an exposé on the group and they scattered.

As different as all of these groups (and countless more) were from one another, they all shared a less "official" and more heinous rule, which was to forbid or strongly discourage the use of any psychiatric drugs, which some members had decided were a violation of sobriety. Just what everyone with actual mental illness wants: a guy who owns a Smoothie King franchise in a strip mall prescribing a regimen of AA basics to cope with acute schizophrenia. This lay psychiatry has obvious consequences, and more than one person in AA has killed themselves due to negligent sponsorship.

I've named just a few, but any city will have, if you look hard enough, an AA group of kooks who have made up, from seemingly out of nowhere, a set of inane and absurd strictures you must adhere to in order to get some of that good, pure "old-time AA." Of course, there is another word for these types of things: cults. If you're reading this from within one of these groups and reject my characterization, let me also point out that cults never feel like cults when you're in them. The Manson girls felt like Charlie had some unadulterated hold on the truth, too. AA is close enough to being a cult itself that if you're in a spin-off that's *more* culty, get out and call your mom. She misses you.

These kinds of groups thrive because AA has a power problem and an oversight problem. Undue deference is given to people with "time," that is, people who have stayed sober for sustained periods. An unearned moral authority is bestowed upon members based solely on how long they have stayed sober. "Old-timers" are treated as gurus simply by virtue of their sober date, not by virtue of their virtue. And most AA old-timers are delightful. Many are very wise, a lifetime of applying principles resulting in a keen enlightenment. Some are even guru-like. But many are not. Some are horrific assholes. Some are miserable. A few are even psychologically sadistic manipulators. This is, of course, true of any group of people. Some will be sweet; some will be sick. The difference in AA is, since there is no real central power structure, the power is bestowed upon people with time. They are propped up by a group of vulnerable people looking for answers. What compounds this problem is the lack of even marginal oversight by literally anyone in AA. There is no one watching. No one tracking predators. No one to hear a whistle blow. There is just a reliance on the goodwill of the body politic of AA and that "God's will" shall be done. Abusers and thought-manipulators have been allowed to operate with impunity from mini-cults to huge groups. They can't be stopped, because there is no one to stop them.

I wish I could say I was too smart to fall for these tactics, but I think it was more luck of the draw. None of this kind of militant AA ever gelled in Oakland, and the closest to a culty subgroup I ever found myself in was Young People's AA, a loosely affiliated group of meetings and conferences where people who got sober young could find one another, stay sober together, and give one another hand jobs and amateur piercings.

Young People's AA was a kind of roving family, a sort of recovery Dead tour where the young members of AA from each respective city would travel from place to place, gathering at large annual conferences. We would stay up all night, drinking coffee and energy drinks,* dancing, attending meetings, making out with each other, figuring out how to grow up. These conferences were a social bright spot for a demographic prone to feeling isolated or alienated from their peers for making the choice to be sober. Back at home, most young people got fucked up and most sober people were old. But at these conferences? It was a taste of a utopia that could never exist in daily reality: thousands of young people who were cool, fun, funny, fuckable. A scene. A subculture. Or maybe, depending on how you looked at it, a cult of our very own.

Having gotten sober so young and stayed sober so long, I took on the self-appointed job of keeping Young People's AA in Oakland from careening off the rails into rigidity or chaos. I saw it as my duty as a "Young Old-timer" to stave off the creeping militarism of these spin-off groups while at the same time making sure Young People's AA, particularly in Oakland, remained a place where people took recovery seriously. We would have fun. But we would stay sober, goddamn it.

We were a mighty dysfunctional family, keen on incest, and constantly losing cousins. Being in AA means watching friends die, over and over and over. It means watching people come to AA destitute and desperate, watching them recover, watching them get their lives back, and then watching them relapse and fall into the same destructive patterns that brought them to AA in the first place. It means watching people who had an easy time getting sober decide to drink and then, realizing they've made a grave error, become unable to get sober again. Sober living is heartbreaking living. It is,

---

* It *was* coffee when I first got sober but then Red Bull and Monster Energy drinks pushed the "quintuple espresso" experience out, and suddenly kids were drinking seventy-three energy drinks over the course of a weekend and pushing the definition of sobriety to its breaking point. Are you truly sober if you have a seizure due to overconsumption of Monster Hydro Super Sport Killer Kiwi? The funniest thing about this was that ten years after the energy drink was introduced to sober culture, people who had been twenty were now thirty and had been drinking daily twelve-packs of supercharged soda for a decade. There is nothing like a sober energy drink belly where a beer belly could have been.

quite literally, life or death. And in Young People's AA, these stakes were in the hands of teenagers. There's a beauty to it, no question, but there's a terror to it, too. And so, even as I got older, I stayed around the Young People's meetings, determined to help the people like me find a new way of life, determined to be a stabilizing force, determined to stay as long as I could.

I was the sheriff in that town, and my methods were loved by many and resented by plenty. If a male AA member was fucking someone who was newly sober and vulnerable, I would scare up a goon squad and confront them with a hearty "We don't *do* things like that around here." Sure, I had a cool haircut and liked techno but in practice, I was as much of a conservative AA cop as the people whose unearned power I lamented above.

This all came at a cost. I alienated people who felt judged by me. *Whatever,* I thought, *heavy lies the crown.*

Then, slowly, exactly like Prince Harry, I started to realize that I didn't know if I believed in the monarchy.

It wasn't sudden. It was a process. And, ironically, my departure came as a result of my recovery journey. As I started to get older, the stridency with which I had carried myself was becoming less and less meaningful to me. And more painful. I began to realize that my judgment was holding me back from connecting to people I loved. My best friend started dating someone nine months sober, a clear violation of Sheriff Moshe's rules of conduct, which stipulated romantic relations were allowed only with members who had a year or more sober. When I found out my best friend had been in a relationship for months and hadn't told me, I didn't get it.

"Why didn't you tell me?"

He looked at me confused. "Because I was afraid of what you would think."

This was a tough pill for me to swallow. Somehow, in my quest to help everyone, I had pushed the people I loved so far away they couldn't even tell me they'd found love. This was a small thing, but it reverberated in a million ways. Little things. Small judgments. Someone would not pay at an "on your honor" parking lot and I'd call them out, embarrassing them in front of a group, wagging a spiritual finger. I'd pontificate from the podium, fire and brimstone, and then wonder why some people seemed turned off by me.

I went to a new sponsor, John, a more Eastern religion and Jungian psychology type of old-timer, and asked if he could help me eschew my judgment of others, if he could help me become a softer man. He asked me a simple question: "What would it look like if you never commented on anyone else's behavior, ever?" I'm not exaggerating when I say the thought sent an actual chill down my spine. I never forgot that chill. *That's* how deeply I was tied into telling other people how to act.

This is not to say no one ever needs to be called out for bad behavior; they absolutely do. But a good rule of thumb I learned in AA was, when considering if you should, to ask yourself these questions:

1. Does it need to be said?
2. Does it need to be said right now?
3. Does it need to be said by me?

It almost never needed to be said by me. This is the big problem with being a judgmental prick. After a while, whatever you are saying, righteous or not, can be dismissed by the person you are saying it to as a manifestation of a pattern of you not minding your own business.

So I set out on a mission to rid myself of commenting on other people's behavior, and the journey was miraculous. At first I found it agonizing torture. I would see an infraction at an AA meeting and look around in a panic thinking, "I need to say something! If I don't, every teen in AA will drink within a fortnight!" I'd catch eyes with my sponsor, who would shake his head no. I'd think, "Fine, then whatever comes of this is on John's hands. I hope he can cleanse his fingers of the blood of Oakland's youth." I'd bite my tongue, hands shaking, teeth clenched.

Months went by.

Now I'd see an infraction, know it was wrong, judge it in my head, but think, "Phew, they are FUCKING up. But I won't say anything. Let them die, it is not my place to stop it." It was getting easier to watch the obvious sins of my peers, the flagrant moral code violations, and not say anything.

More months went by.

Now something unexpected occurred. Not only was I easily able to hold my tongue, but I also found my tongue no longer needed holding. I had stopped caring what other people were doing. When something happened that I would not have approved of in the past, I either didn't care or didn't notice. More than that, I didn't even think it was wrong any longer. I'd moved from "Isn't that awful?!" to "Isn't that interesting?" Surprising no one but myself, I found it a much easier place to be.

But there was another, even more unexpected place I found myself in, having worked through this know-it-all-ism. The softness I found on the other side of it became the small thread I pulled in the holistic worldview I'd been clinging to. If the sky didn't fall when someone decided to fuck that newly sober girl, or text through the meeting,* or lie about this or that, then maybe none of the absolute truths I found in AA were as absolute as I'd thought.

And that was it. That is the problem with fundamentalism: Either all of it is absolutely true, or it becomes possible that none of it is. Sometimes I think if I'd been able to join AA with more of a "wear it like a loose garment" relationship, I'd have been able to stay. Most people aren't burdened by this absolutism. Most people approach systems of belief like a buffet where you take what you want and leave the rest. But, as I used to scream, heavy with judgment, from behind the podium in AA: The part you leave might have been the part that would have saved your life.

So I took it all. Until I couldn't take it anymore.

---

* Speaking of texting through meetings, one of the best things I ever saw in a meeting was a former member of the Sex Pistols speaking at a meeting and going apoplectic when talking about people texting at meetings. He was screaming "This is AA, damn it! You don't text through the goddamn meeting!" It was the most un-punk-rock thing I have ever seen or heard in my life. Fuck it, keep texting, Anarchy in the AA!

. . .

For years after that, I felt my connection to AA slipping away from me. It was imperceptible at first, and for a long time I couldn't or wouldn't admit to myself that what was happening was a slow-building crisis of faith. Ironically it was faith itself that led to my breaking point. Specifically, it was the Lord's Prayer.

One thing I forgot to mention in my description of the typical AA meeting, perhaps in an effort to be charitable, is that yes, they begin meetings with the Serenity Prayer, but in many meetings, they end with the Lord's Prayer. You know, the Lord? Jesus Christ? When I first entered AA, this prayer was jarring. As a Jew, there was no way I was going to be saying that. Reciting the Lord's Prayer is less Jewish than eating pork belly while playing polo on the Sabbath. But after a while of being sober, out of my desire to fit in and adhere to AA's cultural norms, out of the social pressure not to "make myself different from my fellows," I relented and made my ancestors roll over in their dusty graves.

For years I chanted this prayer, but once I pulled that thread I mentioned above, I began to question its appropriateness again. I lived in Oakland, where there were Muslims and Jews and atheists and Buddhists and Wiccans getting sober. Never would we end our meetings with a Wiccan invocation to the trees. Never would we scream "There is no God but Allah, and Muhammad is his prophet!" at the close of a meeting. It began to drive me a little crazy, what an obvious barrier to people of other faiths this prayer was and how willfully ignorant of that conflict people in AA seemed intent on staying.

When I brought it up, particularly outside of the Bay Area, I'd generally receive an eye roll and an admonition that we say that prayer because "that's the way we've always done it." This infuriated me. Isn't changing to make sure we help the most people the way we'd always done it, too? Isn't that the actual reason AA split from the Oxford group and Christianity in the first place, a desire to break down barriers imposed by affiliation to religious groups?

It became my pet issue, my cause. I'd put *so* much of my time and energy into AA that I *had* to be able to effect some change. Right? No. No one was interested.

I tried making the issue heard at a national level by jumping through the arcana of AA's policymaking process, a system so opaque and boring you should be thanking the guy who wrote the Lord's Prayer I'm not going to describe it. It failed to even make it out of the Oakland meeting to be heard at a regional level.

So I wrote an impassioned letter to the AA publication *The Grapevine,* trying to get a dialogue started. It was never published. Now, look, I've been a writer for long enough to know that not everything you write gets published. Nor should it. But this is the AA *Grapevine,* not *The New Yorker.* It's not exactly a sexy publication filled to the brim with submissions. This is a publication where literally every issue has a multipage spread of full-color photos of empty rooms where meetings are sometimes held. They have the space. I knew why they didn't publish me. They either disagreed or didn't want to enter the fray. Okay. I gave up. The message coming back to me was clear, and I could accept defeat.

Then I made the mistake of going to AA's world convention again. I headed to San Antonio, hoping that maybe I could relive that glory moment in San Diego fifteen years earlier. Maybe that would jumpstart my reconnection to this thing that had meant so much to me for so long but was increasingly feeling like a stranger to me.

I sat in the main meeting at the Alamodome Sunday morning, and at the end of the meeting, the chairperson announced that we'd rise and say the Lord's Prayer. I mean, look, it was in Texas, I shouldn't have been surprised, but the previous world convention had been the first to abstain from the Lord's Prayer altogether and end every meeting with the Serenity Prayer (surprise, it was in Canada).

The fact that they were saying it again meant that either a) they were appeasing Texans (always a good idea considering open-carry laws); or b) that people had complained after the last conference and that "Old-time Religion AA" had won again. It was a regressive move and one that disappointed me. But it didn't crush my spirit. I would have been okay. It was what happened next that was a crushing blow.

The cadence of the Lord's Prayer, which I know better than I should as a Jew, is a big part of it. The Catholic version does this weird rushing thing toward the end. The Protestant version, aka the Oxford Group version, aka the AA version, has these little pauses built into it. You've probably heard it:

Our Father (pause), who art in heaven (pause), hallowed be thy name (pause). Thy kingdom come (pause), Thy will be done (pause), on Earth (pause) as it is in heaven (pause).

Right at the "heaven" pause, in a stadium full of sixty thousand people, with a Jew in the nosebleeds pressing his lips closed in a silent and impotent protest, someone else was lodging a protest of their own. Right in that pause, a voice erupted, clear as crystal to everyone in that stadium, a scream, "THANK YOU, JESUS!"

Look, I have no issues with Jesus. I really hope it doesn't seem like I do. This isn't about Christianity, of course, but about its place at the AA table. That scream, that "wrong place, wrong time" prayer to the Christian God, slammed down on me like a guillotine. I'm sure that that lady was just overcome with emotion. She was probably having a moment like I had in San Diego at the same conference, fifteen years earlier. She was having her own conversion moment.

Most likely her sponsor elbowed her to shut up, and they laugh about it to this day: the time when she was so overcome at an AA meeting, she yelled to the Lord at the top of her lungs like she was at Joel Osteen's house of embezzlement.

For me, up in the stands, I was having a different experience. I felt something break. I looked around and for the first time since I'd gotten sober, the first time since I'd found this new way of life, I felt like I didn't belong.

As I melted down, someone from the podium, I'm not kidding, started to sing "Amazing Grace."

I was in Texas, in a convention hall where we were praying the Lord's Prayer, thanking Jesus, and singing "Amazing Grace." This was church.

I didn't belong here.

That wasn't the last meeting I went to. Not by a long shot. I kept attending for a couple of years after that. But it was the last meeting I was able to convince myself that there was nothing frayed about my connection to AA. Now I could say it out loud. Something was wrong.

It felt a lot like what I imagine a spouse feels, fifteen years into a relationship, waking up one morning to realize they don't have the same feelings for their partner they once did. Or perhaps a more accurate comparison is, it felt how I imagine a church elder feels when they realize they are simply not a true believer anymore. Where do they go? What do they do? Do they pretend to believe to protect their soul and their way of life? Or do they acknowledge what is happening? Do they face their fear of the unknown? Do they find a way to walk alone? In AA, an often-heard admonition is "Don't leave before the miracle happens," but the miracle had happened for me fifteen years ago. Am I supposed to wait for it to re-happen?

AA tells you what to do when you feel these things. Call someone. Go to a meeting. Read two pages from the Big Book. Jerk off until the edge of cumming and then back off slightly. Strike that last one, not sure what that was doing in my notes for this book.

But the feeling that you've simply moved past AA benefiting you is as close to a total taboo as you can get. You'd be more well received at a meeting telling everyone you're planning to take LSD *that night* than to intimate you've reached a point where you need to move on from AA. You'll often be told such thoughts are the product of a diseased mind. But I'd been in AA too long to feel terribly frightened by that stuff. I used to be the one telling people that. The fact was, I would attend meetings and feel more anxious afterward than I did when I went in. I'd read through the AA book with people I sponsored and realize I was starting not to believe the things I was telling them.

More than anything I stopped knowing for certain that I was an alcoholic.

AA has this idea of the immutable state of the alcoholic. It is a permanent state; it exists like a fly in amber. Or, as cute sassy ladies in Florida AA meetings say, "You're a pickle, hun!" Because, once you're a pickle you'll never be a cucumber again. This immutability is vital to the AA understanding of alcoholism, because it gives a very clear picture of what to do: Never drink again. But it was this immutability I stopped feeling like I could believe in.

After Texas, but unrelatedly, I had a number of dear friends start drinking and getting high again. These were not tertiary people; these were my core sobriety friends. People I had been sober with for years, for decades. These were my fellow "AA Young People" who I'd trudged with, lived with, struggled with, cried with. These were people who I'd *known* to be alcoholics just like me. They were my brothers and sisters in arms. They were just like me. And they decided they were no longer alcoholic and drank again.

The results were decidedly mixed.

Some were fine and remain fine to this day. Some were bad off and should never have tried drinking again. And some, mystifyingly, just kinda reverted back to being hard-partying, not particularly out of control but not particularly temperate types. In other words, they were kinda like regular young people. Except now they weren't so young.

What I came to realize is that AA doesn't make space for these types, because it can't. In AA they say bluntly, "Once an alcoholic, always an alcoholic." In AA, if someone relapses and they are fine, they are excused as never having been "real alcoholics." If they relapse and have bad consequences, they are held up as proof of the AA conception of alcoholism. If they relapse and are fine but years later lose control, it's pointed out that it's never safe to drink again.

AA suffers from the same problems that plague a lot of systems, which is the inability to contend with the power of a world that's more chaos than it is order. AA has binary rules about drinking and sobriety and the state of alcoholism and addiction, because nonbinary rules would simply not work. There is a message in "Once an alcoholic, always an alcoholic." There is no message in "Once an alcoholic, it's possible, even likely, that you will have to be vigilant about substance use in the future, but hey you never know! You might be fine but also there's a large possibility you'll be dead in a year after you start drinking again, but people are different so who knows?"

How's that for a pickle?

AA is an attempt to save the most people the most quickly and for that, the message of "never again" is the most effective. I understand why. I just don't know what I believe about myself anymore. I got sober at fifteen. Fifteen years old. What else about me was immutable from the time I was fifteen? My impeccable sense of style and little else. This whole book is a record of how changed I have become. How flexible life has asked me to be. Everything changes. Getting sober so young, I would be willfully non-introspective if I never entertained the idea that yes, in fact, my problem drinking was a phase. I was a child.

But then there's my habituation in sobriety, my sexual compulsivity, the bag of thirty kinds of vape juice I used to carry around. I quit smoking, then went to vaping, then nicotine gum, then nicotine toothpicks, then nicotine pouches. Clearly I don't have zero addict in me.

There aren't easy answers, especially with residual thought conditioning still swimming around in my head. It's not so much that I no longer think I am an alcoholic; it's that I no longer think I have a clue what the term means once a person stops drinking. Within AA, when you are sober for a long time, the term *alcoholic* becomes like a reverse panacea. Since you are no longer drinking, it's not that which makes you still an alcoholic: It's your thinking, your alcoholic way of being. It's a spiritual state. One that hangs on an edge, buffered from peril by spiritual works and fellowship. It's the way you think. It's the way you interact with the world. It's you. It's everything. Alcoholics are artistic, we are sensitive, we are brittle, we are wild, we are intelligent, we are unique, we are the only people who can save one another. A guy in a meeting might describe throwing a bottle at someone in a road rage incident, saying, "I'm still such an alcoholic." Sir, is it possible that that was less about alcoholism and more about you being an asshole?

AA offers no worldview where it's healthy to say, "I used to do AA but don't need it anymore." A person who stops going is a dry drunk, guaranteed misery and always at risk of relapse and, of course, as it says in the Big Book, "And with us, to drink is to die."

In other words, be afraid. Stay with us forever or you will die. Fear was not a healthy enough motivator for me to stay anywhere anymore.

And so, after much agony, much soul searching, after so many years in AA where I would grit my teeth waiting to fall back in love with it, I stopped going.

It's been many years since my last meeting. I miss it. Well, less that than I miss how it used to make me feel. Life in AA was exciting. I was on a mission, and every day was another chance to save a fellow alcoholic. Life's primary purpose was clear. As the circumstances of my life ebbed and flowed, as my career waxed and waned, I could always say, "This is nothing. This *means* nothing. My real mission in life is to save people." Five times a week I would gather with other like-minded people and we would share in fellowship about this noble mission we were embarked upon. When I stopped going to AA, nothing slid in to take its place. There was an empty spot where all that work had been. Some days I fill it with the beauty and fullness of my life, and some days I fill it with hours of PlayStation. I'm neither miserable nor ecstatic most days. I'm just some guy. Not an alcoholic guy, not a sober guy, not a dry drunk, not a crazy guy. Just a person passing through time.

This last December 25, I celebrated twenty-nine years of sobriety. I'm still sober. Maybe from force of habit. Maybe the way hair keeps growing on a corpse. Maybe from fear of consequence. Maybe because my life is good, and I can't quite see how drinking could make it better. Maybe because I have a family now and every risk assessment has gotten more precarious.

One thing is clear to me. AA saved my life. It gave me some of the best, most exciting times in that life. I love AA and will always be grateful that it was there at the exact moment I needed it. It is deep, powerful medicine, and I still believe it can really work. If you are struggling to stop drinking, AA can be a great place to find help. But I don't believe it's the only way. Even though I used to *know* that it was.

The principles I learned in AA are still the main tools I use to navigate the world:

Be honest. Pause when agitated. Don't allow myself the luxury of justifiable anger. When I'm in conflict with someone, assess what I did wrong without even considering how wrong the other person might have been. Apologize when I hurt someone. Never admit when I cheat on my wife.

Realize my place in the world. Recognize that there are things greater than me. Help people wherever I can. Don't keep secrets. Avoid the deliberate manufacture of misery. Don't take myself too seriously.

Live one day at a time.

Even all these years later.

2 | *Raves, or Notes from the Underground*

In 1989, New York techno legend Frankie Bones was invited to perform at one of the massive British "hangar raves." He left that party of twenty-five thousand dancing revelers deeply affected and changed. Electronic music, something that had started in the United States, had gone overseas and become a new thing, something massive, something culturally subversive. It had become a rave.

Within a few months of his return, Bones put on what is now credited as the first true American rave: the Storm Rave. With this party, a music genre and cultural scene that had been invented in the Black neighborhoods of the American Midwest and then appropriated by Europe, had alchemized into something else entirely, which was re-appropriated into the American cultural milieu. Most early American ravers had no idea that what they were participating in was a homegrown phenomenon. They assumed that it was a benevolent gift from Europe, like horses, muskets, and venereal disease.

The beginnings of electronic music were, much like every popular form of music in the last hundred years, very Black. Detroit. Chicago. Kids from the poorest parts of town were pulling apart the meaning of what synthesizers were supposed to be used for and creating something new. Something from nothing. Or, rather, from the ashes of something else.

In the mid- to late 1970s, disco was king. It had congealed the pre-AIDS sexual permissiveness and the vestiges of the love-everybody hippie movement into a dance club culture where the only important thing was feeling good and dancing better.

With the full-frontal assault of the disco hit machine taking over, music tastemakers rebelled. Then came the backlash. No doubt fueled by antagonism toward the Black and gay subtext within disco music, "true rockers" began to thumb their meth-addled noses at the simplicity of message in disco.

The death blow was dealt on July 12, 1979. The Chicago White Sox, faced with declining ticket sales due to the fact that they were losing games and the fact that baseball is a crushingly boring sport, reached out to notorious anti-disco crusader and shock jock morning DJ Steve Dahl to cook up a promotional stunt to bolster ticket sales.

The premise was to bring a disco record to the doubleheader that night and receive admission for a mere ninety-eight cents. Between games one and two of the doubleheader, Steve took to the field and wheeled out the pile of records (which, by the way, contained plenty of non-disco records . . . many were just records made by Black artists. Close enough! Stay classy, Chicago!) and literally detonated a bomb on the field, destroying the records while the crowd of fifty thousand anti-disco White Sox fans rushed the field with their battle cry falling from their lips: "Disco sucks! Disco sucks!"

The ball field was completely fucked due to the fact that they had DETONATED A FUCKING BOMB on it, and the White Sox were forced to forfeit the second game of the doubleheader. Disco music had lost, too. Steve Dahl and his rockers had broken America's disco fever.

Disco was soon thought of as a minor and laughable blip in music history. Silly, meaningless, and very gay. But on the South Side of Chicago, the shards of those exploded disco records were being slowly pieced back together into a brand-new, homegrown music form. Enter: house music.

It would be hard to overstate how "underground" a music form this was. No one cared. No one was listening. The artists in the early years of house music were children, sitting in their basements, looping bass lines from classic disco tracks and adding booming drum kicks from a Roland TR-808 drum machine.

The music was future primitive. It was beyond simplistic. This was not music made for the mind; it was music for the body. As Eddie Amador said in his famous track "House Music": "Not everybody understands house music. It's a spiritual thing. A body thing. A soul thing."

And as Joe Raver said: "Omfugking god I'm so high this music is melting my braaaaaaain."

Something happened in those basements that was really inexplicable. The sound produced by those first kids in south Chicago, artists like Chip-E, Jesse Saunders, Frankie Knuckles, Joe Smooth, and Marshall Jefferson (along with the singers, sometimes known as "divas," who would shape house's sound—women like Martha Walsh, CeCe Peniston, Robin S., Crystal Waters, Barbara Tucker, and many more), tickled some deep part of people's brains and turned them the fuck on.

In Detroit soon thereafter, a similar group of young Black teenagers, in particular the infamous Belleville Three—Derrick May, Juan Atkins, and Kevin Saunderson—influenced more by Kraftwerk than Donna Summer, were taking things a step further and stripping away the warm and lush disco sediment and just keeping the machines.

This was robot music. This was techno.

With the one-two punch of techno and house, a new American music form was born. Electronic dance music.*

The problem was, almost no one in America was listening. It wasn't until the music made its way to Europe that its very obscurity would become its defining principle and codify it as the new music of the underground. Europe also provided one essential element in

---

* House and techno provided the first two dishes in what would eventually become a buffet of EDM. From there came acid, ambient, breakbeat, bass, drum and bass, downtempo, dubstep, electro, garage, glitch, grime, hardstyle, hardcore, happy hardcore, juke, trance, trap, and on and on forever (I'm trying to include every subgenre I can think of to ward off attacks by unseen EDM nerds).

the metamorphosis of "new genre of music" to "a scene," the epidural of the birth of the rave scene: MDMA, or ecstasy.

Once the music hit England, they took to it like it was a subcontinent prime for colonization. Soon after that, Frankie Knuckles, Marshall Jefferson, and some other early producers from Chicago got an offer to play their music in the north of England. To play their fucking bedroom tunes. Imagine their confusion when their tiny record label, Trax, which was essentially some sketchy local dude mashing new music onto used vinyl, called and was like, "Uh, we have an offer for you to play . . . England?"

Off they flew (some of them for the first time in their lives) and arrived in Manchester to find a sold-out show of white Europeans screaming in recognition of the tunes. The juxtaposition between their status at home and their reception in England blew their minds. It was like a dude clanging a fork on his pot in a hobo encampment and then finding out that in Nepal the Sherpas were all about "the fork master."

Somehow this strange cocktail of American electronic music and designer drugs tapped into the whole of the unease of England's youth. Rife with the anti-establishment sentiment of the punk scene and sick to death of the repressive regime of the Thatcher administration, England's cool kids were thirsty for something that could unite them, something less angry than punk, something filled with love. And with that, house music and ecstasy sparked a new cultural epoch. Fuck the system but love your brother. The rave baby was crowning. And with one synthetic push, it was alive.

It spread through England powerfully and quickly. Raves were held illegally in abandoned warehouses and in empty fields in the English countryside. Anywhere where the cops weren't looking. In England these now-legendary "parties in a field" quickly got noticed by authorities. All round the M25 highway that surrounds London, thousands of MDMA enthusiasts would pick a dairy farm at random (I just assume all fields in England are on dairy farms and I'm not looking it up; I'm tired of looking things up), hoist up speaker stacks, and run interference on whichever *Downton Abbey*–looking man in rubber galoshes and foxhunting garb came to complain. England being a smallish place, the cops figured out what they were doing and in short order moral panic set in. Members of Parliament were freaking the fuck out about raves and the commensurate decimation of Stilton cheese production that was sure to follow. They hastily rushed through a bizarre law called the Criminal Justice Act that, to this day, outlaws any unpermitted gathering of twenty or more people listening to music whose "sounds [are] wholly or predominantly characterized by the emission of a succession of repetitive beats." They outlawed raving, and an already-underground scene dove deeper beneath the surface. The parties didn't stop, of course. They spread. That's when Frankie Bones took that chance trip to Europe and, like a sailor taking shore leave in a red-light district, he brought something home and infected people.

After the Storm Rave in New York, the scene swept from New York back into Chicago and Detroit, then marched across the United States just in time to meet me in San Francisco in 1995.

My first party. My first rave. I had seen a special on 20/20 a few years before I attended. Some vaguely alarmist journalistic fluff piece about the new, scary ecstasy parties taking place in warehouses. I was intrigued, but I was also eleven. Then when I was twelve and I got into drugs myself, I was far too interested in pretending to be a gangster to involve myself in anything as soft as a techno party.

Then I got sober. And went to those AA dances. Then I started trying to dance. For a fifteen-year-old white fake gangsta, there are few positions more compromising than dancing. The real and palpable terror of engaging in dance and exposing your goofball, *White Men Can't Jump* two left feet was a risk not worth taking. Don't get me wrong. I had danced before that, but in a single, extremely safe style. I called it the Booty Grab Slow Dance.

It was a technique that I learned in middle school. It was the way anyone could dance and look almost cool at the same time.

It worked like this: You'd dance with a girl, as close as you could get, and stomp around in a circle. Her arms on your shoulders, your arms on the small of her back. Bend the knees. Lower. Lower. Get low, motherfucker! As you sunk into the circular groove of this foolishness, your hands would slowly, painfully slowly, creep down and down until you were just about to reach out and grab her butt. Just seconds, milliseconds really, before you took that deep, trembling breath and fully committed to this low-grade sexual assault, her hands would dart, quick as a jaguar, down to yours, pull them back up to the safe zone, and the dance would start anew.

Foiled again.

Every time I tried this, I'd look across the room and see a cool Black kid, decked out in Guess overalls with one strap hanging down, or a hot pair of Z Cavariccis and a rayon paisley print shirt; his hand firmly attached to the ass of his partner, a willing participant in the booty dance. I'd die with middle-school jealousy.

In AA I learned to respect women and to not grab their asses without permission, so that left me with very few dance options but the "butt clench." Instead of clutching others' butts, I just clenched my own. It was a lonely time. I'd stand at the wall of the AA dance as the music slipped from "Funkytown" into Nine Inch Nails' "I Want to Fuck You Like an Animal," a sure sign that the AA dance had transitioned into the risqué final quarter of the festivities. I'd clench my butt cheeks to the beat, each bass drop a new clench. It was the best I could do.

Then the DJ at one of those dances dropped Crystal Waters's "100% Pure Love," a house track that had somehow made it onto the radio and therefore onto the playlist of the glorified wedding DJ at the Danville veterans hall that night. My feet started to move a little. This was the first time I'd ever moved my feet to a beat without a girl next to me. What was I doing? I was moving. I was dancing. Had you been at that dance, watching me groove my way from what I thought was gangster caterpillar to dancing butterfly, it likely would have looked to you like a barely moving brown moth, wings weakly fluttering. But it felt like a huge, sweeping flap of the wings.

A few months later, I picked up a flyer to the Coolworld Cyberfest '95 rave at a record store in Berkeley. I still remember that flyer.

It was huge and colorful, a cybernetic beauty graced the entire front of the thing: a future woman, her head covered in robotics and circuitry and metal spikes. On the back was a list of countless DJs I'd never heard of. This was a massive rave. A huge lumbering mega party, sagging under the weight of its own commercialism. Promised were experiences of unimaginable delights like Kubla Khan's stately pleasure dome. Ferris wheels and slides and other ding-dong bullshit. It sounded fucking amazing.

I decided to go.

I don't know why I made that choice. I didn't know a single person who was into that kind of shit. Maybe it was that Crystal Waters song shaking my feet into action. Maybe it was that 20/20 special. Maybe it was that stupid sexy terminator lady on that flyer. All I knew was, I had to go. I scraped up some money and bought a ticket.

I started the evening by attending an NA meeting across the street from where the party was. This was in downtown Oakland at the Henry J. Kaiser Convention Center, and the meeting that night was not filled with burgeoning rave children. I raised my hand and explained to the room of fifty-year-old Black and Latino recovering addicts how my journey of recovery had allowed me the freedom to attend the psychedelic drug and techno fest across the street.

No one had a clue what I was talking about. But fuck 'em. I was ready to rave.

Only problem was, I didn't know how. I didn't exactly cut a swath as a techno party participant. I had my hair slicked back under my hat and wore sagging pressed khaki pants and a Fila shirt in honor of the company that had given me my identity. Back then, I was known as "Fila" by the other young people in AA due to, you guessed it, the amount of Fila gear I wore. Every day I wore a hat that spelled out FILA in big bold block letters that spilled down onto the brim. I needed everyone to know that *this* was the Italian sportswear company that defined me.

So that night I wore my ubiquitous cap and sagging pants and brought with me, in my bag, a full bottle of the cologne I slathered myself with daily: Escape by Calvin Klein.

I rooted through my bag and decided that I'd need weaponry that night to protect myself against unknown enemies. This was my modus operandi. Wear Fila, talk Southern, have weapon. To clarify, I have never used a weapon on anyone. But it felt really nice to pretend.

And I *was* from the streets!

Only, not really.

Until just recently I'd been a very liberal N-word user. Not in the extremely bad racially hateful way, just in the also extremely bad only maybe not quite as bad but hey maybe just as bad racially confused way. The user-(un?)friendly version that ends in an "a." That is to say, I used it as "an ally." I figured I had enough Black friends to have gotten a pass.

One day, outside of a meeting, my friend Larry threw me up against a wall and revoked my pass. Larry was Black and older than me and I looked up to him as someone who had been sober a long time but was still pretty young. He was my friend. He threw me up against that wall and got in my face: "N*gga, stop saying n*gga, n*gga!"

I was taken aback. "Okay, I'm a little confused by the context switches in there, but I believe you are telling me to stop saying the N-word? You know I don't mean anything by it. It's how I talk. Just some North Oakland shit."

"Stop saying that shit, too. You ain't from North Oakland, you're from *northern* Oakland. You live on Piedmont Avenue."

This was (and still is, even though I'm forty-three now) a true bane of my existence. Piedmont Avenue, the street I grew up on, the place my mother rented a $400 flat paid for by her paltry, state-supplemented SSI check, was a nicer part of town, and it also happened to share its name with the pathetically suburban, lily-white rich-kid city next door: Piedmont, California. As a result, even though I slogged through Oakland public schools and had been rejected as a nonresident when I tried to do a district transfer into Piedmont High after running out of educational options during my drug days, everyone thought I lived in Piedmont because I lived on Piedmont Avenue. But I lived in Oakland, goddamn it! Just not really, in any way, a truly rough part of Oakland.

"Well, Piedmont Avenue is technically North Oakland, it's just a little nicer . . ." I meeped out.

"Stop saying n*gga, stop claiming North Oakland. Next time I hear you doing either, I'mma beat your ass."

I stopped that night. Some personal growth spurts happen slowly, over time, as the universe reveals its will for you and your mind blossoms like a lotus. Sometimes a kid who's bigger than you threatens to beat your ass, and you change all at once.

Larry graciously put a stop to my highly suspect word choices, but he couldn't take the streets all the way out of me. So back to the rave prep. Mission: weapon.

I took that bottle of Escape cologne and stuffed it down into a sock. I took the potpourri-scented blackjack into my hands and gave it a couple of good swings. "Just in case I have to crack a *n-* . . ." I stopped myself, reconsidering. "Just in case I have to crack a *muthafucka* over the head tonight."

Feeling safe against no one in particular, I headed into the party.

By the way, I'm not setting this weapon thing up as some kind of Chekhov's gun foreshadowing device. The Escape bottle never gets used. I never had to crack a muthafucka. I just want you to understand the brain I brought with me to Cyberfest that night, want you to understand my process. I want you to see the conditioning I'd been shaped with that would make fashioning a weapon even seem like a reasonable necessity. I had been so thoroughly through the emotional gauntlet that I was fried. Spiritually crisp. I couldn't have told you then, but even at that point, months after I had gotten sober, I was still terrified. Terrified of my heart, of being seen for who I was: a severely damaged kid who had never had a chance at a normal childhood. I was too busy running from my life to have had an opportunity to experience it. I never could have told you that what I needed most of all was a chance at another life. Not to build from where I was, but to smash into nonexistence the foundation of my old life. To dig below the firmament of that life and inspect the wooden pylons beneath the earth that had been holding me up: rotten wood, scored through with the termite damage of drugs and violence. Soggy, dank, stinky wood that was barely supporting me. I needed to dig down deep and throw that shit away. I needed to build a new foundation.

I needed rebirth.

I dropped the Escape sock in my bag, sealed it, and walked into the womb.

The Henry J. Kaiser Convention Center is an ugly utilitarian building now shuttered from years of neglect. Bare, stark, and devoid of life, the walls are shot through with exposed steel beams and the most function-first kind of architecture. But what I walked into that night was a dream. A transformed shock of a space. A portal to another zone. A fucking Cyberfest!

Sharp green lasers darted around the room and strobe lights flashed, creating a stuttering silhouette of the thousands of people dancing. *Thousands* of people dancing. The hall was filled with shapes, images of people, huge pants, colorful backpacks, some people wearing huge Mickey Mouse hand gloves that pumped the air in excitement. Some wore fairy wings. Some wore Cat in the Hat hats that bobbed and dangled off of their heads. People sucked on pacifiers and danced. I mean, they fucking *danced*. They jumped and shook, they moved violently. Focus your vision and individuals moved hard to the beat, widen your aperture and the whole crowd became a throbbing entity. A gyrating mass of thrill and energy.

My God. My God.

My God, these people looked like fucking idiots.

But I never noticed. I was too busy getting mauled by the speakers.

The speakers were enormous columns of sound that crawled to the roof like the Tower of Babel. They kept the secrets of Babel, too. They spoke unknown languages. They screamed at me, they pulsed at me. I'd never heard anything, never seen anything like this. It was pandemonium. It was bacchanalian. It was a true goddamn rave. I set my bag down, replete with weapon, never to see it again.

What was happening? My heart was being punched by the music, but that wasn't it. I seemed to be moving. Something strange. I was being thrown around. Why was I moving?!

I looked down at my feet. My God, I was jumping. I was shuffling. There was no concrete on my feet anymore, there was only air. Only light. I was moving. I was moving. I was dancing!

The individuals surrounding me melted into a single unit, and I melted into it, too. I was in the crowd. I *was* the crowd.

Somehow, in the course of a few hours, I'd gone from gangster to ballerina. I swear to God by the end of the night, I was skipping, prancing, doing pirouettes. A gay couple, out of their faces on ecstasy, approached me from either side, picked me up, lifted me high, and kissed me on both cheeks when they dropped me down to the ground. "You dance beautifully!" they told me.

What the fuck were these motherfuckers doing? Touching all on me. Kissing all on me. Didn't they know I'm a fucking G? Couldn't they tell? Couldn't they smell the dangerous combination of foot sweat and Escape emanating from me? Well, I'd let them know. I knew what I had to do. I grabbed both of them by their heads, pulled them toward me, and hugged them close. "You're beautiful, too!" I yelled.

Pretty much everybody has an image in their minds when they hear the word *rave,* and I'd wager few conjure up an image of the kind of transmutative elixir I found that night. People mostly scoff at the notion of the *rave* and the *raver.* But when I stumbled into that party, I encountered something still quite alive and potent, still laden with its cosmological forces. Today the shreds of the rave scene have been overlaid on music festivals and the techno beats of action-movie soundtracks. But at some point it was alive. I had the rare privilege of observing the heights and the death of the American rave scene all while completely clean and sober. The sobriety is significant only in its deviation from the norm and my ability to have observed the scene crumble from its roots as a genuine form of cultural subversion into an overwrought neon underage sex and halter-top celebration.

I honestly can't tell if the rave scene still exists in some different form and I am unable to identify it due to a curmudgeonly perspective warp so pronounced that when I see what "kids these days" call a rave I feel like I'm a Bill Haley and His Comets fan listening to Black Sabbath and declaring, "That's not rock and roll!" I just know when I see a DJ in a Halloween mask pressing PLAY from behind a laptop during an afternoon music festival sponsored by American Express, when I see a seventeen-year-old girl vomiting up Heineken and Molly pills in the corner of an inflatable Red Bull TECHNO GIVES YOU WINGS tent, it just doesn't feel like what we were talking about back then.

Although there are certainly people who'd scoff at my claims of being some kind of old-school expert on the topic myself. I remember at one of my first parties in 1995, I was talking to a British guy on a patio who was looking around, shaking his head, and telling me he couldn't identify with what the scene had become. He was among the first generation of people who had brought the rave scene into the Bay Area, and what he saw that night was unrecognizable; it was big and dynamic rather than small and totally secret. To him, its very vitality was a death pang. I still remember looking at that guy and wondering why he couldn't see the beauty around him. It was like we were looking at the same painting and while he sneered at the banality of the *Mona Lisa,* having moved on to the modern art section of his art history class, I was standing there, staring at her sexy little smirk and the hot hot heat of that brown robe gripping her medieval Italian titties.

Perhaps that's just the cycle of things: Someone invents something new and fresh, and it keeps shedding its skin into something slightly different and slightly bigger until, eventually, the inventor cannot identify his creation and a new squad of tinkerers convinces themselves they are, in fact, the masters of the new creature until they also cannot tame the beast.

That's my claim when it comes to electronic music. I wasn't there at the beginning; I was there at the beginning of the end. I was there at its underground apex, the moment before its slide, the last years before it burst above the Earth's mantle and made it possible for Paris Hilton and DJ Pauly D* to see electronic music as some sort of

---

* In 2013, Pauly D, the man best known as "the guy with that hair" from the hit MTV prestige drama *Jersey Shore,* was ranked number fourteen on *Forbes* magazine's list of the fifteen highest paid DJs in the world, pulling in around $16 million that year. He rated above Diplo, the guy behind M.I.A.'s sound. This is somewhere akin to a pile of burlap earning more for playing guitar than Eddie Van Halen.

viable career extender. It never occurred to us back then that anyone could or would make real-world money on this stuff. The highest heights that we could imagine with raves and electronic music was that, someday, someone in the mainstream would catch the interest of the world and act as a translator, allowing the masses to understand what we saw in the repetitive throb.

One of the most baffling aspects of the rave scene to an outsider who didn't understand what we were doing was our worship of the DJ. The prominence of the DJ as the alpha performer at most raves was evidence that the emperor of our electronic kingdom was wearing no clothes. "So you go to watch a person play other people's music? That's not musicianship. That's a guy playing records." It just didn't make sense back then (and to some people now) how you could even compare a DJ with a band whose members were playing instruments, creating the sounds, playing songs they wrote. At least with hip hop you could look at the cutting and scratching as a sound that was being made *by* the DJ, independent of the record itself.

The misunderstanding comes from looking at a digital scene with analog eyes. The electronic music DJ wasn't a person who played an instrument. They *were* the instrument. Producers made their music to be mixed. They made their records for the DJs. The record wasn't just a record, it was a string on the guitar. Unlike the musician, who makes something from nothing, the DJ took two somethings and made a third thing. So the complaint that the music was too repetitive and simplistic was based upon a fundamental misunderstanding of what the point of the music was. It was repetitive by design, not by lack of musical capability. The DJ is a fundamental interchange. When the DJ takes two house records and slides the crossfader into the middle of the mixer so that both records are playing simultaneously often for minutes at a time, the sounds you hear have never been made before. It's a third thing. A creation. A collaboration based on blind trust. Record one might've been made by a bedroom producer in Berlin, record two might be a classic from a long-dead Chicago house icon, and the person who stands behind the decks, playing them together, has created a temporary, momentary homage. He has done his due diligence. He has changed the air in the room.

After that first party, I was never the same person again. It was an instant and extreme change. I caught the bus home in the morning after Cyberfest '95 with the music still pounding in my ears. I held an elaborate burial ritual for all my Fila gear that night. Never again. I needed pants. Big ones. Goofy ones. Rave ones. Thanks be to Allah, Ross Dress for Less had caches of rave clothes that could be obtained on a pauper's salary. The Ross philosophy is to sell clothing that only the very poor or the very blind could love. Irregular mismanufactured T-shirts with pant legs accidentally sewn onto the sleeve, turtlenecks designed for giraffes only, Mickey Mouse boxer shorts with Mickey's hand raised in a Nazi salute, that kind of thing. One buffoonish item at a time, I built an identity.

JNCO brand jeans were the preferred pant selection for the proper raver.

The JNCO family is an old and storied clothing manufacturer. Its patriarch, Salvatore Jnco, was a master tailor in Monaco and hand sewed the most famous harlequin costumes of his age. Sadly, when Mussolini came to power and outlawed the Italian circus, the Jnco family loom came to a grinding halt. Salvatore died of a broken heart a year later. His son, Giuseppe Jnco, took the family secrets and boarded a ship to America with dreams of fashioning oversized garments for the hardscrabble Yankees, who he figured must be in need of pants forty-seven sizes too large. Day and night he sewed those pants in obscurity until, finally, techno parties made such culturally oblong garments a must-have.

Absolutely none of what I just wrote is true. But what is true is that I had to have JNCOs, and they had to be big.

There is much debate on exactly how ravers cracked the code on dressing so poorly. Whether a by-product of psychedelic vision quests or simply the unlucky result of a social scene that takes place in mostly dingy, poorly lit warehouses where people take drugs that affect their visual acuity and make them think everything is fucking beautiful, ravers have long been the vanguard of taking a rather Ringling Brothers approach to street fashion. Huge pants, chain wallets, and childish iconography were staples of raver fashion. But just when you thought it couldn't get worse than a pair of pants more suitable for a "before" photo on an advertisement for gastric bypass surgery, the ravers took it a step further and invented kandi. A sort of fashion-based, imposed infantilization that took the form of piles and piles of charm bracelets, stacked and layered around the neck and wrists like a kind of Mr. T of the homosexual child community.

I got big JNCO jeans and corduroys with huge paisley inserts sewn into the seams to make them comically flared and large. I bleached my hair white blond and sprinkled glitter in it. I'd bought a packet of baby barrettes and clipped them into my frosty blond locks. I curled my hair into little Björk buns. My brother was away at college and returned for a visit about a month into my raver re-branding.

"You *look* like my brother, but I guess you're my sister now?"

Nothing he had to say bothered me. I knew I looked foolish to other people, but I just didn't care. For the first time in my life, I didn't care. I'd been stripped of my callous Oakland exoskeleton, and the soft tissues of the little worm I actually was were exposed to the sunlight. Exposed to the air. I loved how it stung. I loved how it burned. I crawled to the next party.

My second rave was a wholly different affair from Cyberfest. It was an underground party. And it created yet another transformation in me.

This guy Jeremy, an older, more experienced raver who had recently gotten sober, too, whispered the secret of this party into my ear at the tail end of my last ever AA dance. I was still split in two. All dressed up with nowhere to rave. Posters for Cyberfest had been stapled on every telephone pole in Oakland and tickets were available at Ticketmaster. Easy to find. But I didn't know how to get to another. Some raver I was. Big pants, big dreams. Still no plans better than an AA dance on Saturday.

Jeremy smiled at me. "You look like you know how to dance. You go to parties?" he asked.

"Well, I've been to one and bought these pants, which have essentially alienated me from all my old friends, so I'd say yeah, I go to party. Singular."

He laughed. "What party did you go to?"

I shuffled, embarrassed. "Cyberfest?"

He laughed again but kindly. "C'mon, dude, lemme show you a real party."

We piled into his car and took off. The moon shone bright and full in the suburban sky. That was significant. I just didn't know it yet.

The full-moon parties were a pivotal party in the San Francisco rave legend. Every month a crew called Wicked threw renegade gatherings under the light of the full moon. They were outdoor parties that you'd chase down via rumor and voicemail messages instructing you on where to go. Call the number. A click. A pickup. Over the phone you'd hear music play. If you'd made it this far you were almost home. A British accent, a voice dripping with secret possibilities, said nothing but an address. A street corner. An intersection.

Start the car. Drive. Be cool. On the corner was a man holding slips of paper. He handed one over with a wink. Almost there. The small note read "Bonny Dune, Santa Cruz."

As we rounded the bend on California State Route 1, it was nearly two A.M. The cars parked on the side of the road told a story I liked. Alien heads and psychedelic flower stickers stuck to the rear windows meant we'd arrived at the right place. We parked. Opened the door to the car. Heard the throb. Somewhere nearby there was a party. We just had to follow the sound. That far-off pulse of a party happening without you is one that nostalgic ex-ravers know well. It was like a bread crumb trail for Hansels and Gretels hungry to dance. We followed the trail. Walking through the brush and the clifftops of the beachhead, we peeked a hundred feet down to the beach below. The moon lit the way like a disco ball suspended in air. Way down by the water, five hundred, maybe a thousand kids crowded around an altar built in front of the DJ. Huge speaker stacks raised the question, How had anyone dragged those things down that far? I yelled, "See you down there!" to Jeremy. I took off running. Down the sandy dune as fast as I could go. Sand flew up the enormous opening in my newly purchased raver pants. I didn't care. It was time to dance. Two A.M. seemed like a nice time to start the real party.

The scene couldn't have been more different from Cyberfest. These kids were hippie ravers, psychedelic denizens. The DJ stood tall, long dreadlocks tangled up in his headphones. The music was slower than at Cyberfest, *deeper,* it ground down into the beach below. This was the psychedelic disco sound that the San Francisco rave scene was underground-famous for. This was a real fucking party. The wisps of the original flames that lit England ablaze burned bright here. If Cyberfest was Kenny G, this was John fucking Coltrane.

Let me stop here. Let me go back a bit. Actually quite a bit.

Let's go back to 1979. Six days before that shock jock DJ poisoned the well of disco, I was born in Queens, New York. According to Jewish custom, the firstborn son is to be named by the mother. The second belonged to Daddy. My older brother was David. I was number two. My father stepped forward proudly upon my birth and declared my name: MOSHE!

"No way!" My mom laughed. "We can't call him Moshe! That's a ridiculous name. It sounds like Moose. We'll call him Mark." Let's all keep in mind that my mother is deaf and has never heard the word *Moose* and cannot hear the name *Moshe* (pronounced MO-shuh) or the name *Mark*. But for some reason, against the rules of logic and tradition, my mother won the argument that day. The name on my birth certificate: Mark Moshe Kasher.

When my parents split, the one small battle my father never stopped fighting was over that name. He never referred to me as Mark. To him I was Moshe. To my brother, I was Mo. To my mother, I was Mark Moose Kasher.

I never identified with the name *Mark*. Never. But I was hardly brave enough to step into an Oakland public school classroom and declare, when the teacher called out roll, "Actually, if you wouldn't mind calling me by my biblically mandated name, *Moshe*, the patriarchs and I would really appreciate it."

So I stayed Mark. I stayed Mark even when it became a commonly used hip hop slang insult. A mark was a bad thing to be. It was a nerd, a fool, a coward.

"You a mark, Mark," the kids yelled at me and howled in laughter.

"Hell yeah, you a mark ass busta!"

"At least I'm not a moose!" I snapped back to the confused silence of my tormentors.

And the truth was, I was a mark. I was a fool. I was a coward. At least I felt like one. Always. I'm telling you that, always, I felt like an oblong, misshapen fool.

Then I found drugs and booze and forgot about my shape altogether. Mark went from a fool and a coward to a fool and a criminal. He ran like hell to outpace the crushing reality of how he felt.

There is a videogame, a real classic, called *Katamari Damacy*. In it you play a prince, small and insignificant, who rolls a little sticky ball in front of him as he runs through the land. The ball is so sticky that it picks up everything in his path. Small things at first, thimbles and threads, pieces of straw and dander. It gradually gains in size and scale until it's picking up buildings and mountains and the heavens themselves. Eventually that ball is so big and powerful that it's used to rebuild the moon. And that night, under the light of the real moon, the full moon, I stopped pushing my ball for good.

You see, I was just like that little prince. I started running and gathering everything in sight that could cover up the little Mark that I was. Small things at first, an embarrassed swallowing of the pride, a slight change of my accent, until eventually I was snagging everything in sight. Trauma, court cases, drug addiction, all of it. Then when I got sober, I pushed that ball into the AA meetings with me. It had swelled and ballooned to unimaginable size. There was much more ball than there was me. I was all ball. I got swallowed up in it, too. It towered over me, threatening me with each massive rotation.

The first thing people asked me when I arrived in AA was, "What's with the fucking ball?"

"You're asking me? That thing is why I came here in the first place! What do I do?!"

"Stop running!" they said.

I was shocked. "But if I do that, it will run me over!"

"You'll be fine!" they yelled back.

"I'll be fine? You sure?"

"You'll be fine," they reassured me.

I stopped running. I stopped pushing my ball. It stopped short. It teetered. It groaned. It rolled back toward me. It ran me over. I was flattened by that fucking thing. Like Wile E. Coyote creamed by an Acme Co. steamroller, I was ground into the dirt. It nearly destroyed me.

"Why did you tell me to stop running?! That hurt like hell!"

"Ha-ha, yeah, it does hurt!" They laughed. They laughed! They knew this would happen!

I got up. Puffed some air into my flattened body. Brushed the dust off.

"Well, what the hell do I do now?"

The ball had stopped moving, but it was still there. Looming. It was a relief not to have to keep pushing it, but it still defined me. Still surrounded me.

"I said, what do I do?" I was pissed now.

Somebody in AA walked over, handed me a small hammer and a chisel, and said, "Get to work."

I'd been chipping away at that ball ever since. It was smaller these days. Smaller every day. But it wasn't gone. Remember, just last month I'd reached into the ball and pulled out a bottle of cologne stuffed into a sock. My mighty weapon.

Despite my Jesus-in-the-desert moment at Cyberfest, that ball still followed me down to the beach that night. It was raving right beside me. But I was ready for a change.

I sat down with Jeremy at a bonfire as the party raged around me. He introduced me to a friend of his. The most beautiful woman I'd ever seen. Hell, every woman here was the most beautiful woman I'd ever seen.

"I'm Alona," she said. "What's your name?"

"It's . . ."

I looked at the ball.

"It's . . ."

I heard the music.

"It's . . ."

I looked at the full moon, felt its light. It seemed like maybe it needed to be rebuilt.

"My name is Moshe."

Jeremy smiled and hugged me to him. "Well, all right!"

Alona smiled, too. "It's nice to meet you, Moshe!"

"Oh, have you met my ball?"

I looked over to where that ball had been sitting. Hmm. It was gone.

The moon seemed a little fuller than before.

I have never gone by anything but my real name since.

Never seen that fucking ball, either.

Physically rebuilt and spiritually reborn, I was now truly bathing in the reality of my new image. I was a raver. I had never had so much fun in my life. Every weekend was spent chasing down the next party. All week long I waited for the weekend. I began to lose weight, too. There are few fat ravers. Something about the combination of amphetamine drugs and twelve-plus hours of hard-charging warehouse cardio dancing will melt the pounds away. Of course, I had no amphetamine. But I was kept moving by the psychic amphetamines of the new community. Their energy seeped into me. I really think I was as high as anyone else.

There's an old joke about the rave scene that is really an old joke about the Grateful Dead:

Q: What did the raver say when he sobered up?

A: This music sucks!

But it didn't. Not to me. I was sober the entire time I raved, and I loved every second of it. Loved every mechanical *bleep* and *blorp* I heard. That experience I was having didn't exactly translate or make sense to the other sober people in my life.

I brought this kid, Casey, to one of my earliest parties, a rave called Chrysalis that took place in a small warehouse loft space in downtown San Francisco.

After an AA meeting one night, I told him where I was off to and invited him to join me. We jumped in his car and crossed the Bay Bridge. The moment we entered that loft, we were slammed with a wall of heat and moisture, stink and sweat. You put enough dancing kids in a loft space meant to hold forty people and you are quite literally going to change the atmosphere. Casey thought he was on his way to a nightclub that night, because that's the only thing he'd really have to compare it to. A big technologically savvy space with lighting trellises set up by interior design engineers. Girls dressed up in heels and halter tops, ready for a "night on the town." But what Casey saw that night freaked him right the fuck out. Twacked-out hippie kids with their heads stuck literally all the way into the speakers, screaming in demonic orgasmic delight. Girls with their shirts off, walking freely, no one giving them a second look. Crowds of people standing in awe around a single doofus with a couple of glow sticks in his hands making the light dance in the air. Nag Champa incense burning from an altar that hung from the ceiling, statues of Shiva and Vishnu bookending an array of Native American smudge sticks and Santeria crosses, the confused spirituality of the hippie rave movement on full display. He saw all this stuff, and it didn't compute. But worst of all was when he walked into the chill room and saw me. I'd become one of them.

Chill rooms were a ubiquitous part of the raves back then. They were quiet, calm spaces for people to come lie down and ride the rest of their psychedelic trips out. The chill room DJ's sole job was to create a music and atmosphere so relaxed and trippy that the partygoer forgets he's at a party and thinks he's on a one-way spaceship trip to Andromeda. If all that wasn't trippy enough for poor Casey, there were also the cuddle puddles. I really am sorry for the name, but that's what they were called! And honestly, as corny of a name as *cuddle puddle* is, there is no better phrase to describe them.

Ecstasy makes touching things feel great. Kissing, touching, hugging, massaging, every one of these experiences feels like God's reaching out and touching Adam's finger. Shockwaves. When enough people at a rave are high enough on ecstasy and wander into the chill room at the same time, it reaches a critical mass and the gravitational pull is simply too much to resist. The cuddle puddle would congeal organically in the chill room with two people, then three then six people reaching out to touch one another in whatever way felt safe and good. From people staring deeply into one another's third eye all the way to sticking their fingers into one another's second hole, nothing was taboo. It felt totally regular, despite the heavy drugs everybody was on and the open displays of sexualities. It somehow felt totally innocent.

With Casey upstairs wandering around dazed, I ran straight into the cuddle puddle and joined the writhing mound of love that was undulating and shifting the subspace between bodies at the loft that night. I connected deeply to a stranger in the puddle, and as we touched each other lightly and absorbed into one another like a Changeling connecting to the Great Link in *Deep Space 9*, the puddle began to chat, as one, "PLUR! PLUR! PLUR!"

PLUR indeed.

PLUR (Peace, Love, Unity, and Respect) is an absurd acronym that was the unofficial core philosophy of the rave scene. The great irony being, of course, that it's nearly impossible to *respect* someone who yells "PLUR, man!!" at the top of his lungs when a DJ drops a particularly "dope beat." Nevertheless, at the time, the PLUR code was taken pretty seriously. Everyone was welcome at the early parties, whatever your race, whatever your orientation, whoever you were, you were welcome to rave. The dance floor provided a safe space of nonjudgment and equanimity. There was no hierarchy here; we were just there to dance. Sadly, over time, PLUR became a mostly forgotten relic of a scene that got commodified. It now exists only in tattoo form, a painful reminder to people who got a little too swept away by those early parties. A guy I used to rave with once pulled off a fresh bandage and proudly showed me his new ink. It read: 100% *San Francisco Raver, PLUR!* He looked in my eyes expectantly waiting for the "Fuckin' right on, man! Your commitment to this scene is incredibly admirable. Before I thought you might have been as low as 75 to 80 percent San Francisco raver, but now that I see this incredibly large and permanent logo you've affixed to your forearm, I realize my folly!" Even then, as swept up in the raver madness as I was, I recognized that tattoo as a fatal flaw in a person's long-term hopes for success. I hope I'm wrong, but I imagine that guy today, every time that tattoo flashes past his eyes, just thinking, "Shit, I haven't been to a rave in twenty years. I should've gone to law school."

Anyway, beneath that throng of humanity, I peered up and saw Casey looking for me. I yelled out to him, "Casey! What's up, dude?" He looked around, confused. "I'm down here, dude! Look under the guy in the fluorescent soccer jersey, just to the right of the butt cheek of the gal sucking a Kermit the frog pacifier. See me now?"

Casey squinted, then his eyes went big. "Moshe! Hey, man, what are you doing?"

I smiled. "Getting my cuddle puddle on!"

Casey nodded, clearly thinking I had relapsed in the car on the way over the bridge. "Uh . . . I think I'm gonna take off. This isn't exactly my scene," he said. It was at this moment that I realized that what I was doing was a refined experience, not for everyone. Casey left and I kept cuddling, kept connecting, kept raving.

In very short order, AA meetings took a serious back seat to parties. I adorned myself with kandi jewelry, bought a pacifier,* and

---

* The pacifier was a common accessory at early raves. Its purpose was twofold: It was a part of the infantilized aesthetic that was typical of the rave scene back then, but more important it was a tool designed to give your mouth something to do other than grind your teeth into rave nubs when the ecstasy made your jaw vibrate with agitation. Now, as for me? I had a pacifier. A Tweety bird one, in fact. But of course I was sober. I didn't do ecstasy. I sucked on a pacifier simply because I thought it looked cool.

started bringing a stuffed monkey puppet with me to raves. I softened. Deeply.

I also started meeting and hooking up with girls at these parties. The rave scene had much of the free love of the hippie movement laid into its foundations. The bacchanal of that first night didn't wear off at all. Sex was everywhere, and it was wild, easy, fun, and exciting. I was *young,* sixteen when I first started going to parties, and the girls I was meeting and making out with were nineteen, twenty-one, twenty-three . . . and so *beautiful.*

Prior to the raves, my sexuality was largely informed by lessons gleaned from West Coast gangsta rap. The first Too $hort song I heard made every sex ed lecture my mom ever gave me fall entirely out of my mind. I mean, who knew more about fucking, Too $hort or my mom?* As a result, all I really understood about sex was that at the end I was supposed to say, "Awwww, yeeeeeeeah!" and then leave. I knew and understood nothing about sex, sexuality, women, pleasure, and what they had to do with one another. AA helped a lot by introducing me to strong, powerful women, some of whom were instrumental in helping me get sober. None of whom had the slightest bit of romantic interest in me. Even in Young People's AA meetings, the average woman was much older than me, and so I made many older sisters but no lovers. And it's not like I was particularly attractive back then. Pimply faced, angry with an attitude, I greased my hair with Three Flowers (a Mexican hair product), talked with a Southern accent (a Black affectation), and was loud and obnoxious (a white behavioral tic). I sweated the Three Flowers onto my face, which created a ring of acne around my chin. I guess what I'm saying is I was chronically unfuckable when I got sober.

Underage, unattractive, *and* ugly tempered? That's a combo every woman in Oakland AA was able to resist. Which was nice. Everyone treated me like a little brother. All the women babied me, picked me up for meetings, spoke to me kindly. It was a kind of healing. I

---

* After doing extensive research for this book I found the actual answer to be about even.

slowly learned about treating women with respect by learning to respect these recovering women. Then, when I started to drop the more unattractive aspects of my personality, shed some baby fat by dancing all night, and took the grease out of my hair, girls started to think I was cute. By the time that unexpected bonus of life came around I was transitioning into semi-nice-guy territory. My personality was also coming alive. I was starting to feel comfortable in my own skin. I could be funny and charming.

The rave scene was oozing sexuality. Everyone was down to fuck everyone. Sure, it wasn't completely healthy and there were some scabies outbreaks here and there, but it was just part of the big incestuous family I had just joined. So what exactly is therapeutic about a sixteen-year-old kid getting laid after a big warehouse party where he spent the night dancing and lying in a pile of people out of their faces on Molly and ketamine? It was, through admittedly unconventional means, rewiring me, re-creating me, and forging a new identity that would last me the rest of my life.

Looking back, I now understand the dolls and the glitter, the free love and the pacifiers, the cuddle puddles and the infantile fashion, the fingering and the fucking as a lay experiment in a neural rewire. What the rave scene did for me was similar to the work the people at MAPS* do with MDMA, the drug of choice of the rave scene and PTSD-addled combat veterans. In a calm setting, clinicians give the former soldier a dose of MDMA and slowly, as the drug comes on, guide them back into the mental space of where their trauma took place, opening it up, letting some sunshine in, breaking down the barrier, and allowing them to reframe their world going forward. The Molly breaks down their fear of approaching the trauma, trauma so deep that to even look at it will spiral them into a rage or a breakdown of terror. It's the kind of trauma something like the twelve steps can't sufficiently heal you from; it's radioactive, charged with mental explosives that any approach will detonate. The Molly acts as a MacGyver, sneaking past the barbed wire, swimming

---

* The Multidisciplinary Association for Psychedelic Studies. Look into them. These people are heroes of decriminalization and healing.

through the moat, crawling to the explosives, and gently clipping the wire. The drug makes the trauma threat, the huge, dangerous lumbering monster, shrink down to real size. The trauma can then be reapproached; the experience can be reexamined, reexperienced, reprocessed, and recovered from. Without the MDMA it would have stayed unapproachable for life. It would have stayed trauma. Malignant. Festering. Unhealed.

Pretending to be on MDMA did that for me. Dancing did that for me. Glitter did that for me. And, of course, I know my trauma doesn't compare to an Iraq war vet's, but it still had a stranglehold on my life. I missed so many milestones of development. So many innocent journeys that kids go on to discover themselves were abandoned for a blindfolded cliff jump into the churning waters of teenage drug addiction.

I started molting, shedding old, calloused skin, moving back, back, back in time. As fast as I was developing, I was also de-developing.

The glitter and the barrettes and the dolls and the bright colors and, yes, even the fucking pacifier provided me an artificial, hyperbaric chamber of a second chance at childhood. The cuddle puddles and the dancing and the hugs gave me a new and refreshed idea of manhood and masculinity. The raver girls and the free love and the JNCO dry humps reset my ideas of women and sex and sexuality. Did I immediately begin treating all sexual partners with the utmost respect and communication, never ghosting anyone, never objectifying, always the perfect progressive boy-feminist? Of course not. I was still a heterosexual teenage male, the glitter notwithstanding. It wasn't that I became a perfect enlightened and evolved being. I became how I imagine I would have been had I not fallen into an abyss of addiction, crime, violence, and ethnic hair care products. I was so far on one extreme of teenage life and the rave scene pulled me so far to another that eventually it could swing back to the middle.

I reapproached old ideas and replaced them with new ones. I was made totally unafraid of the process by the euphoria of the cultural contact high. The vibe was my Molly. The scene was my clinician. The future was mine. The pendulum swung into areas that were absurd, sure, and I know that it's not common for a teenage wannabe to find a therapeutic breakthrough with a gorilla hand puppet on one hand and a glow stick in the other, but that's what happened to me. This community, these people, these drugged-out scenesters, were just as significant for me as AA was. They saved my life, recovered my mind, and spun my perspective 180 degrees. As cheesy a credo as PLUR was, it certainly beat "Trust no bitch."

My transformation complete, I quickly had to wrestle with a dilemma. Raves were expensive, and I was seventeen, unemployed, and broke. I needed to either find a way to buy a ticket every weekend or find a way to get in free.

Sneaking in wasn't really my thing. AA enforces a kind of pilpul rule following morality that seems to suggest things like sneaking into raves are a surefire shortcut to relapse. That said, I do know the greatest techniques for sneaking into parties from years of working the door: the box and the moonwalk.

These are not the brutish, "Goths sacking Rome" inelegant techniques of hopping an unguarded fence or finding a group of like-minded goons to run full-speed into the entrance of a party; those techniques are for barbarians. Barbarians are not my people. I prefer the sophisticated technique of the sneaky thinker. I like elegant attempts so nimble they are as akin to psychological experiments as much as they are attempts at trespass.

"The box" relies on simple consumer psychology. People want to feel like they know what's going on; confusion or uncertainty is embarrassing. Put simply the box is . . . a box. A plain cardboard box will do, but a milk crate full of equipment-like stuff works even better. Make it big, big enough to slightly obscure your face but *not* cover your eyes. Your eyes are important. They do the talking for you. You simply put the box in your arms, walk right to the entrance of the rave or music festival, and (this is incredibly important): *look like you and your box have an important function inside the party.* Something about a confident person walking with purpose with a box in hand renders a door guy incapable of saying anything door guy–ish like, "Hey, what are you doing?" "Where are you and that box going?" "Does your box have a ticket to get in?" or "Cool box but no dice, Buster!" Door guy can only stare in admiration and think, "That box and its handler need to get somewhere. I better not get involved."

The other ultimate sneak-in technique, the moonwalk, is my favorite because it incorporates psychology, illusion, and kinesiology in a grand and elegant dance. The technique is simple. Walk to the *exit* of a party, where a throng of ravers are walking *out* of the party, making their way home or to their car to grab more pacifiers. Now, flip around so your back is to the exiters. As the crowd moves outward in one direction, you slowly and seamlessly walk *backward* into the party using the forward movement of the crowd the way a cheetah uses tall grass on the savanna to obscure its movements. This illusion creates a nickelodeon type of movement: You move backward but no yellow-windbreaker-wearing security guard is capable of seeing you. It's amazing and works 100 percent of the time and absolutely *cannot* fail.*

None of these techniques were for me, but that didn't mean I couldn't admire them. Also, observing them from afar set me up for the years I would work the Gate at Burning Man, searching cars for stowaways, but we'll get to that later. Since I wasn't down to sneak in but absolutely *had* to rave every weekend and absolutely did not have money to pay for admission, I needed another way.

I had a major realization, one that sounds like a monologue from a David Mamet play: There is an invisible line in the population at every rave, in every scene, maybe everywhere. On one side of the line are the people who paid to get in, the masses, the throng that pays for everything to get done. They aren't cool but they are necessary; without them the show can't go on. On the other side of the line is a much smaller group: Those who don't pay. They, for whatever reason, have figured out some way to get in free or even make money from the party they are attending. I wanted to be on that side

---

* There is very little data available to support this, but trust me, it works. Try it and if anyone stops you, tell 'em Moshe sent ya.

of the line. I wanted to be a professional raver. Over the years, in scene after scene, I would hop this invisible line repeatedly, the one from participant to professional, from patron to paid; again and again I would have the same realization often coming too late to do anything about it: Once you come into the "free zone," the spell is broken. It's like being on the guest list to a magic show, but the only way to get to your seats is to walk through the backstage, watch the magician mid–costume change, a huge metal contraption affixed to his waist that, when covered with velour, looks like a floating orb but from back here it looks like a cheat. Being a pro in your scene is cool and exciting—it pays well in social currency and power and eventually even real money, but it strips away the thing that made you love the scene so much you wanted to turn it into a full-time pursuit in the first place.

But I didn't know all that then. I just knew I needed to get to the other side of that line. I started passing out flyers for the following weekend's party at the exit where people, if they were smart, were moonwalking past me. I did this long enough to want desperately to have my own party. Nothing on Earth seemed cooler and more important to seventeen-year-old me than to have a rave of my very own.

I approached a slimy businessman / bar mitzvah DJ I knew in AA who owned a sound system with a proposition for the ages: If he'd invest in my rave production company and foot the entire bill, I would give him . . . and the Jew in me is very ashamed to admit this . . . 100 percent of the profit. He eagerly agreed. I would do all of the work, book the DJs, hire the lighting guy, pass out the flyers, promote it with the skills I'd learned at the exits of the raves I'd been handing out flyers at, and he would get literally *all* of the money.

It took me years to look back and realize how profoundly un-ethical you'd have to be to hear a wide-eyed seventeen-year-old's pitch to work hundreds of hours in exchange for absolutely nothing and shake on it with a smile. You'd think he'd have at least peeled me off a few hundred bucks but no, he had his mark and to be fair, I conned myself. It was my idea.

My first party was called Meridian and the flyer I designed used,

I believe, a stock image of dancing figures I found on a clip art website. Under the block letters MERIDIAN was a laughable if laudable mission statement: "Dedicated to Taking Our Scene Back." Back from what? I was seventeen, had been attending raves less than a year, and already wanted to "take our scene back." Back to, I guess, nine months earlier when raves were still underground. Ah, the salad days of that past September.

Saturday, April 27, 1996. I found a small warehouse space South of Market in San Francisco. A "virgin" space. Ravers were obsessed with this, with popping the cherry of an abandoned office building or former lumberyard. The sound system would be provided by my investor over at "Hava Nagila Inc." I would book the DJs and the nitrous dealer. I actually got in a little trouble for this. As a sober guy, I was somewhat lost when it came to the drug options for my potential guests. I wanted it to be "as rave as possible," but apparently nitrous oxide (or "Hippie Crack," as they called it) created a vibe of fiendish ravers lining up, desperate to get their balloons filled, waving them in the air like refugees waving immigration paperwork at a border. It was a gray-area taboo. I knew none of this. I was aware that alcohol was forbidden. I know, hard to imagine, but at early raves, booze was a social no-no. Ecstasy, ketamine, and GHB were warmly welcomed as consciousness-expanding drugs, but booze was looked at as a kind of "bad vibe" drug of mainstream society. Instead of alcohol, makeshift bars at early parties would serve "Smart Drinks," smoothies that were stuffed full of amino acids and herbal supplements that had supposed psychedelic drug–enhancing properties. This is all before the Jamba Juice–on-every-corner revolution, man. That's right, folks; I remember smoothies back when they were still underground. That's how cool I really am.

Entrance was five dollars before midnight and seven after. Though you'd have to pay me exponentially more with each passing minute to get me to arrive at a party that late now; the peak hour of a rave was way past the witching hour. Two A.M. This is when you'd have your best DJ, this is when the people would be highest on whatever drug they were on, this is when the vibe would explode. We went all night long. We raved till dawn. We moved until we couldn't move. We beat the sun. Any real raver worth their salt will tell you the most euphoric feeling back then was dancing and dancing and dancing until, from the eastern corner of the warehouse wall, soft, pale fingers of light drew themselves onto the shoddy cracks in the corrugated steel walls of this most incongruous of dance spaces. The light spread across the room until it became a participant in the party. Until it became the reason we partied. We danced until the light was there.

That's how we danced.

As the party approached its peak, its, forgive me, *meridian,* I walked down the hallway connecting the main dance floor to the chill room at the back of the warehouse. A guy I knew from the scene approached me and gave me a hug, his kandi necklace grinding into my collarbone. "This is the best party I've ever been to, man! Thank you for putting it on. PLUR, brother."

I couldn't believe it. I couldn't believe I'd done it. On the dance floor, three hundred kids writhed and pumped to the DJ, perhaps having their own pupa-to-butterfly moment like I'd had at Cyberfest. In the chill room, smiles were huge and the puddles were a-cuddlin'. I'd done something special. I'd made a rave. This was, without exaggerating, the first thing in my life I'd done right. Middle-school dropout, rehab flunker, teenage drug addict, but now: rave promoter (unpaid).

The party went off without a hitch. It was a huge success for my investor and a huge moral victory for me. I was now a rave promoter, and that meant I was now on the side of the "doesn't pay" line. But I was also on the unemployment line. I decided I would become a full-time rave promoter and, inspired by the cool figures I danced in front of every weekend, a DJ. One small problem was, of course, I did not know how to DJ. DJing required expensive equipment. I threw another party, this one with slightly better terms for me, and with the money I made I was able to buy myself two Technics 1200 turntables and a mixer.

Now it was time to practice.

On this front I had a massive advantage: I still lived with my mother, and my mother is deaf. I could spend all day long train-wrecking techno beats* and no one would ever complain. I slowly got better and felt ready to start performing at parties. I hustled my way into a few gigs playing in the chill rooms, which had a lower barrier of entry than the main dance floor lineups. I understood the irony of a two-years-sober guy, still attending AA meetings, stealing off on the weekends to sonically guide people peaking on acid or writhing in MDMA euphoria. I loved it. I would spend my days poring through bins at the Amoeba Music record store trying to find obscure new age music from the seventies like Ray Lynch's "Deep Breakfast" and mix it with a Chaka Khan a cappella track. I'd mix Destiny's Child's "Say My Name" sped up to 45 rpm with a fast ambient jungle track. I'd play Eric B. and Rakim's "Paid in Full" and mix in a DJ Shadow instrumental beat back and forth to make the song last for ages. Over this I might play "Blackbird" by the Beatles. What I lacked in DJ skills I made up for in taking wild, risky mashup swings. I wouldn't say I got popular, but people liked what I was doing because it seemed no one else did it. I started to make a tiny name for myself and got booked more and more. I was a small-time rave promoter, a small-time chill room DJ, and was having big-time fun. I became like the mayor of the San Francisco rave scene. I started to know all the players, and they knew me. Every entrance to a party was like the Copacabana scene in *Goodfellas*, pointing, shaking hands, pressing the flesh.

There was a high-powered rave promoter named Craig who ambled up to me during one of his smaller parties (still five times bigger than the events I put on). After I'd finished up playing my chill room set, he told me that he was impressed with my set and with the fact that he'd heard I was sober. He was, too.

Craig was, let's say, a unique guy. He was built like a ninja, cov-

* Earlier I described DJs as smooth sound shamans, mixing together two separate songs to alchemize a new, seamless creation. But, of course, that describes a *good* DJ; for beginner DJs the more common sound is exactly what you'd imagine two songs playing simultaneously would sound like: a clashing, jangling, nightmare referred to as a "trainwreck."

ered in tattoos, and had a single dreadlock growing from the back of his head.

His car, a 1989 Mitsubishi Eclipse, was hyper-customized to create a "Batman" vibe. Actually, no, vibe is the wrong word. He was trying to build an actual Batmobile on a Mitsubishi chassis. The license plate read BATCAVE and the brake lights had silhouettes of the Batman symbol placed inside the plastic so that every time he tapped the brake to slow down, a shakily cut-out bat symbol would illuminate and announce to the world what his favorite DC Comics character was. The center console was cut and fabricated to have bat ears, fashioned out of fake leather and cardboard. There were secret compartments to hold . . . nerve gas, I guess? Those bat ears should have been a red flag warning me not to go into business with him, but I was seventeen, raves were by far the most important thing in my life, and Craig seemed like the coolest person I'd ever met. He was fucking Batman!

Batman took a shine to me. He told me that he was building a rave empire and that he wanted me to be his right-hand man, his Robin, if you will. He'd teach me all he knew about throwing massive parties and eventually turn the keys to his rave kingdom over to me. He'd also book me on every party he threw and help me grow my name as a DJ. Of course, a guy approaching me, a near stranger, and offering me a full partnership in his business should also have been a red flag, but I'd already ignored the Batman stuff so why not ignore this, too? After all, it was a huge opportunity. Never mind that Craig's former partner, a kid named Slinky, had pulled me aside and warned me that Craig would use me, not pay me, and discard me when I complained about not getting paid, but again, I was already committed to ignoring red flags. Haven't you been listening to me?

Now that Craig the rave king had taken me under his batwing, things changed for me in the scene. I was automatically added to every guest list for every party. I was in the 1 percent, firmly on the other side of the line. The access was dizzying and made me feel important. Every weekend, Craig would arrive approximately three hours after he said he was going to pick me up, not apologize for the tardiness, and we would zoom off in the Batmobile to a rave. We started to plan our first party together, a rave called Second Chakra. He wanted it to be a singular event. Craig, for all of his sketchiness, was an incredibly interesting and creative guy, operating on a much more innovative level than any of the other people throwing raves in the Bay Area. He was kind of a genius.

Most rave promoters kept things pretty simple. They knew that the party existing at all was enough for most attendees and that they really didn't need to do much to satisfy the further needs of a bunch of kids on drugs. Rent a warehouse, a sound system, and some lights barely better than ones you would have gotten at RadioShack, and that would be enough to make people happy.*

Not Craig.

He had a vision of opulence and fun that was positively Wonka-eqsue. His flyers moved away from the then-popular candy-wrapper-and-Lego-inspired renewed-childhood design and instead pulled in Renaissance paintings out of art history class.

Craig would emboss every thousandth flyer in gold leaf, and the embossed flyers would get the lucky recipient in for free, creating a kind of community game with the partygoers. His parties were ornately decorated, semi-Bergdorffian in their attention to detail. I spent hundreds of hours on top of a scissor lift hoisting up a mannequin painted fluorescent blue with huge *Angels in America* wings affixed to its back. Above the mannequin, we suspended a neon yellow baby doll, hanging in midair inside of an atom made of interlocked red hula hoops. This was the centerpiece, and in a line, we hung a procession of bright yellow female-formed angels as if pay-

---

* A similar business principle can be found in most mid-tier cities' kosher restaurants. In big Jewish populations, there are enough Jews for businesses to have to try to actually be delicious or people will go to another place to eat. But in Portland? In Oakland? In Cincinnati? There's usually only one kosher place to eat. Simply being kosher was as hard as they had to try, and as a result, you get a gruff Israeli tossing a plate of baloney shawarma on your table with an expression that suggests you ought to be grateful to be eating at all. Raves tended to be a "one party per weekend" affair. The party that week was the only game in town, and as a result promoters didn't have to try that hard.

ing tribute to the yellow baby and his blue plastic father. It was amazing. No one had ever done anything like this before. All the partygoers were dumbstruck when they rounded the bend into the main room and saw this fluorescent Sistine Chapel. I mean, in reality, it would have been laughed out of any art museum as corny and derivative.

But for the ravers that night, it was a slice of heaven.

Craig threw the coolest parties and I was his number one man, which made me the second-coolest guy in the entire San Francisco rave scene. I started getting booked at parties every weekend. I moved slowly out of the chill room and onto the main floor. Things were happening.

There was only one problem.

Despite the hundreds and hundreds of hours I spent working on these parties, I never seemed to really get paid. Who could have seen this coming!? I was only given an explicit warning that this exact scenario would occur! Craig would give me money here and there—he'd give me a stack of bills at the end of a successful party, for instance—but it never seemed commensurate with the effort that I'd put in. It never seemed like number two–man money. It felt a little more like bottom bitch money.

When I complained, Craig fast-talked past the actual issue, which was to simply pay me fairly, and offered me . . . a different solution. I could join his other enterprise. Not as a rave promoter, but by providing a service just as vital to the rave experience as party promotion. And that is how, in 1997, two and a half years sober and two years after I started raving, I became a small-time ecstasy dealer for Batman.

I needed a job, and drug dealing is a classically well-paying profession. This was a very awkward time in my life. I'd become a petty criminal just after totally turning my life around. The rave scene was so socially all-encompassing that it never really occurred to me that I was putting myself at risk of arrest or getting robbed or anything. It just became what I did. I didn't think about it all that much.

I'd stand at the entrance of every rave and mutter to everyone walking by like a very quiet barker at a Middle Eastern open-air market, "E? E? Anybody need any E?"

Ecstasy dealing at raves is an odd kind of drug dealing because it takes place all at once. Ninety-nine percent of E sales happened upon the phalanx of entry at the beginning of a party. Ravers would walk in with a mission: Find some E, drop it early, and then get the party started. After the first couple of hours of a party, the need for E would plummet to those who got sold fake shit or those who had drug problems and needed more shit.

My shit was good! Or so I was told. I've never even taken MDMA. I got sober too young and missed my chance at all that. But I think I know what ecstasy feels like anyway. I'm guessing it feels "really good" and "like a kind of ecstasy." I was able to use this kind of marketing language to take my biscuit slangin' to the next level. Each pill was twenty a pop, and I got to keep ten. Craig got the other ten. I could make a couple hundred bucks in a night and then go dance once all the partygoers were satisfied.

But those first couple of hours contained chances for very strange interactions. AA people went to raves. How strange it was to stand there, hawking my MDMA, whispering to strangers "E? E? Need any E? E . . . GADS! It's you! From the Tuesday night meeting! How are you, my recovery brother?! Never mind me!"

This kind of split lifestyle wasn't gonna work. I knew that I would soon be faced with a dilemma: AA or raves. But I also knew at that time that my choice would be pretty clear and pretty easy. I wanted to be a normal kid. I was almost eighteen and I'd finally found a scene where people liked me, where I was confident, and where I could meet girls and they liked me, which is really pretty important to an eighteen-year-old. A place where I had social currency and power. Where fun and earning a living happened at the same time. It was no contest. A few months later, I stopped going to meetings and threw myself further into the scene and further into Craig's empire.

The parties we threw together were slowly creeping toward massives. In those days there were really two kinds of parties: undergrounds and massives. Undergrounds were smaller affairs, a few hundred people, a lesser-known DJ lineup, and a general desire to stay connected to the PLUR roots of the rave scene. They were small, vibey affairs where you'd manage to hug or dance with most everyone at the party. They vibrated with peace and community. They were *not* thrown for the money but for some kind of allegiance to the scene. Originally these were the kind of parties I threw and the kind I liked to attend.

Massives, on the other hand, were . . . massive. They were thrown with the explicit mission of making money and putting on an awe-inspiring (if not love-inspiring) good time. They were permitted by the city and often had off-duty cops working security. Massives were thrown in gigantic warehouses or convention centers, fairgrounds or airplane hangars. They were what you think when you think *rave*. Lasers zapping, sound system throbbing, thousands and thousands and thousands of people gyrating. They had their place. The first party I went to, Cyberfest, was a massive.

Then there were the hybrid parties, which were essentially small massives trying to be two things at once. Intimate and authentic affairs that were still moneymaking enterprises with thousands of attendees. The ultimate example of this was the Gathering, a massive party by any estimation, but one that had been around San Francisco for so long that it got a pass in pretending to be underground. These hybrid raves were what Craig had been trying to do with his parties. I respected the vision of what Craig was trying to do. I found his ideas exciting and, if I'm being honest, I was excited by the idea of becoming more powerful in the scene. My little underground parties had been amazing. They kept me buzzing for weeks, but there were only a few hundred people there. And they kept getting shut down by the police. Here was an opportunity to take the thing I loved and bring it to scale. Here was my chance to really become a full-time DJ. Here was my chance to make my rave dreams come true.

Craig had bigger dreams yet.

The next party we put on would be a legit massive, in partnership with another production company, but together we worked on a brand-new idea: a massive that spanned genres. Not allowing the lineup to be limited by electronic music, we'd book hip hop acts for what I think was one of the first of its kind. This party was called Planet Rock, and rather than the typical rave acts the headliners were hip hop legends Afrika Bambaataa and Grandmaster Flash.

In hindsight, it was a watershed event. Until that time, even with raves as massive as they were, the idea of nonelectronic musical acts was sort of taboo. I mean, sure, there was the night that Yanni played his weird pan flute in the chill room, but I might have imagined that. Prior to this party, if you wanted a "really big act," you'd book one of the underground superstars of rave legend, like Frankie Bones or the Detroit innovators of techno Derrick May and Juan Atkins. Or perhaps you'd book one of the European mega DJs like Sasha, John Digweed, or Sven Väth. Are you recognizing any of these names? No? Good, that's how we liked it!

Planet Rock ripped down that invisible fence between genres and, I would posit, signaled the beginning of the end of the era of the "true rave." Once the seal was broken, all bets were off, and the scene slowly began to morph into the era of electronic music festivals. Afrika Bambaataa wasn't exactly a household name—he's more firmly in the "legend" category—but after this party came parties with KRS-One and the Black Eyed Peas. This isn't *that* odd; hip hop and dance music have a lot more in common than most people from either scene used to want to admit. In the early days, there was even a subgenre of both music forms called "hip house," where rappers rhymed over banging disco beats. The most famous track from this mostly cringey subgenre was "I'll House You" by the Jungle Brothers. There was "ghetto house," a house subgenre championed mostly by a guy called DJ Funk who played slammin' house with absolutely *filthy* rap samples laid over them. There was "Jungle/ Drum and Bass," which is essentially double-time hip hop break beats that often had MC's rapping over it. Hip hop and electronic dance music had *very* similar musical roots both culturally and technically. Both used drum machines and turntables, both relied on DJs to get the party started, both were pioneered by bored Black teenagers in the inner city. But mostly, they'd gone their separate ways and were now coming back to meet one another. It wasn't out of no-where, but it was unexpected.

Eventually someone thought, hey, why stop at hip hop? Why not rock? Why not pop? Why not leave the warehouse altogether? Why not be Coachella? This kind of evolution was inevitable. It is a mark of maturity and age. Promoters grow up and move beyond their dreams of being kings of a tiny scene. Eventually they want to make real-world money and do real-world things. Promoters want to send their kids to college, too. And I hate to admit it but eventually you need more than house and techno.

But anyway, back to the party.

Planet Rock was huge, but it was also a disaster. There was a point in the night when the line grew so long and the rate at which people were being let in was so slow that it reached critical mass. I was standing there, staring at the fence as the crowd grew and with it their impatience. Here's the closest I get to mysticism in life: I be-lieved then and I believe now that the *intention* of the promoter of one party or another has a direct effect on the demographics and the vibe of the crowd that shows up to that party. If the intentions are pure, the party, even if it's a massive, will feel pure. The crowd in-gests the energy of the party itself and manifests that.

Planet Rock was thrown for money and size. It was a mic drop, a dick-measuring contest. As such, the crowd was greedy, impatient, and unwilling to pitch in with good intentions when logistics broke down. I don't blame Craig. But I understand why the next thing happened.

The crowd started undulating forward, pushing on the fence, shaking it, and yelling "Let us in!"

They pushed farther. I stood there in shock. I'd helped put this party on—and it was quickly becoming a riot. I tsk-tsked the crowd yelling, "This isn't who we are! PLUR everybody! Remember? PLUR!" A moment later, the twenty-foot chain-link gate buckled and fell to the ground and thousands of ravers charged at me like a scene from *(b)Raveheart*.

Okay, so they didn't remember PLUR.

"Fuck this," I shouted and ran in toward the production office. Craig was in there with a look I'd never seen him exude: fear. I lit a cigarette, trying to calm down and catch my breath, when another producer of the party came in. "Some teenage girl just OD'd. I think she's dead."

I was stunned. What the hell *was* this party? Had I contributed hundreds of man-hours toward something that had ended a life? And why? For what? Didn't I do all this rave stuff because it was my community? Didn't I do it from a place of love? Could I really look around at this party, bloated with commercialism, turned violent and dangerous, and say I was here for anything resembling a good reason? Could I really claim I was the good guy and Craig the bad?

The girl survived. The crowd was eventually calmed down, and order was restored. But something had changed in me.

Planet Rock was a financial nightmare. The promised return for Craig's investors didn't come through, and he suddenly went from being the rave king to persona non grata. This is the unfortunate reality of doing business in the legal gray area of "underground" scenes. People are often living hand to mouth, event to event, and their fates pivot quite quickly. It took only one party to end him.

The rave king was deposed.

He needed his number two as his public face. This was my moment to finally take center stage. He explained the terms to me: The next party would be my party. I would be the face of it. I had to be. And it was also going to be a fundraiser for Craig. Specifically him. *He* was the cause. Getting his Planet Rock investors paid off was the mission of this party that I would be assuming the risk for. He would get the money, and once again I would be paid in enthusiasm. The *next* next party, the one *after this one,* that's when the access codes to his rave kingdom would *really, really* get turned over to me. That's the party where I would get paid, would get my accolades, would get all the direct contact with the investors and the people who made all the decisions. I wasn't getting conned; I was getting pimped.

But I was already in this far. I said okay.

The party was called Pangea, and it was the first of Craig's parties to be thrown by my production company Bay Area Underground. The people (just me) who brought you Meridian! My long-lost credo "Dedicated to Taking Our Scene Back" would be included on the flyer for this party but with a slight edit. It read "Dedicated to Paying Back What's Owed, to Those Who Make Our Scene Happen." It might as well have read, "Dedicated to Paying Craig's Investors Back." Why did I like getting ripped off so much?! My only defense was that I was really young (this defense worked better when I was fifteen), in over my head, and a middle-school dropout.

Pangea was a great success. Big but not overwrought, intimate but still raking in the cold hard cash for good (?) ol' Craig. After that party, right when my time to truly take over had arrived, Craig did the opposite of arriving.

He just disappeared. Poof.

With him gone, my DJ career began to slowly dry up. I hadn't realized how many of the gigs I got were just from being connected to him. My underground cred was shot by association, so I couldn't play *those* parties anymore, and my massive party cred was shot by the same association, so I couldn't play *those* parties anymore.

I still got in free to any party I wanted, I was still on that side of the line, but I would mostly go, stand on a wall, and roll my eyes at the changing demographics of the scene. It was getting *so young* and so . . . I hate to use incendiary language but . . . *mainstream.*

When I'd begun to go to parties I was sixteen. I was the youngest person I'd meet at most raves. By the point I was grumbling on a warehouse wall, sixteen was the median age. Or at least it felt like it was. Did I want to make a living throwing parties for high school kids? Was I Spicoli?

My connection to it all entered a rapid decline. I would get a gig a month, then a gig every few months, and then it had been a long while since I'd been asked to play anywhere. I would walk into record stores in a good mood, look at all the rave flyers for upcoming parties, realize what I already knew—that my name was not on those flyers and that I didn't really know these people—my blood would begin to boil and I would leave in a terrible mood.

• • •

By the summer of 1999, I was a soaky mess. I took baths. Like, a lot. I guess you might call it a depression, but I just thought I was suddenly enamored of getting really, really, like, super clean. I'd wake up at around three P.M., "the crack of evening." I'd lift my little head up and look around. "Nothing much to do today," I'd reason and go back to sleep until my body screamed at me to get up. Then I'd draw a bath and get in it.

There are three reasons to take a daily bath: 1) You are a menopausal woman getting back in touch with your body; 2) you live in the year 1813 and your only possibility of getting clean is for the local saloon to heat up a wooden barrel of water and give you a scrub brush to wash the trail dust off of your back; or 3) you are a depressed twenty-year-old clean and sober ecstasy dealer who hasn't been to a meeting in a year.

Ding-ding, that's me, number three!

I'd draw the bath and get in and immediately fall back asleep. You know that thing where you stay in the bath so long that your fingers prune up like a real cutie patootie? Well, if you stay in long enough that process continues until the pruning cracks and rips your skin and when you climb out, your hands and feet feel like you've run them over a cheese grater. That process would serve as my pain alarm clock to get back up and out of the bath and face the day. Except the day was over. I'd face the night! I'd clean up and put on some clothes and get myself to a rave or a club and I'd stand in the entryway, with a pocket full of ecstasy pills. I was *that* guy. I'd become *that* guy.

I'd thought I'd left this life behind, but somehow this thing that had been like a portal to a new life, this scene, this olive branch from the social universe, had swallowed me up and had curdled around me. It wasn't *fun* anymore. In a lot of ways, I felt like I was right back where I was before I had even gotten sober. Cynical, jaded, distrustful, angry. Apart. The fact that I was right back there while still sober was alarming.

The last straw was when I saw a flyer for a party featuring a DJ with a rather familiar sounding name, "E-Moshe." I kept reading the name over and over again. It did not compute. E-Moshe? What the fuck? I'd been playing and promoting parties for years at that point. How could this guy not know that he was naming himself after an established DJ, added an E, and decided to make his debut? I couldn't go down to Altamont, call myself E-Mick Jagger, and play "Start Me Up." What the fuck was wrong with this guy?

I decided to find out.

I went to the party this charlatan was performing at (got in free, felt nothing), waited for his set to end, and walked right up to him. "Hey are you"—I had a hard time even saying it—"E . . . Moshe?"

He smiled, "Yeah, that's me!"

I cleared my throat "Okay. Well, uh . . . my *name* is Moshe. I'm a DJ here in the SF scene. Have been for a while."

"Yeah!" he said. "I've heard of you!"

You don't say, I thought.

I started pulling out reams of flyers of raves I'd performed at. "Here I am at Mega Buzz, here at Open, here I am at Acid Breaks, Second Chakra, it goes on and on. I've been performing at raves for years."

He smiled again. "That's so fucking cool, bro!"

Was he fucking with me? He really didn't seem to be. I continued, "I, uh . . . I'm saying I don't think it's cool of you to have a DJ name so similar to mine."

He frowned now. "Oh. Shit. Okay."

I stared at him. "So . . . you'll change it?"

"Sorry," he said. "No."

I felt like pulling my fucking hair out. "Dude, this is the first party you've ever played at. Like, what are you even walking away from? Is Moshe your Hebrew name or something?"

He shook his head, "Oh no. I'm not Jewish."

My eyes went wide. "Well, then, why did you choose this name?"

He thought about it for a second. "I just thought it sounded cool."

My eyes went wider still. "It does sound fucking cool! It's my fucking name!" I was losing it. "Look," I said, getting desperate now, "I will battle you for it."

He was confused. "What?"

I dug in. "I'll battle you for it. We will throw a party. Both do a set. Let the crowd decide. Whoever wins gets to keep the name." I was going old-school now, *Electric Boogaloo* style. I'd take this dispute to the rave streets.

"Oh," he said. "Nah. I'm good. I'm just gonna keep the name."

I now had two choices. Accept this fucking weirdo having my e-name, or beat him to death. I didn't have my Escape sock anymore. I'd left it at Cyberfest. I gathered up my rave flyers and walked away. And for the first time, I had the conscious, previously unthinkable thought, one I would one day come to recognize as familiar, "Maybe I don't belong here anymore."*

At the same time, another unthinkable shift was happening. Electronic music acts were becoming mainstream stars.

In 1990, house music had its first real hit with Deee-Lite's "Groove Is in the Heart," but the truth is it could only nominally be called house music. It was a fantastic song, playful and dense, layered and absolutely (de)groovy, but really it was a pop song with some house elements. Prior to that, C+C Music Factory and a couple of others had had some songs approaching hits on the dance charts, but really no artist in America could crack anything like mainstream success. In Europe dance tracks charted regularly, but Europeans also loved Speedos and spandex shirts, so who could trust them? Largely, record companies had given up on electronic music and in some cases were even openly antagonistic toward it because of its association with the moral-panicked view of raves as drug dens. If artists did get

---

* By the way, I never saw a flyer or heard of a party where the infamous DJ E-Moshe was playing again. He simply showed up, pissed me off, and disappeared. To this day, I cannot be sure he was a real person or just a guardian angel—sent to help me with my transition from the underground to the world beyond.

signed, it was to indie dance labels or deep-sub labels of the big conglomerates. Occasionally house music legends would remix some famous mainstream musician's single into a "club mix," but it would be little noticed and mostly heard only at the actual club.

Then something shifted.

People started to notice electronic music. Underworld, Fatboy Slim, the Prodigy, the Chemical Brothers, and more all had albums that if not chart topping were at least chart bottoming. And then it happened: Daft Punk released an album called *Homework* that was absolutely massive. The second single, "Around the World," dropped and you literally couldn't step into a dance club or mall without hearing it. All of this was unimaginable and exciting.

Moby had been a rave legend, DJing at warehouse parties through the 1990s. His "big hit" before the shift was a track called "Go," which was a hauntingly beautiful and simple rave anthem. Don't worry if you haven't heard it; it wasn't his time. Then came "Feeling So Real," a hands-in-the-air hardcore track that seemed made for the Berlin Love Parade. Again, don't worry if you haven't heard it; it still wasn't his time. My point is Moby was huge in the rave scene, all of the aforementioned artists were, and no one outside of our little culture had heard of them. Then came Moby's album *Play*, a record that, if you watched a commercial in the year 2000, you for sure heard. It exploded. It was his time.

These artists were all "real ravers," pioneers who'd been grinding their heads into the buzzsaw of the music industry for years. They'd been kept financially afloat by the scene, by the raves and clubs. They were underground kings finally getting their due. These were *our* superstars. I don't mean to suggest these acts were obscure. They weren't. They'd headline raves in the United States and music festivals in Europe, they were wealthy and successful, but compared to any real chart-topping act, these groups were all still a part of our little secret.

Huge DJs like Carl Cox and Sasha could sell out large venues and a group of them could sell out a massive warehouse. But an arena? No one could do that. We only had one "superstar" DJ and that was a colorful character named Superstar DJ Keoki who was a superstar only because he kept telling everyone that's what he was. Then Paul Oakenfold, a legendary British DJ who'd been around dance music since the earliest raves, since *before* that, remixed a track for U2 that got more play than the original. He went on tour with the band and brought some version of the rave to Wembley Stadium. Then DJ Tiësto, a Dutch trance DJ with a massive following, embarked on an experiment: He'd try an arena tour. And it worked.

Now we had *actual* superstars.

With the true commercial success of these rave legends, these people who we felt "deserved it," something started to change. It was slow at first, imperceptible, the artists ascending to rock-star status, but it didn't affect us. They floated into rarefied air and the underground tipped its cap to them and kept on raving. But as they garnered more and more acclaim, the music they made started to sink into the ears of America and the world. They too had their "'100% Pure Love' at the Danville AA Dance" moment. They, too, were metamorphosed.

Within ten years, the rave scene would essentially be gone, replaced in full by music festivals so massive we never could have seen it coming. Never in a million years could I have imagined two hundred thousand kids at a festival and they were *all* there to see the DJs. Back then three thousand attendees was a massive. Never could I have imagined the 2013 Outside Lands festival, where I watched as tens of thousands of kids streamed from the stage where Nine Inch Nails began their set—the audience confused by what they were listening to—toward the real reason they came to the festival: to see a German pop techno DJ named Zedd who'd done tracks with Selena Gomez and Ariana Grande. Never could I have imagined driving down Sunset Boulevard and seeing billboard after billboard advertising the DJs playing at the biggest casinos in Las Vegas, their draw becoming as profitable for the city of sin as the gambling tables. Never could I have imagined looking at the top twenty DJs in the world and not only barely knowing who any of them were, but that they'd be worth a hundred million apiece. Martin Garrix, one of the biggest and highest paid DJs in the world right now, was *born* a year after I attended my first rave. The way he fell in love with this music was not at a dingy warehouse, its padlock cut open by an angle grinder and a pirate sound system set up in a hurry for hungry ravers. He was watching the opening ceremony of the 2004 Olympics and saw Tiësto, the world's first rave DJ stadium act, spinning records to the assembled Jamaican javelin team. Martin Garrix doesn't care about the underground. How could he? His entire vision of what the "scene" is launches from literally the biggest stage in the world. He isn't "dedicated to taking our scene back" like little Moshe throwing his first rave in 1996. To him, there is no back. Back to where? The Sydney Olympics? When he thinks of dance music he doesn't have to envision a future where the world finally "gets it." He was born into that future. His context is different. This is not negative. This is not a lamentation of "what has become." This is what must be and what always happens. The moment something is created, it is also given away, willingly or not.

The rave scene and dance music does not belong to old-school ravers, and, justly or not, it doesn't belong to the people who started it all; it doesn't belong to Derrick May or Jesse Saunders or Kevin Saunderson or Larry Levan or Frankie Knuckles or Frankie Bones or Paul Oakenfold or Tiësto or the Chainsmokers or Martin Garrix.

It belongs to whoever wants it. It belongs to whoever is there. To whoever finds it. To whoever chooses it. To whoever dances.

For a time, it belonged to me.

3 Deafness, or For Whom the Bell Tolls Unheard

My mother has no boundaries.

The deaf are not known for their social graces. In deaf circles, it's known that, if it's been a while and you've gained weight, you are likely to receive a hearty greeting of "Hello! Oh my! You've gotten so fat! Why?" from a deaf person.

I've never been able to figure out exactly why that is, why the lack of hearing leads directly to a razor slicing through the bullshit, right to the meat of the thing. This can manifest in a few ways.

Deaf people fart. Or maybe it's just the deaf people in my family.

Without the ability to hear the trumpet blast embarrassment alarm, just about every deaf person I know lets it rip with abandon. They are never embarrassed about it. They hardly even acknowledge it happened. Without the full scale of exposure to the specific stimulus that one is embarrassed about, one apparently just can't muster the will to *be* embarrassed.

It's not that they don't know farts are embarrassing to hearing people. Deaf people are not some pure, naïve souls, levitating above the brown cloud we occupy. They live in the same world we do. They know all about the rules in hearing society. They've just set up a separate society within the foolish, delicate castle of manners and convention that we hearing people fortify with our bullshit. They know hearing people have decided that a fart is considered worse than a yawn; they just don't really care. I'm not sure if they are right and we are wrong. All I know for sure is that my mother farts in public.

But my mother goes beyond the cultural relativist dance I'm describing and into the realm of the shockingly inappropriate. Maybe all those farts have blown down the walls that we've built up around every social agreement. The foremost among them: the line of appropriate sexual communication between mother and son.

Hang on to your hat, this will get uncomfortable. But just imagine how uncomfortable I was (am).

My mother loves masturbation. It's kind of her *thing*. Farting and masturbating. In my house growing up there was always a prominently displayed Hitachi Magic Wand hanging out on her dresser with zero self-consciousness or any attempt to hide it. Do I have to mention that the Magic Wand is the loudest vibrator available? And that my mother has no relationship to the concept of sound?

Right next to it was always a large purple bottle of Astroglide lube. I could never use Astroglide myself. Beyond its horrifying viscosity and ectoplasmic makeup are the terrible images in my imagination of my mother slathering the stuff onto her wall plug-in vibrator whose low, deep humming kept me awake at night and infiltrated my dreams; boogeymen whose spoken language was a mix of Hitachi-esque Japanese and guttural vibratory buzzing.

Let me say this again . . . I can't use Astroglide *because it reminds me of my mother.*

My mother was thrilled by my sexuality. She was determined to make sure I had a healthy and open sex life. How I longed for the sex education that most of my friends at school got: Anecdotes passed down from *Hustler* magazines to older brothers and then to the playground. Third-hand misinformation that had gone through amazing telephone game transformations and left us with advice like "Always wear a condom every day, all day; that's the only way to avoid AIDS" and "Women give birth out of their assholes" and "Women actually have a thing called the clitoris" and other such playground legends.

I knew way too much way too fast. Regular sex-ed lectures from my mother broke down the labia minora, the labia majora, and the uber-rare "labia menorah," a vaginal lip seen only on Jewish women for eight days a year around Christmastime.

I knew about female orgasm and read books with tips for masturbation. I tried one that suggested using the inside of a toilet paper
roll as a homemade masturbation tool. I found my eight-year-old
penis woefully lacking the girth for what I imagine is an entirely
unpleasant experience even for a full-grown penis. Hard edges and
all that. Use it vigorously enough and turn the whole thing into instant papier-mâché.

A few years later, when my mother found pornography in my
room, rather than yell at me, she took me shopping at a local feminist vibrator shop with aisles and aisles of dildos and throbbing
dolphin clit ticklers, and, shudderingly, in the corner, an entire mon-
ument to the Hitachi Magic Wand, apparently the Eames chair of
vibrators. She pointed me to the literary section and allowed me to
select volumes of Anaïs-Nin-without-the-writing-skill feminist erot-
ica. I guess she wanted to be sure that if I was going to dabble in
porn it would have at least ninety pages of expository prose poetry
before we got to the good stuff.

Eventually I started bringing women home. Mother was thrilled.
Once, when I was sixteen, my mother walked in on me and a girl. I
was facedown with the covers pulled up just over my head, lying
fully prone on my belly as I experimented with such advanced
mother-taught cunnilingus techniques as "the turtle," "the butterfly," and "the Michael Douglas," where you eat so much pussy you
nearly die. I was prostrate before the temple of goddess worship
when I heard the door to my bedroom open. My mother had walked
in. Again, I was entirely prone. Flat on my stomach. Picture it. Picture it. You have to because I've had to. This belongs to you now,
too. Like the video in *The Ring*.

Using core muscles I didn't know I had, I catapulted myself up
from my entirely flattened position, the blanket pulled tight around
my neck to protect my nakedness. I leapt up and flew through the
air, flew over my terrified lover, the blanket billowing behind me like
the cape of a pussy-eating superhero, and landed on top of her, covering us both with the blanket. I held my breath. I heard the door
close again.

Many mothers would have been mad or, at the very least, concerned with what was happening under their roof, but my mother simply told me later that day that she was "sorry she interrupted my private time."

That was it. She apologized to me!

Well, that was *almost it*. My mother told my grandmother about the incident and my grandma cornered me the next day to have a little chat.

"I've noticed you've started bringing girls around," she started, looking deeply into my eyes, probing for something. "I just hope that you've been satisfying those women."

"On what level are you saying that, Grandma?"

"Oh, on a sexual level! You know your grandfather made me climax every time we made love and I just think . . ."

"Grandma, never, ever speak to me about this again!"

That kind of conversation leaves a ton of emotional scar tissue. I still deal with it. It's been twelve years since my grandmother died, and I still can't achieve orgasm with a woman until I yell, "You just got Grandpa Kashered!" and then dump a bag of Werther's Originals on top of her and run out of the room.

Sometimes, when I meet a nice Catholic person whose ideas of sex have been destroyed by parochial shame games, I get a little jealous. You mean your mom made you feel ashamed to masturbate?! She didn't buy you special Kama Sutra brand jerk-off lotion when she learned you were just getting into it? She told you God was watching and was mad about it?! You lucky dog!

And I'm sorry to trivialize anyone's sexual trauma; I don't want to do that. I certainly realize that the trauma of feast is preferable to the trauma of famine, but I wish I'd had just a teeny bit less to eat growing up.

And yet, despite how weird it all was, there's something kind of heroic about it. My mother. The wildly sex-positive, deaf single mom, raising me in a household devoid of sexual hang-ups and patriarchal ideals of sexuality. In a world of slut shaming and sexualities so twisted by embarrassment and religious dogma they can hardly be discerned from psychological disorders, my mother was offering me the opportunity to be exposed to sex and embrace it as normal.

And I think it all goes back to her deafness. She farts because people fart. She fucks because people fuck. I mean, she might have heard that we are supposed to keep both things quiet, but she couldn't care less about that idea. Where you find a "You've gotten so fat, why?" so too will you find a "You really need to buy a Hitachi Magic Wand because it will make you cum like crazy."

Because it's just the truth. She did fart. You did get fat. You would cum like crazy.

She still has the Hitachi, in case you were wondering. It still sits there, in its place of honor next to that horrible purple bottle of lube, daring someone, anyone, to say, "Can't you just, like, put that in one of the drawers? It's sitting on top of a bunch of drawers."

My mother is seventy-five now. I'm sure when she's getting close to the end, and almost all of her strength has left her and she's ready to pass over, I'll come visit her in a hospice center and be able to find her room by listening carefully and following the sound trail of a low robotic humming followed by a deep, orgasmic, Earth-shaking fart.

I am a CODA, a child of a deaf adult, which, I guess, makes my mother a COHA, a child of a hearing adult. Two actually.

One was her father, Dick Worthen, a man's man, a house builder, a World War II airplane mechanic, an English professor, a bastard. My entire life, I never heard my grandmother speak a single positive word about Dick until that day she told me he made her shudder with orgasmic bliss every single time they banged. Dick fell asleep at the switch on parenthood. Dick's only child, my farting mother, Beatrice, was born deaf, her eardrum ballooned up into non-functionality. And Dick, a prominent English professor in the Bay Area, an activist for the advent of the modern community college system, and by all accounts a remarkable and passionate advocate for the importance of the mastery of language, never learned sign language. Until the end of his life, his communication with his only child, my mother, was limited to a mix of cartoonish gesticulations and scribbled notes. The master of communication couldn't communicate with his own child. Which is tragic, but also tragically common. The vast majority of deaf people are born to hearing parents, and a heartbreaking number of those parents never bother to learn the language that would enable them to have a relationship with their children.

My grandmother, Hope Worthen, receiver of Dick's seemingly magical dick, was the "other way" this story can go. She was a public school teacher in the Oakland public school system. The moment she realized my mother was deaf, my grandmother quit her job, went to graduate school in deaf education, and eventually went back to work for Oakland public schools, leading their program teaching deaf children. In other words, she did what mothers do. She put her child first, and my mother reaped the benefits.

This question is raised every time two unwitting hearing people give birth to an unexpectedly deaf child: "What are we going to do?"

Their answer to that question decides not only their relationship with the child but also forges that child's destiny, determines if they will be a professional or a pauper, illiterate or enlightened, independent or subordinate to state-sanctioned "help." The decisions of people with zero experience in the deaf world, who have never really thought about deafness in any way, shape the future of the deaf, again and again.

Though Dick's neglect is common, more common still are passionate parents who only want the best for their deaf children. But a parent's love for their children is not a guarantee of sound decision-making. In many ways, it can have exactly the opposite effect. People's love of their children is so overwhelming it can become impossible to recognize the choice you are making *for* that child is actually a gateway to their downfall. This kind of destructive, "best interest" parenting is made more acute by faulty information. Sometimes this information comes from a QAnon adherent, convincing a parent that the polio vaccine is filled with the spinal cord fluid of enslaved unbaptized babies, and sometimes, in the case of the deaf, it comes from the inventor of the telephone.

• • •

Young Alexander Bell was born with a chip on his shoulder. Unlike his brothers, he had been born without a middle name, and he pleaded and petitioned his dad for the dignity afforded a three-named person. On his eleventh birthday, Daddy Bell relented and gave him the gift of the middle name Graham. This just goes to show you how poor and bored people were in the mid-1800s: You could delight a child with a birthday gift of being named after a cracker. You know Alexander Graham Bell as the man who invented the phone. But to the deaf community, he is more than that, a self-appointed Moses, a boogeyman, a Pied Piper, playing a flute no one could nor wanted to hear, guiding the deaf to their educational doom.

Bell was, like me, the child of a deaf mother and was married to a deaf woman. You'd think that would ingratiate the deaf to him, that his connection with that world would be, as mine is, tender and loving and filled with a fierce loyalty. And maybe Bell felt that loyalty, but tender and loving he was not. It is not hyperbole to say that, in some ways, he wanted to eradicate the deaf from the face of the Earth.

Like most hearing people throughout the history of the deaf, the way he proposed to do it was to "help" them. Without even asking if they wanted that help, he would insert himself into their world, slam a railroad switch into the track of their emancipation, and force a crossroads where before there had been a straight line. He was, for all intents and purposes, an imperialist, considering his superiority objective and decreeing the great tragedy it would be to deny it to a primitive culture. And, just like standard-issue imperialism, the savages he wanted to liberate were unaware of their savagery; they were whole and complete, not in need of rescue. The liberty he offered would quite quickly prove itself to be a prison.

Before Bell imposed his will upon the deaf, they had been on a one-hundred-year journey out of darkness. Their own self-initiated liberation was a dramatic tale of impossible odds, Napoleonic violence, Catholic education, and three singular geniuses living at the same time, in the same place: a tale that eventually led to the founding of the National Institute for Deaf Children of Paris.

Prior to the establishment of the school in 1750, the station of the deaf in France (and the rest of the world) was largely a dire one. We're talking old-school "bath a month" France, so let's be real: The station of everyone in France other than powdered-wig, paint-a-mole aristocrats was pretty dire.

But if you were born deaf? You were fucked.

Often, you'd be born poor in a village where you were the only deaf kid. The only language you'd ever receive or experience was whatever gesture you and your family invented in order to get you to understand when Papa said, "Pass the ratatouille." You'd be born in the dark, destined to destitution, largely wordless and language-less, an island of deafness alone in a sea of the hearing.

But what if luck smiled on you and the genetic deafness in your family tree produced more than one deaf kid? At that, your chances of intellectual freedom exploded. You and your deaf sibling could pass language back and forth, building on it an increasingly complex structure. With the simple power of one peer, a peer who defaulted to your natural state of communication, you could, quite literally, create a new language. A language of two. With that, you could unlock your mind, learn to communicate, and step out into the light.

A pair of siblings just like that met a Catholic priest, Charles-Michel, abbé de l'Epée, "the abbé," in 1770 and changed the destiny of the deaf in France and then the world.

Prior to this meeting, the intellectual status of the deaf was in question. Aristotle himself thought that the deaf were incapable of reason or complex thought. He claimed reason without hearing was an impossibility. The truth is, it is not hearing but *language* that unlocks reason, and deafness at that time had the profoundly destructive effect of cutting people off from language. But like two male velociraptors in a Michael Crichton book, deaf people (like all people) "found a way." They created language from nothing, and it was this language that the abbé encountered in a Parisian slum in 1770. Struck with the hand movements he saw exchanged between two deaf sisters, he knew that he was looking at language and, at that moment, he dedicated his life to finding a way to use those signs to educate the deaf, and to allow them salvation.

Salvation was most of his concern. The abbé intuitively saw that deaf people had no less ability to reason than anyone else but, if they didn't have language, they could not be given the sacrament and were therefore damned to hell. This makes perfect sense of course: an almighty God, looking down at the deaf and saying to the devil, "Look, if they could *talk* I would grant them permission to eat my God-Body biscuits but, with things as they are, my hands are tied. They're all yours! Into the eternal hellfire they go!"

From this religious instruction, and these two signing girls, the first free school for the deaf was formed, the National Institute for Deaf Children of Paris. The abbé began to gather deaf students from around France and to teach those children.

The abbé was a teacher, but he learned as much as he taught. As he was taught by his students how to sign, he reciprocated by using those very signs to teach them French, how to take the sacraments, and indeed how to acquire the knowledge that had been withheld from them behind an unscalable wall of spoken language.

In other words, the students taught him how to weave rope and the abbé taught them how to form it into a ladder that they could use to scale the wall. Over the years the signing system, aided and added to by all of the gathered deaf students there, formed and shaped by the collective body of the deaf in Paris and the teachers at the school, became increasingly complex and sophisticated, and by the time Laurent Clerc, the father of modern American Sign Language, arrived, fresh from a French village and hungry for language, there was language waiting for him.

Born in 1785 in a village outside of Lyon, France, Laurent Clerc became deaf after an accident when he was one year old. He was lucky enough to be the son of the mayor. If he'd been the son of the baker, odds are we'd have never heard of him and he'd have died in that same village, making baguettes in a languageless world.

I know that France is so charming that it's hard to paint a tragic picture by saying "this poor guy might've been living in a rustic French village, pulling crusty bread out of an oven and spreading it with fresh-churned butter made from the milk of the cow that lived next door." But for Clerc and the world, it would have been a tragedy, because when Clerc left that village for Paris and the school for the deaf, he began a journey toward changing America, changing the world, and changing my life.

When he arrived at the National Institute for the Deaf and was met by the staff there, they quickly recognized what they had. A genius. More than that, a genius they could use to further their cause. This was the basic business model for the national institute: Find exceptional deaf students, teach them French and French Sign Language, and send them around the country and the world to perform exhibitions of the deaf showing off their language skills.

This was entertainment in the 1700s. A traveling road show of deaf people just being like "Hey, yeah, we're deaf but, like, we're smart, too." The exhibitions were smashing successes, standing-room-only affairs praised as nothing short of miraculous. The format was simple but dramatic, made all the more so by the low expectations of the audience. An audience member would ask a question to the panel of assembled deaf students or administrators, some French-ass question like "What degree of suffering can be borne by man?" or "How many creams is *too many* creams for a ripe Brie?" A hearing administrator like the abbé would then sign the question to the assembled deaf presenters, and one of them would get up and write an answer in perfect French on a blackboard: "Trois crèmes."

People lost their fucking minds. This was real-time, mind-blowing, miracle shit. It was a true revolution in the way people saw the deaf. For the first time in history, the now-obvious realization that deaf people can learn, can reason, can feel, was made on a societal scale.

The abbé was lauded as a hero, a humanitarian genius who went mining in the depths of the human experience, grabbed the deaf, and dragged them out into the light. Now, thanks to sign language, the deaf could be offered salvation, education, and dignity. Both the state and individual donors threw money at the cause. Again, this was France, home of Rousseau, and Rodin's *The Thinker*. There was an appetite to fund enlightenment for its own sake. Had the abbé done these exhibitions in America, a P. T. Barnum–type would have immediately franchised the show and created a traveling deaf circus.

There was one type of donor from whom the abbé would reject a donation, and that was a visiting leader from another country. If such a leader, inspired by what they saw at the exhibition, offered to fund the school, they would be turned down and given a simple request: "Send an educator to come to the institute and learn how we sign, learn how we teach, and learn how to repeat it back home."

Within one hundred years of the founding of the institute in Paris, there were more than one hundred schools for the deaf in Europe. Most had deaf professors, themselves born into linguistic darkness, now making a living as lamplighters—showing their brethren the way out of the cave. The revolution had come. Clerc was recruited by an ambassador visiting from America named Thomas Hopkins Gallaudet who, in true American fashion, didn't go the route of learning everything another country had to offer, and instead offered to buy one of the "pre-learned" French folk. Is anything more American than that? Gallaudet offered Clerc a job in America and, just like that, a once-languageless kid from a village in France started his journey to become the father of an entire language, the tongue of my mother and my mother tongue, American Sign Language.

Before Clerc's arrival, deafness in America was much like that of "pre-institute" France, isolated pockets of homegrown language and deaf people largely suffering alone in languageless circumstances. With one unique exception: the current vacation destination for the Eastern Seaboard's elite, Martha's Vineyard.

Martha's Vineyard wasn't always just a place for Kennedys to fuck their mistresses. For a long time it was a hardscrabble fishing and whaling island with one odd facet. It was home to one of the largest concentrations of deaf people in the world. The reasons for that are genetically complex but suffice it to say, when it came to sex, the Islanders didn't have anyone but one another and maybe the occasional sea cucumber, and as a result, the genetic pool got as small and murky as a bowl of New England clam chowder. Someone moved to the island with a recessive deaf gene and then a hundred years later, 1 in 155 Islanders were deaf. In one town, Chilmark, up-island and cut off from easy transport to other villages on the island, the deafness rate was 1 in 25. This means that almost everyone on Martha's Vineyard was related to a deaf person. The numbers are shocking, but the consequences *of* those numbers created an egalitarian linguistic utopia for the deaf that's never been re-created anywhere.

If I haven't made this clear yet, when it comes to deafness, the real disability is not the lack of hearing but the lack of access to communication. The hearing loss is incidental; the linguistic isolation is monumental. So when you have a place where there are so many deaf people that *everyone* speaks at least a bit of sign, you pop open the ability for the deaf to communicate and truly participate in society. In this way, the acquisition of sign language by the hearing has the real effect of destroying the disability of deafness, crushing the isolation, and proving that the deaf can participate equally in society.

Almost everyone in Chilmark signed fluently, hearing and deaf alike. It was like speaking French and German in Switzerland, just considered one of the things you need to know if you want to be part of the place. Hearing people would sign to one another at church or the grocery store. Deaf people were universally understood when they signed. The result? The deaf of Martha's Vineyard operated at a more or less equal level to the rest of the barnacle scrapers on the island. They worked, worshipped, married, and lived just like everyone else. The proliferation of deafness was considered about as remarkable as a proliferation of sensitive skin or that weird thing that Kennedys have going on with their faces.

This was unique among the experiences of any community of deaf people in the world. And I will take it a step further: Chilmark might be unique among the experiences of *any* minority community in the world. Because on that island, at that time, what was occurring was not an affirmative action, a compensational equality working overtime to make up for some oppressive wrong done in the past. What was happening on Chilmark was honest and organic—an equality of synthesis—one that rolled out into the community slow and thick in the blood. No one on the island would have said that the deaf were treated equally. Instead, they would have been perplexed by the question. That's real equality. Not "We treat them the same as anyone else" but "Who are 'them'?"

The homegrown language on Martha's Vineyard had a fertile pool of signers to bandy about tales of mermaid sightings or nor'easter gales or whatever it is that fishing people from Cape Cod talk about. As a result of this, Martha's Vineyard Sign Language became more than a home signing system; it became a creole, a pidgin that would provide a framework for the new language that was about to be born on American shores.

As American Sign Language ascended, MVSL receded and so did the deaf of Martha's Vineyard. Intra-island transport, an influx of newcomers to the island, a nearby school for the deaf on the mainland, and the birth of a new sign language meant that, in a short period of time, the deaf of Martha's Vineyard began to leave the island and their deaf utopia behind, matriculating into the body politic of the American deaf. They took their sign system to the new schools for the deaf and the community. The moment Clerc landed in America, MVSL was doomed to be absorbed into ASL's dominance. MVSL was a temporary gift, a spool of thread woven into the American Sign Language linguistic net. Today, not a single person speaks MVSL and nothing remains of the deaf community of the island. But in every ASL user, every native signer, every interpreter, in my own fingers, the legacy of Chilmark remains, forgotten but not gone. ASL is three parts French Sign Language and one part American original MVSL.* And it still smells faintly of seafood!

Back in France, Gallaudet and Clerc boarded a boat together in June 1816, and by the time they landed in America fifty-two days later, Gallaudet had taught Clerc English and Clerc taught Gallau-

---

* Speaking of American originals, there were other homegrown sign language systems that make up ingredients in the bouillabaisse that is ASL. Home signs from various deaf families and communities were subsumed into the body of ASL and the sign systems of the deaf and non-deaf Native Americans, in particular PISL, or Plains Indian Sign Language. These are the sign systems you may remember from Western movies, designed to be an intra-tribal trade language between bands that didn't share a common spoken language. That might be why there are more than one hundred ways in ASL to sign "Don't trust the white man."

det how to sign. In April 1817, the first school for the deaf opened in America.

Within a few years, schools around the country began to open, all taught in the new language of the American deaf, ASL, and often taught *by* the deaf. By 1864, there were schools throughout the United States and, finally, a first of its kind: a university. Declared into being by Abraham Lincoln, the first university for the deaf was established in Washington, D.C. They named it Gallaudet University. The arc of deaf history had moved from languageless darkness to higher education in fewer than a hundred years. Gallaudet University instantly became a symbolic institution of this journey. It became the Vatican of deafness, a fortress of the opposite of solitude.

Almost as soon as the institute in Paris began with a sign-centered curriculum, there emerged voices from the hearing world that demanded that the deaf be taught exclusively in spoken language.

This is the birth of oralism.

Oralism is a pedagogical idea that the deaf should be taught to speak and lip-read rather than to sign. It's a cold irony, when you think about it: Sign was the only reason hearing people ever even realized the deaf could be taught at all, and the moment hearing society realized this, they demanded sign be outlawed in exchange for something they themselves already understood. It became an obsession, a need for the hearing world to accomplish the impossible, to eminent domain the minds of the deaf.

To make them hearing even if they couldn't hear.

What oralism really wants is not that the deaf thrive, but that they make us feel comfortable. So the search is not necessarily for the best system in which to enrich their minds, but rather the system in which they will become the most like us. In this way, "success" is marked by the ease with which they are able to interact with the hearing world surrounding them and, by extension, the ease we feel when interacting back. Oralism hasn't been looking for the best system of education for the deaf; instead it has been, for two hundred years, searching for a miracle, a way to turn them into us, to make them hearing, no matter the cost. Of course, the deaf aren't alone in this search for liberation through assimilation. Native American kids in the United States being sent to finishing school, Yemenite children adopted to wealthy European families in Israel, aboriginal people fitted for three-piece suits in Australia: The helping hand of colonialism is always gloved in chauvinism but called benevolence.

This impulse is understandable. I get where it comes from, which is our own disability: the mental inability to look at a world different from the one we know. We know spoken language and hearing and really can't, even the most sensitive of us, even me, a person surrounded by deafness for my entire life, comprehend a world without sound and speech, and thus the help we offer is help born of that mental insufficiency. It makes sense to us. But it's not about us. And unfortunately, for most deaf people, the thing that makes sense to us simply doesn't work.

To try to understand how wrongheaded and doomed to failure the oral approach is, ask yourself this: What's happening in your brain when you read this book? (Disregard this if you are listening to the audiobook, you cheater.) If you're familiar with my stand-up or podcasts, maybe you hear my voice when you read the words. And I do hope for your sake that's true: It's butter smooth, deep, and inflected with slight Jewish undertones and the top notes of a man who could make you multiple orgasm.

But maybe you don't know my work and got this book from a friend with great taste. Then maybe you hear your own voice as you read the words. Maybe you hear the voice of the Abrahamic god. The point is, you *hear* a voice reading each word with you, correlating it to the sounds you know that word makes. You have a "mind's ear" that allows you, in real time, to hear along as you read silently.

But imagine you were born deaf. Imagine you'd never heard a single one of those words. Never heard a voice, a sentence. Not even, as shocking as this is to imagine, a podcast. You've never heard a single sound. When you look at these words, no commensurate sound accompanies it because no sound can be formed from memory because no memory contains any sound.

So how do oralists suggest deaf people learn spoken, sound-based language if they don't soak it up passively through their ears? Please brace yourself for my attempt to explain color to the blind. (That's you. You're the blind.)

A teacher shows you a card with a D on it and makes a DUH DUH DUH sound waiting for you to catch on. You can't hear the "duh," but she wants you to mimic the lip movement of her DUH, in the hope that that will be sufficient for you to eventually correlate the shape of a D with the sound a D makes. Sometimes she might even stick her fingers in your mouth, pushing your tongue up to your hard palate, manually forcing your tongue into the D zone. But it's worse than that. It's not just the correlation of a D to the DUH sound you're supposed to be learning. It's its place in the word D-O-G. First you learn D=DUH somehow, then O=AH then G=GUH and then you string three sounds you've never heard together in order to form another sound you've never heard: DOG. It's only then that you correlate *that* sound to the live dog in the classroom that your teacher kidnapped for this demonstration and you put it together: The dog is connected to the shape of the letters on the flash card which is connected to the mouth movements your idiot teacher is making.

Compare this to how *you* learned language. You knew "dog" meant the animal that lives with you and eats its own puke way before you ever knew what a D was. How? You heard your mom call it a dog. So your process is one of simply applying that which you already knew and heard and assigning letters to it. You apply the sound you knew *long* before you learn letters, and every time you see the word D-O-G you hear, in your mind's ear, the word *dog*.

But it's worse than *that*. This all starts when you're an infant, *before* you know any shapes or creatures or anything.

It's a miracle that oralism leads to anyone learning anything. As Oliver Sacks wrote in his book *Seeing Voices,* this approach is like trying to learn Japanese from within a soundproof booth while a person on the other side of the glass shows you flash cards of Japanese characters and makes mouth shapes at you. Take a moment and truly imagine how far you'd get with this approach.

Then there's sign. A language system that requires no interlocutor, no phantom mind's ear. It is a language that develops normally and naturally using your eyes as input instead of your ears. It's a direct engagement with the language. It's immediate and requires no special dispensation. Your mind's ear is suddenly needless; your eyes do the work. Now as you learn language in that incremental, piecemeal way that babies do, you can eventually, after learning the handshape for the English letter D, and the knee slap that is the sign for dog, make the connection; "Oh! D-O-G is English for knee slap! It means:

Doesn't this seem like a better way to learn language? Well, tell it to these motherfuckers. . . .

In Milan in 1890, at a convention for educators of the deaf, a vote was held: oralism or sign? The deaf teachers were not allowed to vote. And hey, why would they be? After all, if it was speech that was going to be taught to these kids, it certainly couldn't be taught by deaf people who could not themselves speak intelligibly. These masters of sign, these great thinkers of the deaf, these products of the hundred-year enlightenment brought about by the abbé and his institute, by the early deaf professor pioneers, by Laurent Clerc, they were locked out of a vote on their own destiny.

The oralists won.

And with it, one hundred years of progress was cut off like a French guillotine to a royal neck. And it was Alexander Graham Bell's fault.

Alexander Graham Bell was all grown up now. He'd invented the device that would eventually house TikTok in its digital display, and had taken a wife, Mabel, herself a deaf woman. It was now that Bell could return to his great obsession: that of finding a way to teach the deaf that would make them more like us. Bell was, in this way, a typical white fella of his time (and most other times): convinced of his supremacy, unconvinced by any evidence suggesting something couldn't be done. He'd just done the impossible, hadn't he? He'd invented a machine that could carry a voice over the air and into your ear. If he could do that, teaching the deaf to speak shouldn't pose a problem. Because Bell was a great man of the Americas. A man in the tradition of Lewis and Clark and the decimation of the Native Americans, of the transcontinental railroad and the expulsion of the Chinese who built it, of the Bill of Rights and the slave trade. Bell refused to relent on his obsession no matter the human collateral. He did it to help, never imagining that help could do anything but. Like a sexually frustrated wife, Bell tirelessly campaigned and advocated for the oral method.

Naturally, he was a product of the racism of his time too. This is old school, vintage racism; racism with nuance, racism so specific it's hard to even make sense of. We soft woke folks of the twenty-first century think we understand racism: white people oppressing Black people, true patriots hating Muslims, everyone hating the Jews. But this is hacky, broad racism. Simple to understand. Try the racism of the 1800s! Protestant Swedes hating the Welsh Catholics, Puritan Germans hating the French fur trappers, everyone hating the Jews. There came an idea, in the American consciousness of the time, that these small categories of immigrants carrying on the subcultural traditions of their homelands was beginning to have a corrosive effect on Americanism—the tradition of nontradition—the immigrant soup.

By staying walled off in their respective cultures they were creating an America of ethnicities. They were speaking in their native languages, printing newspapers in those languages, praying in churches with liturgy in those languages and re-creating ethnic villages within America. That is not what we want. It's un-American. This attitude became prevalent in the time of Bell and is the reason that we don't have Welsh rarebit with every meal. Bell and others looked at the deaf in much the same way people looked at the Italians, the Jews, or any other ethnic minority setting up camp in the American experiment. They were othering themselves and making blockades in the nativist dreams of America.

At the same time, the pseudoscience of eugenics began to take an intellectual foothold in the United States. The idea was that the undesirable traits of society could be bred out of existence by enacting strictures on breeding. The proposed strictures were vast and included many groups with "undesirable" traits: people with low IQs, criminals and deviants, people from ethnic minorities, and, of course, the disabled.

Bell applied homegrown xenophobia and pseudoscientific breeding programs to his view of the deaf and their signs. He wanted to assimilate the deaf by stamping out their otherness. He used all the substantial financial resources at his disposal to push forth an agenda of a future for the deaf that would slowly remove their deafness from the equation. ASL was an othering force; it needed to be banned. He believed that deaf people signing would keep them from learning to speak and thus, in his view, keep them forever in ignorance. For him, the opposite of ignorance was not education but assimilation. Being like everyone else.

In 1890, Bell founded the American Association to Promote the Teaching of Speech to the Deaf (now the Alexander Graham Bell Association for the Deaf and Hard of Hearing), which had the stated goal of eliminating sign language education and, in fact, sign language altogether.

It also had the less explicitly stated goal of discouraging deaf people to marry each other. The hope was, much like the ethnic eugenics fever dreams of the time, that eventually, if the deaf were taught to speak like us and to reproduce like us, they would become so much like us that they would evaporate, and the deaf dilemma would be solved by no longer existing.

If this all sounds barbaric and draconian, you'll be shocked to hear how popular it became. Never quite able to get deaf people to stop fucking each other, the oralism movement was nonetheless incredibly successful. Despite not actually working.

Hearing parents of deaf children were understandably seduced by the message and the messenger. Here was a famously brilliant American genius telling them, "If you follow my suggestions, not only will your deaf children be educated, they will become 'normal.' They will become like us and they will cease to be deaf at all." He preyed on the hopes and fears of guilty and scared parents of the deaf who had no context for the value of sign language. All they wanted was for their children to be okay. In his defense, Bell wanted this, too. But his "okay" only ever meant "more like us."

So yeah, Bell won. How could he not? He tantalized society with the promise of a "cure" for deafness. By learning to mimic the mouth shapes of speech and to generate sounds, the deaf would be able to speak. By learning to read lips, they would be able to understand. Combining these skills, they would be, finally, normal.

In the wake of this, ASL was not only rejected as an educational modality, it was lambasted as a low form of communication, not even worth using in private. It was simian and base; the exaggerated expressions and gesticulations were vulgar. Indecent, even.

ASL became banned in residential schools. In 1867, there were twenty-six American schools for the deaf, all using the sign educational tradition that harked straight back to the Institute in Paris, from the abbé to Clerc to Gallaudet. It was a golden age of sign and deaf education. Half of the teachers were deaf themselves, passing on the educational oxygen tube they had learned to breathe through.

By 1907, there were 139 schools, and *none* of them allowed sign. Deaf educators now numbered only 17 percent of the faculty at schools for the deaf and most of them didn't teach academic classes. They'd been moved to vocational classrooms to ensure hearing parents didn't object to their children being taught by deaf teachers who had never learned speech themselves. This number continued to dwindle until there were almost no teachers of the deaf who were themselves deaf.

The tradition of deaf educators, their very existence proof to their students that great things were possible, was broken, gone, lost, supplanted by the unrealistic dreams of hearing parents and a misguided education system that felt if they could just try hard enough they could perform a dark miracle: erase deafness from the face of the Earth. Thus began the dark ages of ASL. The bell was rung.

Bell's victory would prove an educational disaster. One that would plunge the deaf back into an imposed ignorance, back to isolation and intellectual loneliness. A fog rolled out over the minds of the deaf. For fifty years the only deaf people who would make it out of the educational doldrums would be those who were so gifted that their innate intellect could supersede the deficits of oralism. Like many minority communities in educational deserts, if you were deaf, you had to be wildly gifted in order to fight your way to even being average.

My mother was gifted, lucky in her station of birth. Bright, curious, born to a public school teacher and a professor of English. Books lined the walls. Ideas abounded.

If you were to see her sign, if you were to really and truly understand the linguistic sophistication of the ASL she uses, then you'd see her for what she is: a woman with a master's degree in education, a wise, worldly woman, an educated woman, an equal.

However, if you were to read her writing in English, if you were to assess her competence based on this alone, you would be forgiven for thinking she was uneducated. Simple even. Charming in its broken syntax, her English reads like the Italian chefs in *Lady and the Tramp*. I love the idiosyncrasies of her text messages, and yes, I laugh at the bizarre language choices she makes.

Sometimes it's loving, like when she texted the whole family:

Sometimes it's critical, like when she texted me a huge picture of an "F" and wrote:

You get F as bad son!

But hidden behind the amusement is a tragedy, a failing in the American education system. Her writing reads like it was written by a foreigner because that's what she is: a foreigner in her native country. Bell's dream may have partially come true, but it did nothing to erase her otherness. It just served to stunt her acquisition of information until she was old enough to strike out on her own and seize it for herself.

My grandmother faced a heartbreak similar to millions of parents in America each year. She had a baby—her only child—and played and cooed to her just like every parent does. She talked and read to her, sang lullabies and told her stories. Only, something seemed wrong. It took a while to realize a dropped dish wouldn't elicit a startle reaction, a song wouldn't soothe. She took my mother to a doctor to find out what was wrong but was assured everything was normal. After all, babies aren't generally known for their back-and-forth communication. Reassured, my grandmother went back to a largely "Rock a Bye Baby"–centered educational program. But she saw no improvement.

Finally, my grandmother put my mother in a car and drove her from Mesa, Arizona, to the John Tracy Clinic in Los Angeles, a clinic founded in honor of the deaf son of famed actor and model for the old guy from *Up,* Spencer Tracy.

They confirmed her fears: My mother was profoundly deaf. This is a heartbreaking moment for hearing parents. Not so much for deaf parents; in fact, people are often shocked to see deaf parents high-fiving and busting out cigars when a diagnosis of deafness is confirmed. But for my grandmother this must have been a rough realization.*

The John Tracy Clinic is a staunchly oralist clinic and, while confirming my grandmother's fears of my mother's deafness, did not even mention as a possibility the use of ASL as a linguistic tool. Back into the linguistic darkness plunged my mother as my well-meaning grandmother took a year off to get a master's in deaf education at Columbia.

Are you following what's happening here? Everyone had the best interest of my mother in mind. Everyone wanted her to succeed, but while they ran around trying to come up with the best solution to educate her, she aged in silence. One year, then two, then three, and finally by the time most kids are starting to speak, receptacles of the passive acquisition of language that your ears provide for, my grandmother returned from Columbia with an idea of how to communicate with her daughter. She was older than three when she was even shown her first "word" and this was simply English text printed under a picture with my now Columbia-educated grandmother hoping she could get her only child to decode the letters.

If only she'd been granted a reprieve through the use of sign, my mother could have been communicating using language instead of pointing to pictures and gesturing. This wasn't meant to be.

My mother didn't start signing until she was thirteen years old and enrolled in the California School for the Deaf. It's funny, despite all the professionals and clinicians that had surrounded my mother for her entire life, the reason she is who she is today, an educated

---

* Hearing parents have tried to cure their children's deafness through various methods, most of which never had any hope of success, but the coolest of which has to be the "deaf flight." Offered near the advent of airplane flight, someone posited that a flight, replete with plenty of loops and dives, could jar the ears into working. Before Charles Lindbergh became a professional anti-Semite and then died, he offered hopeful parents such flights at fifty bucks a pop. As far as anyone knows he cured no one. But, wheeeeeeeeee!!!

and proud deaf woman in full mastery of her native language, has nothing to do with any of them, and everything to do with a deaf shoemaker and his sad tale.

This shoemaker was poor—very poor—but every night, a bunch of playful elves would . . . wait no, wrong shoemaker. This shoemaker was someone my grandmother went to for . . . shoe construction, I guess? Is that what people go to shoemakers for? At this point I'm feeling self-conscious about how many times I've used the word *shoemaker* so I'm going to stop now.

My grandmother, through some random chance, found herself talking to a deaf man, a *cobbler,* who'd been reared in the same oralist system my grandmother worked in. He was lonely. His speech was unimpressive, but his story made a huge impression: Despite all the intervention of the oralists, the system had failed to make him hearing, failed to make him "normal," which, of course, left him out of step with hearing society, never truly one of them.

But he'd also never been exposed to the deaf world, never learned to sign, never met and spent time with people like himself. As such, here he was, a grown man, fully reared in the dream of Alexander Graham Bell and yet still fully locked behind the walls of isolation Bell had hoped to destroy. He was all alone, friendless, without a community, hammering lengths of leather with nary an elf to talk to.

My grandmother had a profound paradigm shift after talking to him. She decided that her daughter would not end up like him. She enrolled my mother in the California School for the Deaf, one of the "residential schools" for the deaf.

The residential schools became a rite of passage in the deaf world, a cross between boot camp and a language intensive. These schools became islands of deaf culture. At some of these schools, of course, sign was banned. If caught signing, the kids would be punished, sometimes forced to wear big cloth mittens like an oven mitt, tied together at the wrist like a pair of handcuffs. A dunce cap for the hands.

But in the yard? Between classes? The kids were like prisoners passing the contraband of ASL. No one could stop them from using their language. They became the holders of the secrets of Clerc and co. This became a truism that could not be stopped: When deaf people got together, regardless of indoctrination or enforcement, they would default back to their language, back to their natural mode of communication. They would sign and be themselves. They knew what they were doing was banned; it was wrong, but it felt right—it felt like being themselves.

My mother walked into the California School for the Deaf in Berkeley at thirteen years old, having never signed, having never even seen sign language. Her mind was blown. In three months, she was *fluent* in ASL. Three months! How can you say this was not her native language?

Of course I knew none of this growing up. I missed the gap my mother experienced in her linguistic upbringing. To me she was always a powerful communicator, fluent and in command of her language. She was an activist, a member of the board of directors for Berkeley's Center for Independent Living, a graduate student putting herself through night school to get a master's in deaf education as food stamps put meals on the table. To me, my mother was only ever a powerful example of never letting your circumstances determine your destiny. I never saw her as a part of a lineage of oppression, a success due only to her innate intelligence and educationally privileged upbringing.

How many deaf kids were born to families that due to lack of resources or lack of interest simply didn't put the work into finding the best path for their education, delayed or not? How many deaf kids fell into a languageless world because their parents simply never knew better, never met a cobbler, never got their teaching credential from Columbia? How many?

A hundred years' worth.

ASL had never actually died; it just went underground. And in going underground, it crystallized the deaf as a people apart, a distinct minority that deserved dignity and respect. More than that, deaf people became (or maybe always were) *proud to be deaf*. This is a fact that always surprises people when they find out. Deaf people not only don't feel *bad* about being deaf; most of them wouldn't have it any other way. In my experience, most deaf people don't want to be hearing, don't consider themselves disabled, and identify strongly as members of deaf culture.

My dad was an exception to this.

He had speech that would instantly be identified as that of a deaf man, but if you *really* tried, you could understand him. He also had minor residual hearing. He took these two facts, and his ability to lip-read, to mean that he was "not like other deaf people." He never identified with the deaf community, and never declared his allegiance to ASL. Though he used it and was far more proficient in ASL than he was in English, his connection to his deafness was mostly through how "not deaf" he appeared.

He'd make a show of wanting to go to the movies. This was in the days before movie theaters offered portable captioning machines for deaf people, those little screens that you jam into the drink holders on your arm rest that display subtitles. No, my dad didn't need those. He could read the lips of the actors. He was basically a hearing person, remember?

We'd sit down in the theater and the lights would darken and from the first line of the movie he'd turn to me with the same look of confusion my wife gives to me when my mom speaks to her, and sign, "What did he say?" And I would, in the dark, sign all the dialogue to my dad so he'd know what was going on. This was my start in showbiz, my first acting role: understudy to Arnold Schwarzenegger in *Total Recall,* signing "Consider that a divorce" in Austrian-accented ASL to my dad.

And for a "hearing person," my dad sure never got far from deafness. When my mother left him, he married another deaf woman.

My stepmother, Betty, a Hasidic Jew, had a different kind of deafness. It was a dominant deafness. A genetic deafness that didn't just run in her blood, it galloped. She was deaf. Her sister, Barbara, was deaf. As were her kids. And her sister's kids. And her kids' kids. And her sister's grandkids.

Strangely, or probably not strangely if you understand genetics at all (which I do not), her brother could hear, and all *his* kids and grandkids were hearing. My father and Betty lived above Barbara and her family. The entire building was a compound of deafness.

Every doorbell had flashing lights attached to it. Every TV had captioning machines, every phone had a TTY (the teletype machine that allowed deaf people to type back and forth using a proto modem system). I have deaf siblings and cousins, deaf nieces and nephews, and a guy who is much like the title of the inclusive mafia movie I dream of making someday: My Deaf Godfather. My entire New York family, the family my father started after us, isn't just deaf. They are avowed deaf activists. ASL purists. All of them except my father.

When I'd go back to California after spending time with him in New York, my father would call me to check in. Not interested in using a TTY, he decided to simply pick up the phone and call.

Perhaps you're already seeing the problem with his plan: The man could not hear. Call me crazy, but I believe the phone to be a heavily ear-based technology. My father would say things to me over the phone and I would scream a response, absolutely at the top of my fucking lungs, then my father would pretend to understand what I said and answer back a totally unrelated topic.

I never quite figured out why my dad had so much invested in pretending he could hear or, at least, that he wasn't "all that deaf." He was not ashamed of his deafness. It's hard to imagine my father being ashamed of anything really. It was more that he pretended that deafness did not exist, at least for him.

But most deaf people I've ever met are more like my mom and my dad's new family, proud deaf people, secure in their identity, a hand to one ear and a fist in the air signing "Deaf power!"

After watching through the 1960s and '70s as community after community fought off their marginalization through protest, the deaf community began to reclaim its self-determination through reclaiming its connection to ASL. Shucking off the taboos of signing and rejecting the mandates of oralism, the Deaf began to reclaim their destiny. But they needed to push further. Deaf people were down to fight for their liberation, but how? Who could they fight? Then the answer came. They could fight their own institution. They could fight home base. They could force change from within the walls of their own homes by ousting the landlords.

On March 6, 1988, the student body of Gallaudet University gathered to hear the announcement from the board of trustees as to who they'd selected to become the college's seventh president. It had been 124 years and they'd never had a deaf president, despite the fact that there were deaf deans at the university itself and plenty of deaf educators with doctorates serving in educational positions of authority around the country.

When the previous president stepped down, the student body made it clear in no uncertain terms that they *expected* a deaf person to be chosen as his successor. The board seemed to heed the warning, and after a nationwide search, the candidates were narrowed down to three, two deaf (Dr. I. King Jordan, a dean of the Arts and Sciences department at Gallaudet, and Dr. Harvey Corson, superintendent at the American School for the Deaf) and one hearing, Dr. Elisabeth Zinser, an academic administrator with zero knowledge of deaf culture or ASL.

At this point you probably know the direction this story is going, so I'll cut to the chase. The board, composed of seventeen hearing members and only four deaf, announced they'd picked a new president. After 124 years, nothing would change: The reins of deaf history would remain in the hands of the helpers. Dr. Zinser was selected as president, and all hell broke loose.

The "who do we fight" question had been answered: Fight the people closest to us, fight for ourselves, fight to take back our home. After more than a century, after Bell and Milan and oralism and generations of patronizing destiny-robbing help, the collective back of the deaf broke. No more. The struggle was summed up in just three words: *Deaf President Now.*

How, after 124 years and with two other qualified candidates, could the world's only deaf university have chosen *another* hearing president, one who did not sign, did not understand anything about the world she was stepping into? Try to imagine this was not a deaf university but Morehouse or one of the other historically Black colleges and universities. Imagine a white dean chosen again and again for 120 years. Imagine there was *still* a white president at Morehouse the year *A Different World* came out! Imagine the creator of *A Different World,* a father figure to a nation, was secretly drugging women and sexually assaulting them! You'd never dream of it. But the deaf had their own timeline, and their revolution came later. This revolution *would* be televised. Almost immediately the campus of Gallaudet was shut down, sit-ins were everywhere. The roads in and out of campus were blocked by school buses that had been hot-wired, moved to the entrances, and had their tires slashed. The deaf community mobilized.

And it wasn't just students. It was the entire community. The board of trustees had miscalculated how deep the frustration and resentment went. A student leadership council emerged making a list of four demands:

1. That Zinser step down and a deaf president be installed, effective immediately.
2. That the chair of the board of trustees step down.
3. That the board of trustees be reconstituted with a 51 percent deaf majority.
4. That there be no reprisals to students or faculty for these protests.

The board flatly denied all of the demands.

Decades of entrenched paternalism don't die easily, but the board miscalculated how sustained the protests would be. The movement swelled and gained traction with the national deaf community. Hearing interpreters from the area arrived to volunteer their time to help the activists conduct media interviews. The faculty lined up behind the student body in calling for Zinser's ouster. Zinser pretended that nothing was going on and, for a few days at least, remained steadfast in her intention to take over a school whose student body and faculty were calling, in one voice, for her head.

Then the board declared their willingness to talk about a compromise. But it was too late.

There was no room for dialogue, no room for compromise; the

deaf had been compromising for more than a hundred years and they were done. They would accept nothing but a total agreement to their four demands.

Nightline broadcast a special episode to talk to the leader of the student activists, Greg Hlibok, Dr. Zinser, and deaf Oscar winner Marlee Matlin. Zinser repeated her defiant stance in the face of the student demands. The nation was suddenly paying attention. For the first time, the destiny of the deaf was in the hands of the deaf, and everyone involved was fighting the power using ASL.

The resistance was gaining momentum.

Zinser withdrew from the presidency the next night.

By March 8, each of the four demands had been met and Gallaudet announced their new president: I. King Jordan. There was a deaf president now. It was over. The epicenter of deafness was in deaf hands. The dreams of Bell had crashed and burned. The deaf community had come into its own. I still remember my mother, tears in her eyes, watching the announcement on the news. Turning to me, signing, "We won!"

This was no longer the world of insecure signers, victims of an imposed inferiority complex. Of hiding signing when the teachers weren't looking. This was the world of fierce, proud signers who had the spirit of the success of the Deaf President Now protests animating them.

This was the deaf world I was raised in.

My childhood was filled with ASL story nights and poetry readings. The ASL I saw growing up was one in the midst of a creative resurgence, a language that had always been poetic and playful was now in a stage of massive identity reclamation. It was similar, I'd imagine, to the Black Is Beautiful era of the 1970s, only it was centered around language. I saw my mother perform ASL poetry and delighted in her storytelling. I was proud to be able to understand it in its unadulterated form. Most hearing people in the audience needed an interpreter to know what was going on. Not me. I was a member of this community. I was a CODA.

For some CODAs, that identity is the most important marker of who they are. Others feel trapped between worlds, never fully hearing because their childhoods were conducted in ASL and surrounded by deaf people, but also never fully deaf because . . . they can hear. I've been asked by other CODAs, "Do you consider yourself to be hearing or CODA?" To me, this is like asking a chimp if he considers himself to be an ape or a primate (never do this; they are very touchy about the topic). So, given the options, I said, "Uh, both?" and the devastated look on my CODA friend's face told me I'd clearly answered incorrectly.

Some CODAs consider ASL their first language but I don't, though I'm not totally sure what a first language is. Is it the first language you learn? If so, then I'm ASL all the way—the fine motor skills of baby hands develop long before the tongue and vocal cords. I was signing well before I started talking. But if your first language is the one you claim mastery of, the one you think in, write in, and express yourself best in? Well, then, I'm a traitor like Benedict Arnold: I sided with the English. You should be grateful for that, since you're reading a book I wrote in English.

When I was growing up, my mother left my brother and me alone at night, latchkey style, driving an hour each way to San Francisco State to get a college degree, first an associate's, then bachelor's, and then a master's, all in night classes. I went to all three graduation ceremonies, and all three were an acknowledgment that she'd broken through walls designed to hold her back. My mother refused to allow her circumstances to dictate anything. She was a part of the vanguard of deaf Americans with a very clear message: I can do anything hearing people can do except hear. And society was finally able to accept that.

Two years after the Deaf President Now protests, the Americans with Disabilities Act passed in Congress, breaking down longstanding barriers for accessibility to the deaf and disabled communities. The right to accessibility was now protected by the weight of law, and it had massive consequences for the deaf.

It had massive consequences for me as well.

One of the guaranteed protections that the ADA provided for was the access to professional sign language interpreters.

I spent my childhood as most CODAs do, in a nonconsensual sign language interpretation internship program. Every retail transaction, every school meeting, every doctor's appointment that didn't provide an interpreter and that my mother couldn't figure out how to navigate on her own would be interpreted by me or my brother. This is the solemn duty of the CODA; you're one part child, one part administrative assistant.

As the years went on, the meetings I had to interpret became about me: behavioral disciplinary meetings, learning disability diagnostics, therapy sessions, and so on. The fun days of interpreting for my mother's gynecological appointments were gone. Now I had to translate to my mother what a piece of shit all my teachers thought I was.

The ADA changed all that. I mean, my teachers still thought I was a piece of shit. But now some other guy had to tell my mom about it. Suddenly there were professional interpreters at every appointment. I saw them at the time—because I was in my hating adults phase—as annoyances, simply another adult in the way. I never would have suspected I'd be in the field myself years later.

When I was sixteen, I got a job working in a bear costume. I was making minimum wage working in a mascot suit, taking smoke breaks with a papier-mâché and faux-fuzz monstrosity balanced akimbo atop my head. Wide-mouth half-liter of Mountain Dew for breakfast. Newport dangling from my lip.

Little kids would walk by and point at me asking, "Mommy, why is the bear smoking?"

"I'm Smokey the Bear," I'd grumble. I was still tired from the rave the night before. Not sure I'd slept.

When my mother approached me about a job opening at the local Oakland community college as a sign language interpreter, I flatly rejected her. For one, I had no desire to cross-contaminate my childhood trauma with my employment goals. And I didn't need a job: Look at my bear head—I was already making a living in show biz.

"They are paying $13.25 an hour," signed my mother. I looked down at my bear paws. I'd been making $4.25 an hour as Smokey. My choice was clear.

I spent the next fifteen years as a sign language interpreter. My first job had been sober ecstasy dealer, second was the bear, third was professional sign language interpreter, fourth was Burning Man gate guard. Fifth was stand-up comic. That's my entire employment history. Kind of has an arc to it when you think about it.

My first boss, Catherine, was a blind and deaf woman who trained me via tactile sign, which is hand holding while someone signs. It was the first time I'd ever held a woman's hand. No it wasn't, but it was definitely the first time I'd held hands with my boss.

The fact that the administrative head of the American Sign Language department at the DeafCan program at Laney College was a blind and deaf woman is the culmination of everything I've written about in this chapter. Catherine was an incredibly talented administrator and could assess my skills without having to "look" at my hands. She felt where I was at. And where I was at was lazy.

When you're a rebellious child of a deaf parent, it's easy for your signing to slip into a kind of hybridized mixture of speaking, home signs that you just made up, and sloppy, understandable-only-to-your-parent ASL. I hadn't been trying to sign for anyone but an audience of one, and Catherine felt it.

She gave me my first assignment: working at Laney College's welding program for a student who already knew how to weld. So really my job was to just sit there, watch real men walk by me with TIG welding guns in their hands, and wait to see if the deaf student had a question. It was an entry-level job.

Every week, Catherine would take my hands and reassess my signing skills. Little by little, my technique was getting sharper, crisper, more formal. It came naturally to me. The fluency poured into my hands like the tungsten arc into a weld puddle, which was a thing I had just learned and somehow still remember.

I got good enough that Catherine decided to let me interpret a class where an actual lecture would be taking place. I'd be working with a "team," a more experienced interpreter who would be watching me and helping me if I needed it. I was in an odd position. I was a seventeen-year-old raver, a couple of years sober, and dressed like I'd just stepped out of Studio 54. I had no actual training, and I had dropped out of school in eighth grade, yet, most of the time, I signed with more natural fluency than the interpreter assigned to train me.

This is a classic dynamic within sign language interpreting. Most interpreters attend years of school to learn the craft. They start at the bottom, learning the basics of ASL and deaf culture. Then, after years of practicing and working their way up the ranks, they begin interpreter training, learning the concepts of language translation, the ethics of interpretation. They do role-playing and run drills on potential scenarios. Then they graduate from their interpreter training programs. They enter the workforce and do a few years of entry-level jobs, slowly building their skills until they are ready for higher level assignments. Finally they can call themselves interpreters. It takes years of intensive training to get to the starting level and even longer to approach anything resembling mastery. And then a seventeen-year-old CODA walks in with no idea what they are doing and signs better than most of the trained people in the field.

On a job, a deaf person will find out you have deaf parents and largely ignore the other interpreter, seeing you as the ally and them as an interloper. That's gotta be tough, but since I was the beneficiary and had completed a seventeen-year forced unpaid internship, I didn't mind so much.

Non-CODA interpreters occupy a strange place within the deaf community. They are both cherished and resented, welcomed and not trusted, needed and not wanted. There's a certain skeptical shade thrown at the people who come from outside the world and, upon graduating from an interpreter training program, begin making more money an hour than many deaf people will ever earn. But interpreting is righteous work, and most interpreters truly believe in the mission of the job.

That job is, simply, to facilitate communication between the hearing and the deaf, to build an invisible bridge between worlds. To become conduits through which equality and equanimity can be made manifest. No interpreter has ever gotten rich from the work.

The most they've gotten is a million hits on a viral video of them pantomiming a blow job at a gangster rap concert.

I got good quickly. By the time I turned eighteen I was making more money per hour as an interpreter than any of my friends who weren't drug dealers. It was mind-blowing: The thing that had contributed so much to my childhood poverty was now the exact thing making my teenage years financially stable. I didn't get rich obviously, but I now had a professional's hourly rate rather than a bear costume.

I left Laney and got sent out into the world of freelance interpreting. Any place in the world a deaf person might have a meeting or an appointment, a class or a job interview, someone like me would be assigned to show up and facilitate communication. I started to learn the deep grammar of ASL, the ways in which it was superior to spoken language and the ways in which it was not.

For example, ASL cannot come close to competing with English when it comes to vocabulary. English is a language with more than 170,000 words. ASL, on the other hand, has only between 10,000 and 40,000 distinct signs for words. Point for English.

But while at a disadvantage vocabulary-wise, ASL has a twofold advantage over English in its *flexibility and fluidity,* which actually allows for a quick adjustment anytime an unassigned word or concept is encountered.

Suppose I was interpreting in a college class on the subject of anarchy. There is no dedicated sign for the word *anarchy,* though you'd obviously assume it would be heavy-metal horns with your tongue flicking up and down like you're eating air pussy. It is not.

The first time we (the student and I) encountered the word *anarchy* in the lecture, I'd fingerspell the word "A-N-A-R-C-H-Y," and then enter into a negotiation with the student to establish what would be, for the duration of that class, our agreed-upon sign for anarchy. I might offer up the sign for revolution, a fist in the air, and rather than use just my fist, I'd use the letter A. A for anarchy, fist in the air for revolution. I'd then see if the student accepted that sign. She might nod, "Yes, that will work" or correct me and give me a better sign to use and then, for the rest of class when the professor said "anarchy," I would use the agreed upon sign and the student would know what was being said.

ASL is nimble and able to pivot on a dime to ensure clarity. But ASL's fluidity goes deeper, into an area of communication that soars beyond the limitations of spoken language.

Suppose the professor, in her lecture on anarchy, describes a skirmish between the anarchists and government forces like this: "*In the middle of a field just outside of the town, a small group of anarchists were totally surrounded by government forces who rushed them and destroyed them completely.*"

Each of the words above does have a designated sign (except *anarchists,* which we've already established). And I could, if the student had asked me to, sign each word in the order the professor said them. But this would not be ASL. This would be a signed translation of English. Real ASL would toss out the vocabulary altogether.

In the air, with my hands, I would establish a great field, more or less "drawing it" in space. On the side of the field, I would point to an area and sign *town.* I now have my field and it's just outside of town. Pointing back to the field I would point to the middle and make a tiny version of the sign for *group* and then do my A-fist in the air for anarchy. This is the small group of anarchists. Now I draw a great circle around the field and populate it with thousands of people and sign *government/soldiers.* I now have my great field and my small group of anarchists that are totally surrounded by government forces. Then I would make those forces run from all sides toward the middle of the field, toward my small group. I might make fierce faces for the government forces and make scared ones for the anarchists, and when they reach the middle of the field, I sign *destroy.*

I have only signed a few actual vocabulary words: *town, group, anarchists, government, soldiers, destroy,* but in ASL, using what are called "classifiers," I have created a temporary, improvised, complex, and sophisticated three-dimensional communication. It is crystal clear what I mean and what happened to those poor anarchists, and what I have done is perfectly linguistically acceptable and accurate. Even though that particular sequence of signs will never be duplicated. It was an improvised linguistic canvas. It was itself a kind of ordered anarchy. It was pure sign.

I got better and better at interpreting. I got to the point where the more sophisticated the job, the more I enjoyed it, and the better I signed. I asked the agency that sent me out on jobs to send me the challenging work. Graduate school and court cases were my favorite. Middle school was my least favorite. Middle school is the worst part of human development. Just peach-fuzz mustaches, bad skin, and a marble rolling around where their brains will hopefully grow. Maybe I'm saying this because the kids in middle schools would openly make fun of me. Mimicking my signs or nudging each other as I walked by, saying, "That's your boyfriend."

"No, you little fucking asshole," I wanted to say, grabbing them by the lapel and throwing them against a locker, "I'm not. I don't date children, I'm too busy making love to beautiful raver women I met at the bottom of a cuddle puddle. In that world I am fucking irresistible."

I never said this. But I did ask to be sent to any job but middle schools.

I started to really enjoy the job.

I'd be sent like a spy into these various moments in people's lives and drop in for an hour or an afternoon, facilitate communication, and then move on. I interpreted for podiatry appointments where the smell of burning toenails being ground into smoke by an electric toenail sander is still seared into my memory. I interpreted graduations and speeches, criminal court cases and job interviews. I watched people's greatest triumphs as they walked the stage to get a diploma and sat in on their biggest traumas as they found out they were dying.

I interpreted for deaf graduate students, nodding along as I barely kept up with the sophistication of the lecture I was interpreting. I interpreted for barely linguistic deaf immigrants—people who'd never learned the spoken language of their native countries nor its sign language. At the meetings that would determine if they qualified for SSI benefits, their survival was, quite literally, in my hands. Their future depended on my ability to use my ASL and negotiate that with whatever linguistic level they were operating at. I was proud when I interpreted well enough that they walked out of those meetings with a ticket to government cheese.

I met a ton of fascinating deaf people. I met a ton of very stupid hearing people, too. Sometimes I'd walk into a classroom, be pointed to the deaf student, and told, "They are working on pre-algebra equations today. Help them finish their work." I'd have to explain that I was not a math tutor; I was an interpreter. Usually this would elicit an annoyed reaction, like I was being a diva.

"Just help them with it; we're understaffed."

"And I'm undereducated," I'd explain. "I dropped out of eighth grade. This student probably knows more about algebra than me."

Sometimes I'd walk into a classroom and a student wouldn't even be deaf. They'd be a nonverbal developmentally disabled kid in a wheelchair, and I'd be told I was going to be their aide for the day. "No," I'd explain. "I'm not."

This might seem harsh to you, but the boundaries I set were due to my abilities. I didn't know anything about special education. Or math. And my boundaries were also set due to a deep frustration with a system that pours all difference into one bowl, and, rather than do the hard work necessary to actually help the students whose care they are charged with, simply hires any warm body they can con into babysitting a student they don't want to have to deal with.

There were depressing jobs. The worst were driving to a far-off school system to meet the sole deaf kid in a rural school system, a kid with no friends to sign with, no peers to talk shit with, no girls to flirt with. I don't mean to suggest deaf kids can't do all of these things with hearing friends—they can and do—but these islands of deaf kids, mainstreamed all alone in their district, often sat there talking far more to me, the adult interpreter hired to be there for just one day, than they did to the kids they shared a classroom with all year long.

I took a job once at Napa State Hospital, a state psychiatric facility that included an Arkham City–style prison for the criminally insane. I was charged with interpreting for a deaf and severely autistic kid who'd been locked in there for years. I had not been briefed as to what I was getting myself into and had no training for this kind of scenario. When I arrived at his cell to interpret for him, I realized that he was about seven feet tall and, as the counselor explained, "He likes to strike males sometimes."

"Cool!" I thought. "I'm a male!" Upon meeting him, he instantly lunged at me, and an alarm went off and ten police officers piled on him, restraining him while I retired to the break room to read a novel for the rest of the day.

Some jobs were really fun, though. There's a rule in interpreting that if you take an assignment, no matter how long it is, and the client doesn't show up, you get paid for the full job regardless. You wait for your client for half an hour and if they are a no-show, you take off and get paid anyway.

One day I accepted an eight-hour job at a community college. These long jobs were rare and great: They'd provide a full day's work that would compensate for other days when you had only one twenty-minute assignment at a doctor's office. I showed up that day for the first class at nine A.M.: nude figure drawing. I sat down in the front row and waited. When the class started a woman ascended the stairs and slipped her robe off, lying down on a platform. My kid was a no-show. All the art students set up their easels and started painting. Not me. I had no easel; I was the interpreter. But I couldn't really go up to the model and say, "Hey, don't worry about my lack of paint. I'm just here to facilitate communication."

So I just sat there, occasionally checking my watch. No easel. Just staring. Still no one to interpret for. At the thirty-minute mark I stood and walked out of the room and into my car, and went to get a cup of coffee.

I wondered what she must have thought. Did she think I was actually an art student, waiting until she did an exciting enough pose to justify me wasting my paint on? "Could we try face down/ass up?" Did she think I stormed out of the room in disappointment? Just a random creep and not a student at all? All I knew was I had just gotten paid three hundred bucks to stare at a naked woman for a half hour.

I spent a decade in freelance interpreting until a breakthrough in technology changed my job. The advent of the webcam. Now I could finally make money putting hairbrush handles in my ass.

Actually, the webcam opened up new vistas of communication for the deaf and new areas of employment for interpreters. When I was a child, the technology did not exist to dial up a sign language interpreter on your webcam and then bring them into your call. Back then it was just some operator reading stuttered text typed into a small interface. This interface was called a TTY, as I mentioned earlier. It had been revolutionary for the deaf.

Prior to that, deaf people could not access anyone on the phone unless they had a hearing person to make the call for them. This kind of thing led to teenage boys being forced to have their mom ask a girl to prom for them. It was a dark time. The TTY, created by a deaf inventor, was far from perfect, but it helped. If a deaf person wanted to call a hearing person, they'd have to use relay services, operators who also had TTY machines and would take calls from the deaf, reading the text to the hearing person the deaf caller wanted to speak with. And that operator is whose voice you'd hear on the phone. This is how I would talk to my mother on the phone growing up:

The phone would ring, and I'd hear a deep booming voice as my mother:

OPERATOR/MOM: HELLO, MY SON!
FRIGHTENED BOY CHILD: God?
OPERATOR/MOM: No, no, it's your mama calling.
CONFUSED BOY CHILD: Mom, are you a Black dude?

On some calls, she was. Sometimes an Indian woman, or a Jersey guy. It was kind of amazing, actually.

Then came the webcam and now an interpreter could see my mother and make the call in ASL rather than read a bunch of broken text. It allowed deaf people to make calls that approached normal in a language that would match their abilities.

I took a job at a relay center. It was a surreal job for me as I had grown up taking calls from operators, and now I was one. Some of the calls were exciting. Most of the calls were boring. And a select number were so horrifyingly, mind-numbingly, *MacNeil/Lehrer NewsHour* boring that they folded back onto themselves and became interesting again.

There was a guy, let's call him Dan, who would call in every day at around four P.M., when I assume he arrived home from his assisted living life skills training program. When any of the operators saw that name pop up on the "incoming caller" field on our computer interface, they would feign shortness of breath or arthritic pangs or any excuse to hit the REJECT CALL button. But eventually, everyone's time would come. You'd click ACCEPT CALL before you had a chance to process that it was Dan. Panicking, you'd sit back and hope to God the internet would go dead. But it never did.

Dan was always wearing the same outfit. Always sitting in the same chair. Always calling the same person. "Amanda." His lover. Well, that might be a bit of a generous term. Amanda and Dan were, as best as I can guess, schoolmates at the assisted living school. Amanda was certainly the leader of the two. She sort of led the conversation. And by "sort of led," I mean she talked incessantly for, literally, hours on end as Dan mirrored, mimicked, and repeated back to her exactly the things she had just said. Due to some strange rule at the call centers, interpreters were not allowed to get off of calls still in progress unless they legally had to go home for the day, and so if you had the bad luck of clicking ACCEPT on ol' Dan Juan, the internet Casanova, at the beginning of your shift, you could literally be sitting there, trapped, signing and repeating the same conversation back-and-forth for eight straight hours.

AMANDA: YOU LOOKED CUTE TODAY.
DAN/ANGUISHED INTERPRETER: Yes, I looked cute today.
AMANDA: Did you like my shoes?
DAN/SUFFERING INTERPRETER: Yes, I like your shoes.
AMANDA: What did you like about them?
DAN/BORDERLINE INSANE INTERPRETER: Yes, what did I like about them?

This sort of question was Dan's Achilles' heel; the kind of thing you couldn't simply repeat back without causing communication breakdown. Amanda, romantic saint that she was, remained undeterred.

AMANDA: OH, DAN, YOU'RE SO SILLY!
DAN/SUICIDAL INTERPRETER: Yes, I'm so silly.

And so on. For, I'm not kidding, hours on end.

Any time you see a Beyoncé concert or a presidential press conference where there's an interpreter onstage, signing along to beautiful music or powerful people, and you think to yourself, "Now, that would be an interesting job!," think of me sitting in a cubicle, interpreting the sweet literal nothings of a young couple in love, praying desperately for a 9/11-style attack on the suburban headquarters of the Sorenson Video Relay Services.

On the other hand, some calls were epic. One day two young dudes popped up on screen and told me to dial the 1-800 number they had plugged into the computer. I should have noticed something was off based on how eager they both looked. Usually people ordering Papa John's didn't have a look of nervous excitement vibrating off of them. As soon as the number picked up, I knew why. It was a recording: *"Tons of fat-titted horny babes are fingering their juicy slits right now waiting to talk to you. Press one and be connected for $7.95 a minute."*

I, of course, was tasked with interpreting the message of the hot fuckmonster on the recording, which only made them more excited, but when it came to pressing one, I had to give these fellas the bad news.

"This is a phone sex line. You have to pay for it. As much as I'd love to watch you two pump your dicks on a webcam, I can't press one to accept the charges. Sorry, boys," I signed.

They looked horrified. "No no no!" they signed. "That's not what we wanted!"

Oh, okay. That made way more sense, this was a mistake, a wrong number, maybe they were just trying to dial customer service for Frigidaire. They clarified, signing desperately, "We don't want phone sex. We want a woman to come here, to our house, and *have* sex with us."

I cocked an eyebrow. "A . . . prostitute?" I signed.

They smiled. "YES! That! We want a prostitute. Do you know anyone we can call?"

It's basically in my DNA to find a way to help deaf people as much as I can. But as much as I wanted to help these guys lose their virginity to a local courtesan, I had to break the bad news. "I'm sorry. I'm not a pimp. Good luck with your search. Try searching 'Escort' in your area." They thanked me and hung up. It breaks my heart that to this day I still don't know if those boys ended up getting laid.

The greatest call I ever made was to the police. A deaf guy popped up on my screen agitated and shifting back and forth. Perhaps in a meth daze, he demanded I dial the number for his local police department's non-emergency line.

"I'm calling the fucking police!" he signed.

"Okay!" I affirmed and pressed connect on my computer's interface.

A slight aside: There are many rules to being a sign language interpreter. There's an entire code of ethics that one must adhere to in order to get and maintain certification in ASL interpretation. Like the prime directive of the United Federation of Planets, the interpreter must not, cannot, get involved. The mission is to interpret only. Not to help, not to assist. In fact, sometimes it had to be the opposite. If I was interpreting a job interview and the deaf person interviewing for the job was saying things that made him or her sound unintelligent or mentally unhinged, it was tempting to clean up what they were saying, to make them sound better and more employable. But if I did that, then I might be helping an unqualified murderer get a job as a local magistrate.

The temptation to help can be brutal. At times it is patently obvious that your client has been taken advantage of. When the Nigerian scandals made their rounds through the human population, burning through the first wave of gullible folks who sent their life savings to Lagos and then the second wave and then people finally got savvy to the fact that a man who can barely pen an intelligible email is unlikely to be offering you a real opportunity to make millions of dollars in secret money, it did what all scams do. It sank deeper into the human population to find people more vulnerable and less aware of the story: the elderly, the uneducated, and then finally, the deaf.

At the call center the people getting scammed were obvious. The line was always filled with static, the conversations always deeply sketchy and involving terrifying things like the deaf caller booking travel to Lagos to receive their plunder in person. I don't know what part of the scam it was to actually get these deaf people to travel to Nigeria, but I very much doubt it included a cool trip to the Olumo Rock for sightseeing.

I complained to my bosses and was told in no uncertain terms that we *had* to facilitate these calls, without interference, at risk of losing our jobs. The idea of what we were doing was to facilitate communication access that was *equal* to that of a hearing counterpart. Just as hearing people could be taken advantage of by Nigerian princes, so, too, could the deaf. This is all a neat philosophical musing, but when it came down to it, I just couldn't do it. I mean, I tried. I'd make faces when interpreting the calls, providing hints like, "He sounds *strange*." When this didn't work, I outright violated the code of ethics, signing "This sounds off. I think he's trying to cheat you." When the caller ignored my unethical warnings, I just started saying I couldn't understand the callers due to the static on the line. When that didn't work I just started pressing ignore when calls came in from Nigeria.

Allowing deaf callers to get cheated rather than get involved shows you how deeply the "Do not try to help" ethic goes in the interpreting field. It is rule number one.

This can be particularly hard to resist for CODA interpreters who, as I said above, have been trained their entire lives to maintain a standby "ready to help" position. It's deep in the blood. Once, when I was at an airport, getting ready to board a flight, I saw, at the Southwest counter, a woman with hearing aids seemingly struggling to understand what the check-in attendant was saying to her. Like a bloodhound getting a whiff of a missing kid, my instincts began to twitch and throb. This is why I am here.

Must. Help. Deaf.

I walked over and signed to the hearing aid user: "Do you need any help?" The woman's face contorted into a confused grimace and she gave me a look I can only describe as "I don't know sign language why the fuck are you talking to me?" face. Deeply embarrassed, I started to back away but the lady working the counter at Southwest wasn't gonna let me off that easily.

"Don't you *ever* bother one of my customers while I'm talking to them!"

This kind of scolding never quite makes sense to me. Admonishing someone in an incredibly specific situation to never repeat it feels like a waste of time. Did she think I spent my days haunting the luggage check-in counter at LAX hoping against hope for an opportunity to jump in and disrupt the notoriously smooth Southwest customer service experience?

"I was just trying to help." I muttered, face flushed.

Our lady of perpetual Southwest was not having it. "Nobody asked for your damn help."

This wasn't exactly true. My entire childhood, everyone had asked for help: my mother to understand the people around her; my teachers to understand my mother; therapists who wanted me to translate the psychological diagnosis they had made of me to my mother; interpreters who had misunderstood what my mother had signed. But this lady didn't seem receptive to me explaining my backstory and the psychological forces and family dynamics that led me to this moment, so I just slinked away. You ever have an experience that instantly turns you into a worse, more callous human being? That happened to me that day at the Southwest counter. I vowed never to help anyone, ever again. That transformation was one of Southwest's lesser-known rapid rewards.

Another important rule in the interpreter's code of conduct is to always speak in the first person when interpreting for a client. Never "He said he wants to order a pizza." Always "*I'd* like to order a pizza." The idea is to facilitate communication as close to normal as is possible for the deaf person. The interpreter is to be invisible, a transparent bridge between the two callers making sure that pineapple and ham, extra cheese, gets to where it was going with as smooth a transaction as possible. When the interpreter says something like "He'd like to order a pizza," it's a banal, infantilizing reminder that the deaf person cannot order a pizza without assistance. Perhaps this has little enough impact when it's a pizza order, but it can become massively detrimental when calling about a job opening. There might not be more of a taboo for an interpreter than jumping into the third person. It's cause to get fired. Got it?

Okay, so back to the guy calling the police. An officer came on the line, "Police department, can I help you?" I gave the standard video relay interpreter's greeting, "There's a person who uses sign language to communicate on the line; I'll be interpreting the call starting now," and with that, we began the call.

My methy deafy instantly launched into a tirade about the police, surveillance, and his feelings on law enforcement. "Fuck you, you fucking pig! Fuck the police, you fucking pig bitch!"

I was in the pocket, interpreting my ass off. I added a little anger to my voice to get the point across. To be honest this was a dream come true. I'd always wanted to call a cop a pig without consequence.

The cop responded, a calm picture of professionalism. "I understand you're agitated, sir, but I don't know how I can help you if you don't tell me what's wrong."

My deaf friend would have none of it "Suck my fucking dick, you stupid pig!"

I was really getting into character now, adding a few pig snorting sounds for some added mise-en-scene. Again, the cop responded with perfect sober composure, "Sir, I'm sorry you're upset. If you'd just give me an opportunity to understand why you are calling I might be able to help."

Then my client signed something I wasn't ready for.

"Fuck. Your. Mother."

I asked him to repeat. He signed even more clearly.

"FUCK. YOUR. MOTHER."

I hesitated, not sure what to do. The deaf client looked at me, expectantly. The police officer asked, "Hello?"

"Uh . . . *HE SAID*, 'Fuck your mother!' "

I jumped out of first person so quickly I almost got whiplash.

The cop jumped out of professional composure even faster.

He exploded in anger. "Fuck my mama?! Fuck your mama, you deaf piece of shit. Come to the fucking station and say that shit again!"

Click.

What a call. What a day. Luckily everyone was so angry, no one noticed I'd flagrantly violated the code of ethics, so I lived to sign another day. Of course, another huge breach of ethics is to violate the confidentiality of the clients you work for and tell the story of when you were able to yell at a cop to fuck his own mother. But I left the interpreting field years ago, looking for bigger and better things.

It's been years since my last call. In that time a lot has changed for the deaf community. Just before I wrote this sentence, I FaceTimed my mother and signed to ask her if she needed anything from the store. She told me she'd just seen me acting in an episode of *This Close,* a show created and starring Shoshannah Stern and Josh Feldman, two deaf writer/actors. She had turned the volume up and my mother could "hear" the audio through her cochlear implant. Robotics have accomplished what Bell wanted, but it still didn't work.

My mother and the other deaf people who choose implants are still deaf; they're just cybernetically modified deaf people. Deaf people are in Marvel movies; in 2022, Troy Kotsur became the *second* deaf actor to win an Academy Award. There are deaf doctors and lawyers, deaf authors and UFC fighters, and deaf professors and scientists. Every passing year, deaf people become less "deafness the disability" and more "deafness the culture."

In many ways the disability was eliminated the moment the language was created. As for that language, since stopping interpreting, my sign has gotten rustier. My fingers do not flow as they once did. But it's still there. Still the native tongue. Still a visual dance that connects me to my family and connects me to that part of who I am. I am a member of deaf culture. A proud son of the deaf. In them I see a people undeterred by a dominant society that wanted to cure them of themselves. If the Jews are a people of the book, defined by their relationship to information, the deaf are a people of the tongue, a people of the hand, a people who eked out dignity where there was none promised. Though a priest was inspired to teach the deaf in order to bring them to the table of Christian salvation, they ended up building their own table.

Because for them, salvation was never a helping hand, but a talking one.

4 *Burning Man, or Staring at the Bright Lights*

On Labor Day of 2020, I was sitting in my house, wearing seventeen KN95 masks, washing a head of cauliflower in an anti-COVID delousing agent, when I realized that this was the first Labor Day in twenty years I was spending at home, not caked in alkaline dust kicked up from the moonlike expanse that is the Black Rock Desert just outside of Gerlach, Nevada. That year, Burning Man, like the rest of the world and an ever-increasing number of men in the entertainment industry, and every other industry, okay let's just say men, had been canceled.

Some people were likely happy about that.

Everyone loves to hate Burning Man. You're probably sitting there reading this and hating on it right now.

In San Francisco, long the population center of Burning Man attendees, the locals hold a festival of their own every Labor Day to celebrate the departure of the smelliest and most polyamorous of SF residents. There are articles written in the local free paper rejoicing in their absence.

Often when I mention to someone that I've attended the festival for more than twenty years and used to work for the organization, I'll get a rolled eye and a remark that they can't stand it. I always ask the same question, "Oh, you've been?" The answer, invariably, is no.

That's not to say every person would like it. I'm not such a naïve acolyte of the movement that I believe that. It's just that Burning Man has such an outsize image in the American consciousness that people have the ability to hate it without really having any idea what it is.

The truth is Burning Man is more awful and more awesome than most people who have never attended (and many who have) could imagine. It is what they think it is and also more, and also less. It is a wild neo-pagan orgy, an ecological disaster, a muddy mess (it was fine, we liked it, stop asking), a tech-infested "billionaires who want to live on the edge" club, a countercultural middle finger shoved in the face of stable society, a drug fest, a spectacular art installation zone, an experiential playground, a new kind of religion, a bureaucratic moneymaking nightmare, a clueless Never-Never Land for white people who think neon-colored dreadlocks will make them people of color, a rave, a drug fest again, a temporary city, an orgy again, an experiment in off-grid communal living, a utopia, a lie, a hypocrisy, a mess, the greatest party on Earth.

When I first attended in 1996, it was almost none of those things. It wasn't sure what it was. And that was okay with me, because I wasn't sure what I was, either.

The reason I first went to Burning Man was simple: I was a raver and I'd heard they had a rave camp there. No bigger mystery than that. No cosmic draw. No conscious seeking. A rumor of a rave at the time was enough to get me to pack my things into a car and drive six hours, unsure of anything awaiting me but a dance floor.

I packed an experimental BBQ called the Amazing Newspaper Grill that my mother had bought from QVC. It could supposedly cook hamburgers in minutes using only crumpled-up newspaper. I grabbed a pound of ground beef from the store, a stack of free weekly papers for fuel, a few gallons of water, and said, "Let's roll."

Four other rave zombies and I packed into a 1991 Ford Escort and tore out. We drove past Reno and turned off of the freeway onto Paiute land. Deeper and deeper into the desert we went, past Pyramid Lake, a body of water that is said to be cursed. According to local legend, the lake teems with malevolent "water babies," the spirits of ancient infanticide victims who will grab the little tootsies of swimmers and drag them down to their doom. Odds that this is just a racist myth told to make the Paiute tribe look bad are high.

We passed through the Paiute reservation and deep into Wild West territory, the kind of landscape where you could imagine a bandit hiding from the marshals. The land started to bleach white, endless cracks of dust stretching before us in all directions. An hour later we hit Empire, Nevada, current population 65, peak historical population 750.

Empire is a former company town for the United States Gypsum Corporation, one of those old-school *How Green Was My Valley* towns where everyone who lived there mined gypsum for the company, and food debts at the Empire General Store could be debited straight from your gypsum-covered paycheck. At this point you are undoubtedly asking, "What the fuck is gypsum?"

The history and chemical makeup of gypsum is exactly what the next thirty pages of this book are about. I'm kidding; google it. Or don't and just pretend I said coal.

Ten miles past Empire is Gerlach, Nevada, a Wild West ghost town that people forgot to abandon that constitutes the last slice of civilization you'll hit before your brain explodes. Ten miles past Gerlach shit starts to get weird.

Out there, in the true middle of nowhere, we saw a hand-painted sign that read BURNING MAN with an arrow pointed down onto the dry lake bed below.

We pulled up to the "box office," a single canned-ham trailer in the middle of the crunch of the desert. A naked fifty-year-old man walked over to us holding a revolver. He grunted, causing his dangling over-tanned penis to jiggle. "Sixty-five dollars each. There's four of you, so two hundred sixty dollars." This Burning Man security apparatus was so cracked out he'd missed an entire person in a very small car. I was such a square AA bitch at the time, so hung up on ethical living, that I meeped out, to the horror of my carmates, all dirtbag rave kids barely able to afford the trip in the first place, "There are actually five of us!"

Naked guy shook his head and refocused his vision, "Oh yeah. Three hundred twenty-five, then." We handed over the cash and he told us, "Reset your trip odometer to zero. Drive straight for eight miles and then veer to the right for three miles. You should find the city."

"What happens if we miss it?" I asked, a little intimidated now.

"Then you get stranded in the desert. It's a hundred and eight degrees right now. Probably not a good time for that to happen. See ya!"

Frightened fingers pressed reset on the tripmeter, threw it into drive, and watched the world slip away.

In the winter, the Black Rock Desert is a boggy, marshy lake with a foot of standing water and a thick sludge of lake mud. When the rains come, they revive petrified fairy shrimp eggs like sea monkeys, and the lake begins teeming with life. During those months it is a buffet-style stopover for hungry migrating birds. In the summer, the lake dries up, cakes over, and becomes a 360-degree moonscape: bleak, dry, and seemingly incapable of supporting any life. It is a vast expanse of white dust, going forever in all directions. As I type this, I can taste the dust, feel it. Once you get out there, the desert gets in you and doesn't leave. The vast dusty nothingness is called "the playa" and it is the landscape where psychedelic dreams come true.

It was into this whiteness that we drove. We couldn't see anything, did not know if we were coming or going, did not know what direction we were traveling in. The tripmeter clicked over from 7 to 8 and we cocked the steering wheel to the right, hoping to find something.

We kept going in the white, seeing nothing, hearing nothing. Sweating now. And then, just as Tan Penis Guy told us, at the 2.5-mile point, we saw, emerging from the dust like an oasis, dots of strangeness. Domes and tents and movement.

We had arrived.

I didn't know what this was but it was no rave, that was for sure. It was one part *Dune*, one part *Mad Max*, one part hippie gathering, and five parts "What the fuck is this?" It was Burning Man. Real

Burning Man. This was what people refer back to when they say they heard it used to be cool.

By the end of that weekend in 1996, it would never be the same again. Nor would I.

Burning Man didn't spring out of nothing. Like every scene and subculture, it is a child of its antecedents. The Towns Hospital to the Oxford Group to local AA to the world AA conventions. Disco to house to trance to Deadmau5. Chuck Berry to the Beatles to Zeppelin to Black Sabbath to Metallica. You get the picture. The progenitors of Burning Man were odd just like the child they eventually birthed.

It probably starts with LSD.

I'll try to do this quickly.*

On April 19, 1943, Albert Hofmann, the inventor of LSD, dropped a bunch on his tongue and went for a bike ride. This is "Bicycle Day," recognized as the day of the first intentional acid trip. This singular experience spun out into a ton of different directions: the new age movement, the antiwar movement, free love, "I'd Like to Buy the World a Coke." Timothy Leary's famous admonishment, "Turn on, tune in, drop out," had different meanings depending on who was hearing it. But most of those perspectives were focused on how beautiful the world could be if we just figured it out.

On the other hand, Ken Kesey and his Merry Pranksters took a perspective that was much more "Everything is absurd" than "Everything is beautiful."

In 1964, they set across the United States on a drug-fueled bus trip dedicated to experiential immediacy and living for its own sake. Meaning was mush; all that mattered was the spontaneous collection of experiences.

Ten years later, tangentially inspired by Kesey's idea, a secret society called the Suicide Club sprang up among the freaks and

---

* If you want a more exhaustive rundown of this, read Brian Doherty's excellent book *This Is Burning Man*.

weirdos of San Francisco's art scene. Their mission took Kesey's one step further: They would not meander around life looking for things of interest to occur; they would manifest them in real time, manufacturing experiences through manipulated experiments in reality.

They began their exclusive club with an act of great danger, crawling down into the Pacific Ocean during a raging winter storm, grasping a handrail for dear life as twenty-foot waves broke over them. It was all about feeling alive.

The Suicide Club would script experiences for its selected members to enjoy, and the absurdity of those experiences was not just part of it; the absurdity was the point. They'd white-knuckle crawl to the top of the Golden Gate Bridge, just to have high tea. They'd take off their clothes and mob a cable car. They'd infiltrate American Nazi Party meetings. These were people interested in experiences on the edge of comfort, both for themselves and the people who witnessed them. The lines between prank and performance, theater and audience, reality and fantasy, all began to blur.

By the time the club disbanded, they'd inspired a new generation of people who wanted to find a meaning of life through examining its profound lack of meaning. These people felt they could push the mission of scripted randomness further than the Suicide Club had. They called themselves the Cacophony Society.

The Cacophony Society wanted to move beyond the Suicide Club's individual experiments cloaked in secrecy. It wanted to provide the kinds of experiences the Suicide Club offered to its members but to bring them to the public. To make them transparent. The Cacophony Society was more elaborate in its experiments, more ritualized and conceptual. And it was all in the service of random, absurd, experiential happenings. Like the Suicide Club, the value of what they were doing rested in the experience of it, not in any underlying meaning.

Imagine you're taking a city bus and at one stop, a fully costumed clown gets on. "Hmm," you think, "that's a full clown. Must be on his way to work at a birthday party. Sad he has to take the bus. Shame he can't afford a tiny car to drive to his gigs." Back to reading your newspaper you go. Then your bus gets to the next stop and another clown gets on. "What the hell? Two clowns?" This is really odd, but your brain wants to make sense of it. Must be a weird coincidence? Another stop. Two more clowns. Now your mind is getting ripped open, it can't be a coincidence, but it also can't be organized, because what would be the point? Oh, maybe there's a clown convention in town, you think. Yeah, that must be it. You ask a clown sitting next to you if there's a clown convention; he says no. But he won't answer any more questions. By the time the bus is filled with clowns you are in disbelief, something is happening, but you have no idea what. That feeling, that "What did I just witness?," is the result of what they dubbed "culture jamming." Culture was stupid. It was based on rot. And the only thing to do with that rot was to kick at it until you caused a collapse of meaning and a swell of wonder.

The cynicism engendered by the cultural emptiness of 1980s Wall Street wealth worship and an endless Cold War left a group of young people convinced life had no meaning other than whatever you could extract from it. So that's what they'd do, strip-mine life for experiences that had no inherent meaning but that they could shake you from the banality of reality and make you emerge changed. This change was correct no matter what it was. The pointlessness was the point.

The Cacophony Society kept churning out these random experiences of ultimate weirdness that would eventually result in the creation of flash mobs and Improv Everywhere and SantaCon (the annual gathering of white people pub-crawling and vomiting on one another in Santa Claus outfits) and the invention of the Billboard Liberation Front.* It even inspired *Fight Club,* whose author, Chuck Palahniuk, was an early Cacophony Society member.

They searched for places to stage more and more elaborate happenings, and this eventually led them all the way out to the Nevada desert, where they found a place so desolate, it could become the canvas for anything they could imagine.

---

* Anytime you look up and see a billboard that has been masterfully transformed from its corporate messaging to read something subversive, you can thank the Cacophony Society.

At the same time as all these culture jamming rituals, another ritual was taking place on Baker Beach in San Francisco.

On the summer solstice of 1986, a man loosely connected to the San Francisco art scene, Larry Harvey, constructed a simple eight-foot wooden statue of a man and invited twenty friends to the beach to watch him set it on fire. It was rustic art, less high concept than a Cacophony Society ritual, but it seemed to do something for the invited guests. As soon as it burned, they resolved to do it again the next year.

That next year, the man they built was fifteen feet tall and a hundred people came. The year after that, Larry, for the first time, called what they were doing "Burning Man." The Man was now forty feet tall and collapsed when they raised it, burning on its knees like a prostitute protesting the Vietnam War. The next year, 1990, Burning Man had two groups crash the party that would change its destiny forever: the Cacophony Society and the police.

A ritual burning of a statue sounded like a Cacophony Society good time and an unpermitted mega bonfire gathering of what was now nearly a thousand people sounded like a San Francisco ordinance violation. Only the cops couldn't figure out which ordinance was being violated. They hadn't made a rule about that yet. When Larry Harvey unveiled the Man, the police told him he could raise it but not burn it, and for the second time in two years the event was a bit of a bust.

It might have all ended there.

They raised the Man, everybody said, "Yep, that's a statue of a man all right," and started to go home. But a representative of the Cacophony Society pulled Larry Harvey aside and told him about a place where they'd started staging rituals, the Black Rock Desert, a place where there weren't enough people to have rules. Harvey and the society agreed to meet there on Labor Day and burn the fucker there.

When they arrived in Black Rock, one Cacophony Society member, the mysterious Michael Mikel, aka Danger Ranger, drew a line in the dust and told the assembled hundred or so people who had come all the way from San Francisco to see who knows what, that to pass that line, to step over it, was to pass into a new realm, to leave the world behind and join the Temporary Autonomous Zone. They passed that line, burned the Man, and the Black Rock Desert merged with the Burning Man and became one.

Six years later, the event I had just driven to had doubled and doubled and doubled again. Nineteen ninety-six was the first year it was something massive. There were eight thousand people in attendance.

It was also teetering on sheer chaos. Its size had reached the breaking point for the kind of anarchy that a bunch of punk art clowns could inject into a festival without consequence. With no rules to abide by and no greater society observing or policing their nihilistic antics, no shocked bystanders to stand agape at clownery, the stakes and the danger of the place just kept escalating.

This works great until it doesn't, and 1996 was the year that it didn't. Infiltrated by word-of-mouth masses, Burning Man lacked the infrastructure to protect its attendees from what we found there. As the back of the ticket read, "You voluntarily assume the risk of bodily injury or death by attending," and before the gates even opened, one man was already dead, his head nearly sliced off by a car he was playing chicken with.

These days, every Burning Man has a theme, a central motif to position the art and performance around. The first few years on the playa, there was no official theme, only the loose, ever-present themes of danger and finding a place to shit. In 1996, Larry Harvey declared the first official theme: "The Inferno," and, by the end of the weekend, it was precisely that.

On Saturday night, we all watched the Man, who was hoisted onto a pyramid of hay bales, immolate and fall, announcing to us all that our big wood daddy wouldn't be watching us anymore.

The entire place suddenly decided it was free to start misbehaving.

If I thought raves provided bacchanalia, I must not have known what the word meant. Guns were going off everywhere, a stream of bullets in the air for no apparent reason. People set fires to structures seemingly at random. A larger-than-life model of the game Mouse Trap sent bowling balls down a Rube Goldberg–like track until one slammed into the windshield of a car, destroying it. A fake mini mall, complete with satirically redesigned corporate logos and storefronts, was set on fire. Gallons of gasoline napalmed down the four-story structure as a man on fire ziplined into a wall of neon from the top of the tower. Flaming art cars drove by and propane-puffing fire breathers painted the night sky orange. San Francisco's drag nuns, the Sisters of Perpetual Indulgence, walked by fanning themselves. Naked hippies writhed in pits of playa mud, caking themselves into tribal-looking tech pagans. A two-story pile of broken-down pianos lay on the desert floor, inviting you to climb them, play them, and get a tetanus infection. A fifteen-foot-tall sculpture of a woman sprayed water out of its vagina, my first-ever female ejaculate shower.

Everything felt like it could kill you or delight you, depending on how you approached it. This was Burning Man at its Cacophony Society peak. The ultimate iteration of what the group could do.

I spent much of my time out at rave camp, a mile outside of the main city, accessible only by car.

They placed us out there due to a general disdain for our music and fashion choices, the underground artists and underground dancers forming strange bedfellows that were only reluctantly accepted. This placement would prove to be a grave miscalculation for the organizers of the event.

In the middle of the night, one of the cars driving back and forth from the city to the rave camp, undoubtedly piloted by a very high or very drunk or very both person, careened into a tent where two sleeping ravers slept, crushing them.

When the sun rose, there were scar marks all over the playa, structures having been burned into the lake bed, causing black wounds to form. Little piles of raver and hippie and techno-punk poo-poo littered the playa, the paltry port-a-potty infrastructure no match for the rectums of eight thousand.

On Monday morning, when the Burning Man organization took stock of their event, they had a grim tally: one dead man, two permanently injured participants, ecological destruction, and a sea of human shit. Local police and the Bureau of Land Management noticed, too. It was clear something had to change if Burning Man was going to survive. That something meant structure. It meant rules. To the Cacophony Society that signaled that Burning Man had run its course. From here on it would only be watered down. To Larry Harvey, it meant they needed to grow up and grow big. The Cacophony Society cut ties with the event after 1996, and the slow creep away from danger began.

I knew none of this at the time. I sensed it was dangerous, but I was sober and knew how to protect myself when dumb shit was happening.

I had the time of my life that weekend.

I explored, danced, drank free chai, lay down in the dust, felt the vibrations of the Earth enter my body from the ground below. Yes, I was sober, I'd been to the inferno, and I loved how it burned, but damn it I was determined to be as much of a hippie as anyone there.

I made love to a woman in a sleeping bag on the open playa as cars zipped past us going sixty miles per hour. I stayed up every night until the sun rose. I felt, as the week went on, a kind of molecular reconfiguration. Raves had prepped me for this but they had not prepared me. The experience of a full-bore gavage of chaos, absurdity, and saturnalia was like a waterboard of wonder. It shook me into the category of freak in a way that felt absolutely permanent. I had been to the crossroads, met the devil, and danced with him all night. I was certain that I'd go to Burning Man for the rest of my life.

It took me five years, but when I returned in 2001, Burning Man was a totally different festival. The Man was now seventy feet tall and attendance was twenty-six thousand. It had matured and become the festival it is today.

If you pull off Nevada State Route 447 onto the Black Rock Desert on Labor Day now, you will be met with a very different experience from mine in the back of that 1991 Ford Escort. The first thing you will encounter will be a very familiar, very "default world" experience: traffic. Miles and miles and miles of cars, two-story hippie buses, five-hundred-thousand-dollar RVs, modified rockets slapped onto tractor chassis, World War II tanks affixed to the back of flatbeds, and every other vehicle you could possibly imagine, all gridlocked into an ingress traffic jam so fantastically slow-moving that you'd think you were in a developing nation that had just paved its first freeway. In that line is the city of Black Rock. The demographic is older than many festivals, and richer. Most people are in their thirties, but many are retired while some are children. Most are white (duh, techno fest in the desert), but that's slowly changing, too.

But the most interesting demographic aspect can't really be quantified. It's ethereal, it's the deep connection people feel to Burning Man. An entire subculture is centered around a single event. These are "Burners." You never meet a Coachella-er. In that traffic line are people for whom this event is the most important time of their year and often of their lives.

That line, during peak times, can take up to ten hours to slowly eke up to the front gate, where every vehicle is searched, tickets are scanned, and Burners are sent into the city. The people searching your car are gruff pirates in black. This is called the Gate, and the workers there are some of the last vanguards of clownery and Cacophony-style antics left at Burning Man. Of course these are the people I eventually ended up living and working with at Burning Man.

The ten-hour wait in Burning Man traffic comes on the heels of a six-hour or more drive, and many people start drinking or getting high right there in their cars, impatient for the party to start. I can't tell you how many confused Burners I have encountered up at the front of this line, who got a little too high in their traffic-jam pregame, wandered off from their car to "explore," and ended up at the Gate, peaking on acid, wearing only a hemp bikini and a pair of butterfly wings, with no clue where their car, their friends, or their tickets got to. Cold and scared, they'd ask one of us for help, and we'd point back at the cars and say, "Your ride is out there." Then, looking back for the first time at the line they'd just wandered down, they'd see the sea of pearls, the headlights of ten thousand cars. Helpless and near tears, they'd wander off, hoping to find their way again.

Once past the Gate things get more pleasant. You think you've arrived but in reality you'd only just passed customs. Now the journey begins.

A mile down from the Gate you encounter the greeters, a far-less-gruff welcoming committee than the Gate. Here you are directed to exit your car, hug the topless greeter in front of you who whispers "Welcome home" in your ear, bang a gong, and, if you are a "virgin" (a first-timer to Burning Man), you will be commanded to get down on your back in the dust and make "playa angels," covering yourself in dust the moment you arrive. And, honestly, you might as well get dirty now, because you're not going to be clean until you get home, and even then, only after a few showers.

Then again, depending on what you do there, you may never be clean again.

Past the greeters, you see, for the first time, the lights of the city. And these days it truly is a city. When erected, Black Rock City, as it has come to be called, is four square miles and is the tenth largest city in Nevada. Population these days is about eighty thousand.

Black Rock City is arranged like a huge clock, with the Man, who has grown closer to one hundred feet, standing at the twelve o'clock position, orienting you to what will be a very disorienting experience.

You find a place to park your vehicle and set up camp. Depending on who you are, where you camp can vary wildly. Suppose you were driving a two-story hippie bus from the traffic jam above. Well, you might pull into the Dr. Bronner's camp, a large dome set up by the tiny-font soap impresarios. We all owe Dr. Bronner's a debt of gratitude for making bathing cool among the hippie community.

Every year they erect a huge dome, and wheel in a shipping container modified to serve as an enormous communal shower. People wait in line for hours to get their single shower of the week. But this is no mere shower. Once you pass the threshold of the dome, you are expected to strip and are then marched, now nude, toward the center of the dome where psychedelic trance plays. Naked dancing toward the shower car is encouraged. They stuff you in, nuts to butts, with hundreds of naked Burners in various states of pungency. When the boxcar is sufficiently stuffed, costumed volunteers grab hoses and, screaming, turn them on the stuffed car, spraying it with thousands of gallons of pepperminty soap. You squirm and slide, using the body hair of the anti-vax Instagram influencer standing next to you as a loofah.

If being stuffed naked into a boxcar while uniformed officials spray you down promising a shower feels vaguely Holocausty, you're not wrong. But it's much more fun. Rarely did they dance to techno at Bergen-Belsen. After your shower, you get tea and, now that you're clean, you can start to scan the crowd for your Burning Man three-way.

But maybe you're not a hippie. Maybe you came in one of those half-million-dollar buses. Maybe you are Puff Daddy or a tech billionaire or a Russian oligarch and don't want to spend your time with the Bronner's-washed masses. You'll probably be driving straight to a plug-and-play camp where massive $50,000 per-person ultra-lux villages have been set up for your convenience. In these camps sushi will be driven in from Reno daily, as will cocaine, as will, in some of the darker corners, women.

These camps always baffled me. Why visit a place where the whole point is to sublimate yourself into an experience that is meant to take you out of reality but pay exorbitant fees to ensure you never interact with anyone outside of the other programmers at your start-up and high-priced Estonian sex workers?

Much has been made of the tech bros infiltrating Burning Man and slowly ruining it with weaponized douchebaggery, but that tells only half the story. Inarguably, yes, Silicon Valley dorks have increasingly made Burning Man a Wild West company retreat; trust falls and team-building have been replaced by doing coke and riding

electric bikes to go dance to dubstep. But the idea that the tech invasion of Burning Man is some kind of new phenomenon is false. Tech
people have been at the burn since the beginning. It is not that tech
has changed Burning Man for the worse. It is that tech itself has
changed for the worse and brought all that energy with it to Burning
Man. And Burning Man, rather than rolling an eye, rolled out a red
carpet.

When I first started attending, tech people were there. At the time,
they were not only a subculture, they were a counterculture, an out-
law by-product of ones and zeros more at home in the universe of
The Matrix than in a boardroom. Then tech took over the world
and the punk-rock programmers became billionaires. The only difference between a tech CEO and a Dupont CEO is that one has had
a ménage à trois. When Silicon Valley decided it was Mount Olym-
pus, Burning Man, like the rental market in San Francisco, got
fucked.

I've tried to avoid wanton bigotry through the rest of this book,
but now I'm going to say something so inflammatory I'll probably
be excoriated and labeled a hatemonger: Billionaires are fucking
dorks. I don't mean dorks like charming, socially awkward weirdos.
I mean dorks like complete fuckwad losers. Maybe Jay-Z is cool.
The rest of them? Peel-my-skin-off-rather-than-talk-to-them, out-of-
touch shit heels. That said, I've never met a billionaire so maybe
they are awesome.

Burning Man certainly thought they were. The festival grabbed
its ankles and bent over to try to court these geeks, allowing them
access to privileges that violated its own supposed core values. It
looked the other way as camps were set up that hired manual labor-
ers from Reno to clean up the expensive trash of the secret aristoc-
racy of Black Rock City. "Leave no trace," a Burning Man–adopted
motto used to ensure the place wasn't left trashed, was slowly adjusted to "Have the guys you rounded up at the Reno Home Depot
parking lot make sure you leave no trace." Burning Man plied the
billionaires with tickets on demand when entrance to the event was
becoming marked by scarcity. Seemingly in the hopes of inspiring
some kind of large-scale funding pipeline, tech magnates were

granted access to the inner sanctum of shaping Burning Man's culture, given unofficial access to Burning Man's decision-making apparatus. And just like that, tech bros became above the law at the burn.*

Why did Burning Man do it? They felt they had to. Burning Man's financial and labor model was wildly unscalable. Even at eighty thousand attendees and a psychological serf caste providing the labor, they needed more money. For a while Burning Man managed this by jacking up ticket prices, which started pricing out the less wealthy, leaving the rich a progressively higher percentage of the population. This changed what and who you saw at Burning Man. The counterculturalism at the core of the event began to rot, and with it, its reputation. Very gradually, yet never entirely, Burning Man moved from a place where weirdos came to feel normal into a place normal people came to feel weird.

Burning Man could no longer raise prices without fully estranging its core demographic, the interesting people who made Burning Man an event where uninteresting people wanted to come gawk in the first place.

So, they made a choice, and a big one: They'd dissolve as a for-profit entity and reconstitute themselves as a nonprofit with a stated goal of accomplishing a fairly incoherent vision: ". . . to guide, nurture and protect the more permanent community created by its culture." This way, they could solicit donations from the Big Tech Burners, write those donations off, and fund the event that way.

Money made the burn better and it made it worse. Money allowed for large-scale art and camps to be built, million-dollar projects funded by Elon Musk or Sergey Brin that operated at a magnitude way beyond anything anyone on Baker Beach ever could have imagined. This was not outsider art; this was opulent excess that used spectacle as its primary medium. The visual scale was breathtaking. But as often happens, the more money you pour into

---

* To Burning Man's credit, in recent years it has copped to this corrosive violation and has enacted steps to try to mitigate the damage and the influence of such people. It remains to be seen how effective this will be.

something, the more soul you suck out of it. Increasingly, Burning Man became a playground for the rich. Art projects became increasingly defined not by sweat equity but by actual equity.

But maybe you aren't in a rich person's camp either. Maybe you're just some schmuck, sitting in traffic, waiting to go to Burning Man for the first time.

You find a place to park, set up your tent, and wander out to explore Black Rock City. When a storm isn't whipping sand at you at sixty miles per hour, slapping your skin with grit and blinding you, the city can be incredibly beautiful. Your eyes and mind cannot compute what you are looking at, what you are processing. It often takes a day or two to even get into the groove of the thing, to stop dropping your tongue out of your mouth in the shape of a staircase at all the glittery naked titties and penises, and actually take in the city.

Much of the municipal action of Burning Man takes place on the Esplanade, the main street of Black Rock City where you will find some of the largest interactive theme camps, from tiki bars to body-washing stations to orgy domes to lemonade stands. And it's all free. No commerce allowed.

You can fight a rival in the Thunderdome, a re-creation of *Mad Max*'s famous "two men enter, one man leaves" gladiator pit. Only you will be fighting with foam bats as a goth siren in two-foot-tall platforms and a cat-o'-nine-tails hoists you up on a bungee cord and releases you into combat. Next, you may find a TED Talk–like gathering of psychonauts discussing the therapeutic power of psilocybin in terminally ill patients. Farther down you may climb into a funhouse maze where, after getting lost for forty-five minutes, you finally make it to the inner sanctum and find the prize in the center: a raucous dance party where the DJ is playing remixes of "Don't You Want Me" by the Human League over and over and over again. Everything is weird, wild, and random, and the number of times your mind will be blown stops feeling quantifiable.

But sitting there with your jaw dropped is not at all the point here. Participation is one of the cornerstone principles at Burning Man. The ultimate insult is to be called a spectator, a person who comes to gawk, gives nothing, adds nothing, takes up space. Participation means a thousand things, and in it are the ghosts of the Cacophony Society. Participation can be simple, targeted, and meaningless.

When I first went back in 2001, I knew this kind of participatory action would be expected of me, so I staged an elaborate "reverse robbery" of the Center Camp Café, which is a central gathering place that, in violation of Burning Man's own anti-commerce rules, sold coffee and tea.* We ran in with a team in ski masks and holding fake guns, screaming, like the opening scene of *Pulp Fiction,* that this was a "reverse robbery." We jumped on the counter and threw money at the cashiers, stuffed gems into people's bags, and took off, tossing all of our equipment, then doubling back a few minutes later to get in line and ask the people what just happened.

Years later, my wife, Natasha, and I took a walk through Black Rock City to take in the scenery. It was her first burn, and I'd dragged her along despite her reluctance. As we walked, we noticed a small whirring noise at our ankles. Pulling up alongside us was a tiny remote-control truck with a tub of guacamole and chips in its bed, along with a bottle of tequila and a sign that read THE GUACA-NATOR. We smiled and kept walking, but the Guacanator wouldn't take no for an answer. It pulled up and cut us off, and the remote operator, wherever he or she was, kind of shimmied the truck back and forth as if to say, "Bitch, you know you want some guac." We knelt down, took a chip and scooped into the bounty of the Guaca-nator. Natasha took a shot of tequila and the Guacanator zipped out into the city to go delight someone else. This kind of tiny-scale offering of absurdity can make the entire experience. It can remind you of the wonders of life.

---

* Burning Man disbanded the café in 2022 in order to cease this hypocrisy, and many Burners, including me, were made very tired and annoyed by this symbolic gesture. I mean, how noncommerce-based is an event where tickets cost $1,200? Just accept the implausibility of your own event and sell me a fucking latte!

Perhaps I'm putting too much significance on a bowl of chips, but I'll never forget it.

Another time, I was walking with a group of friends, late at night, nearly three A.M., way out in deep playa, far past where the action was, where it was just cold and quiet. A thousand yards out, we saw a single pale blue light. Having nothing better to do, we walked toward it. When we finally got there, there was a single man, alone in the dark, no one around him for miles, putting on a tiny marionette show, replete with a little stage and a cast of puppets. He did it for nothing, for no one.

He did it for us.

A friend of mine was once at his camp on a Thursday night, taking a break from the insanity of the city by sharing a drink with his campmates. Suddenly, a tiny alien approached the camp, clearly a kid or a little person in a costume. In his hand the alien held a small glowing crystal.

"Hello!" greeted my friend, trying to be cheerful. Complete silence from the alien. It pointed ominously at the crystal it held and then at the campers as if to say, "Take it." They laughed and said, "Oh, that's all right! We're good." Desperately gesturing, it insisted, pointing at the crystal and then at them. Out of politeness, they relented, "Sure. Thank you!" The alien, seemingly relieved, gave them the crystal and ran off into the night. "That was strange," they thought, and got back to their conversation. A full five minutes later, having nearly forgotten about the alien, a team of men wearing fully functional hazmat suits ran up to their camp screaming, *"The crystal! Hand over the crystal!"* They sprayed the camp down with some sort of old-school pump-action fumigator, trying to get that nasty alien radiation off my friends, reached out for the crystal with two-foot tongs, dropped it in a biohazard bag, and ran off. My friend and his campmates were left feeling just how that woman in the '80s felt when the clowns boarded her morning commute. Delighted, amused, and once again aware of wonder.

But tiny wonders are not all that await you in Black Rock City. You will see some of the wildest, most mind-blowing things imaginable. A full-size electric weeping willow with ten thousand digital leaves, handmade and glowing in fractalated LED neon like an offering from a cyber garden of Eden. A four-pronged, 180,000-pound steel dome with stone slabs hanging off its arms suspended by giant chains, a temple of gravity. An eighty-foot-tall mother made of found metal and rusted-out chains, trailed by her three-story child following along its mom's flaming footprints.

You'll see beauty.

That's what I saw.

At the edge of the city, out at its two o'clock and ten o'clock positions, are what became of the techno ghetto I had to drive a mile to get to back in 1996. It's now the massive "sound camps" of Black Rock City: thousands of revelers throbbing and dancing to absolutely gigantic sound systems and being zapped with laser installations so over-the-top they look like an alien invasion scanning the Earth's defenses. I'll look around and think, *Wow, this party is so insane,* so chock-full of the most beautiful people in the world going wild with revelry, it's exactly what I'd picture a hundred million dollar movie would set design for their big "rave sequence." Then, a hundred feet away, there will be another party just like it. And another. And another.

At night, as the city gets higher, beauty turns to bedlam. Everyone's inhibitions drop further down than any place I've ever been.

Years ago, I was at a party at a camp called Jub Jub, sitting on a couch between two beautiful women who were wearing almost nothing, when suddenly they started to make out, leaning over me and kissing passionately.

"Hmm," I thought, "lucky seat."

They began to rub and fondle each other, collapsing onto my lap. Right there, in front of hundreds of people, these girls began to sixty-nine right on top of me. I reached out to touch them, to join in the fun, when suddenly it occurred to me, "Wait, I don't think I'm supposed to participate in this." Until that second, I had been convinced, in my default position as a man, that I was somehow involved, that I had to get in there, that this was a performance for me, an invitation to join in. I realized suddenly that I'd totally misread. I was not being asked to fuck them. I was being asked to stay still as they fucked each other. I was flesh furniture. Respectfully I stayed there, enjoying the show until they were done, and then got up and went about my night. It was revelatory. Even when you're right in the middle of something, that doesn't mean it's about you. It's important to know that. It's also important to know that I never washed those pants again.

There was a lot of public sex back then. The early 2000s were the peak of raw fuck sessions right there in the thick of the city. I think perhaps it was the last vestige of lawlessness people felt they could engage in as the encroaching tsunami of rules flooded the community.*

Burning Man has had to accept changes to its core culture with increasing frequency since that death in 1996. Every time something new and insane happens, a new rule is instated, so the burn these days is a much more sanitary and safer affair than it was in 1996 or in 2001.

But I did love its wildness.

My crew and I had the distinction of the absolute worst art car in the history of Burning Man. Art cars are the only motorized trans-

---

* And not just public sex. There's sex everywhere. Burning Man sex is always complicated by hygiene. You really have to work at staying clean and sex can be dirty in the best of circumstances. Once, I was walking a woman back to my tent after a night of dancing. We were holding hands the entire mile-walk back because I am a very sweet lover, and just as we rounded the bend to my camp, I stopped in the porta-potty to use the bathroom before I got naked. It was dark in the porta and I didn't have a light and I couldn't see if there was pee on the toilet seat. I decided to grab some toilet paper and wipe any droplets from the toilet seat. It turned out to be a catastrophic mistake. I balled the paper up and made a quick swoop over the seat and credit-card-swiped my hand through a pile of ice-cold human shit. Earlier, someone must have had the same pee droplet dilemma as me and decided to hover rather than swipe. I was now in a panic. I had a shit mitten on my hand and a girl whom I'd been holding hands with for a half hour. I didn't know what to do. I wiped as much of it off my hand as I could, burst out of the porta-potty, and walked/jogged ten paces in front of my hot-burn lover like a very dirty sultan, all the way back to camp, where I doused my fingers in gallons of hand sanitizer and considered a DIY amputation. Then we retired to the tent and had sex while I held my hand outside the tent. You do what you can.

port allowed at the burn since driving was outlawed on the playa after the tragedy of 1996. An art car is a vehicle so substantially modified that it no longer looks like a car at all. It's a lot of investment. Space shuttles, pirate ships, golf carts transformed into unicorns, and a million other creative restructures of vehicles abound. They are called "Mutant Vehicles" and there is literally a DMV, Department of Mutant Vehicles, on-site, inspecting cars and making sure they are safe and sufficiently modified to be allowed to drive in the city. Some become legendary, like the crowd favorite "El Pulpo Mechanico," a two-story articulating metal octopus with eyes that dart around and a body that shimmers while shooting flames out of its head. There's also the Mayan Warrior and Robot Heart, roving dance clubs with a million dollars' worth of sound equipment and lasers welded to the bodies of school buses.

And then there was the Void.

One of my campmates, an East Bay punk-rock-legend-turned-vegan-doughnut impresario, had an old, ugly gray Chevy cargo van. The floorboards were rusted out from discarded doughnut sugar corrosion, the brakes barely worked, the ignition needed to be tripped from underneath the chassis, lying down on your back to kick it on. It was an eyesore. We decided to use it to make the ugliest art car ever created. My campmates lashed two-by-four framing around the sides of the van and to the roof rack, creating a kind of "picture frame" around the entire van on both sides. From there we dropped black shade cloth down over the two sides, effectively creating a ten foot cube of pitch black. The Void was a tremendous hazard, a giant square of black that when parked at night was basically invisible; people would walk or ride their bikes directly into the side. We strapped a sound system to the roof and would drive around the playa at night, blasting Hüsker Dü, Slayer, and Anal Cunt and bringing some much-needed (though not always appreciated) "bad-vibe clown energy" to the event. With a plugged-in mic we'd spot a pile of ravers, out of their faces on MDMA and acid, and pull up, the shade cloth blocking their entire view of the city in front of them. It would be like darkness itself had pulled up. From the PA one of us would ask, "You there, peaking on LSD. Have you ever wondered what happens to you . . . when you DIE?!" Then we'd pull off so they'd have some time to consider the question. How did we manage to get a license to drive such a death trap monstrosity, you ask? We worked at Burning Man, and members of my department, the Gate, kind of did whatever the fuck we wanted.

Since Burning Man loves to pay wages that would be scoffed out of a sweatshop for being unethically low, management often has to find perks to ensure that no one ever throws them into the flames at the Sunday night Temple burn.* Mostly these perks are cheap; aloe-soaked wet wipes to scrub off an inch of dust accumulated during a sandstorm or a patch that says, "I gave up the best years of my life to throw a dirt rave!" or something like that. But there is an occasional "true perk," like stealing off to the secret hot springs of the Black Rock Desert under the guise of "checking the area" for unticketed sneaks. You slip into the piping hot pool, look around, and say, yep, all looks secure here, might as well stay an hour or two to make sure. Or you might be offered a ride in a private plane taking off from the onsite Black Rock City Municipal Airport (perhaps no airport has created more members of the mile-high club than this one: planes are often chartered for this specific purpose; you need only ignore the masturbating polyamorous aviation enthusiast piloting the plane).

There is one ultimate perk, the rarest of the rare, the holy of holies when it comes to staff bonuses. The inner circle pass. It's a badge given to perhaps five percent of Burning Man employees each year. And it is quite a perk. It allows the holder entrance to a dangerously close inner circle of seating for the Saturday main event, the burning

---

* The Temple burn is a second "main event" that takes place Sunday night after much of the chaos is done. Every year an elaborate shrine is erected as a holding place for the loss the community of Black Rock City has experienced in the year past. The design varies from year to year—from the Temple of Honor, a Russian Orthodox–inspired cardboard pagoda; to the Basura Sagrada, a cathedral of recycled, burnable junk; to the Temple of Tears, an elaborate, intricate, interlocked wooden mausoleum. The temple is a receptacle of grief, and every inch is covered in handwritten messages to fallen comrades and loved ones or other losses experienced. On Sunday night, they burn it and, in total silence, the ashes and smoke evaporate the collective grief of Black Rock City.

of the Man. You're up so close that it's dangerous, scary, you can feel the heat of the ten-story fire singe your eyebrows. It's really fucking dramatic. Imagine sitting on the front yard as your childhood home, which was a fireworks factory, burns up. Over the years I worked at Burning Man I was offered this perk for a job well done a few times and I was always honored. I also got in three times through less labor-based methods.

I hustled.

The first hustle was straightforward and what I'd suggest as the easiest way in for the layman. You have to be a lay, man. I just had sex with a fire dancer who had an extra pass and, in thanks for a job well done, she tossed me one on her way out of the tent.

The other time I made it in was more illicit. I traded it for cocaine. Just a little FYI: I hate cocaine. It's always confused me why people are willing to set fire to their personalities for a drug whose effect seems little more than "hypercharged coffee with an add shot of ego engorgement." There is nothing so unpleasant as a person on coke choosing you as the receptacle for their new theory on human potential and monologuing at you for fifty hours. Actually, wait no, there is: It's the "newly on coke friend." The newly on coke friend is an old friend who newly discovers the wonders of cocaine. If you're a sober person like I am, you might not notice your friend is on coke at first. All you notice is that the person with whom you have plans is constantly gone. You turn around, wondering where your buddy went, and suddenly they are back and VERY talkative. When they talk, do they ask you questions about yourself? Oh no they do not! They talk about how cool they are and then, very suddenly, poof! They disappear again. "Brian!?" you ask to the air where Brian used to stand. Boom! Brian's back. But then, bang! Brian has to go to the bathroom or meet some friends or meet some friends in the bathroom or stop by a buddy's tent or run to the car. And then Brian wants to DANCE. Now. This kind of rat-trapped-in-the-maze friendship might go on a full weekend until you, the naïve sober dork, finally realize: Brian's not busy. He's just on coke now.

Back to the coke mission. A man named Clodhopper, whose job was to coordinate the porta-potty pumpers with the potties they had

to pump, had an extra pass and no desire to use it. He was willing
to trade. Barter economy, baby! "What would you like?" I asked,
excited. "A home-cooked meal? Perhaps some chai!?" "Cocaine."
He grunted, "I want coke." "Sure!" I smiled. "I can definitely get
that! Cocaine it is!" I had no clue how to find cocaine. Not exactly
my vibe. My current drug of choice is 7-Eleven-brand sour cherry
balls (the whole bag, one go. I don't fuck around.).

But I needed that pass.

I ended up wandering down the road, telling passersby, "I need
some coke," like a character from a 1990s movie about the scourge
of gang life. Finally, a friend told me she had some and broke me off
a little somethin' somethin'. Excited, I ran back to the commissary
to hand over my baggie and receive my plunder. I passed it to Clodhopper and quickly realized I knew very little about cocaine. The
look of sadness and disappointment on his face was so palpable that
I asked, "What's wrong? Is it PCP? Baby laxative? Dust scooped
straight off the playa?" He looked up at me. "Is this all there is?" I
stammered, "I, uh . . . Is that not a lot?" It apparently was not. I felt
pretty guilty that ol' Clodhopper wouldn't be staring down the barrel of a porta-potty, his heart pumping overtime as mounds of
booger sugar crumbled into the human waste stew below, but I just
sat there smiling, hoping a bump was enough.

Clodhopper grunted and tossed me the pass and that's how I
traded coke for an inner circle pass.

But the first time I got into the inner circle without earning it was
the best and, in a way, a very Burning Man story.

In the early years, the pass to get into the inner circle was just a
simple laminated photo of the Man, worn around the neck and
checked by the Black Rock Rangers.* One gate-mate, Low Rent the
Clown, and his partner in crime, Garagefuck,† saw the simplicity of

---

* The khaki-wearing pseudo security force within Black Rock City who protect
and serve with zero authority other than the power they can muster through calm
dialogue and a pair of sexy legs peeking out from a tan utilikilt. They provide a
kind of stopgap between the actual police and actual anarchy.

† You may be noticing at this point the oddness of the names of the characters
I'm describing. Clodhopper, Low Rent, Garagefuck, Exitwound Crybaby, Phlap-

the pass that represented the last line of defense between the hoi pol-
loi and the VIPs of Black Rock City's working class and were struck
with a very good/bad idea. They had a laser printer/scanner brought
in from the Walmart in Reno, scanned the pass, and began printing
out golden tickets. Staring at the counterfeit passes and comparing
them to the real thing, Garagefuck and Low Rent realized a fatal
flaw. The passes were laminated and looked like badges, and their
printouts were . . . pieces of paper. They hadn't been able to afford
a laminator but, not to be deterred, they spent the afternoon hand-
melting sheets of laminating plastic onto the passes with Bic lighters.
By the time the burn was close, Low Rent and Garagefuck passed
me and my friends our passports. We inspected them, bubbly,
burned, wrinkled, and sure to not work. Then we encountered the
security apparatus of Burning Man. I would say it was not exactly a
crack team, but the rangers around the outer ring of the Man were
fairly cracked out from a week straight of all-night partying and
designer drugs so, yeah, maybe they were. They barely glanced at
our passes and, giggling, the assembled clowns of the Gate crew slid
right into the inner circle. And slid. And slid. Low Rent had passed
out a very large number of passes and, once inside, people were taking an extra off the neck of a friend who was already safely inside
and slipping back out of the ring to go grab their buddy or a date or
even just a random sexy Burner they'd grab, and whisper, "Follow
me for a treat!" By the time the Man was about to burn, there were
probably fifty of us in there, a clown car right in the holy of holies.

Here's the problem with clowns: They are clowns. Even when
it's time to take off the red nose and do a little spycraft, the urge

---

jack, people at Burning Man often adopt a nom de drouges. These are called
"playa names" and serve to further wedge the separation between the default
world and the universe beyond reality that is Black Rock City. Mostly these
names are pretty cringe—a process server who calls himself "Sparkle Lemur" or
a Google exec who's found new life in the identity of "Molly Shark." My brother
had perhaps the worst one of all, "Tuna Bag," so granted due to his unfortunate
habit of carrying around sacks of tuna fish he'd scoop straight from the bag.
When I brought Natasha, she found the whole thing so eyeroll-inducing that she
gave herself the playa name "Amy." What a rebel!

to fuck around is too tantalizing to resist. As we sat there, waiting for the Man to burn, we noticed a distinct figure rise from his perch on the ground, stretching out and lighting a cigar. Even from the back, the cowboy hat he was famous for identified him. It was Larry Harvey, the man who started it all, he who burned the Man in the first place, a demigod among the assembled citizens of Black Rock City. Larry Harvey would inspire awed whispers in whatever cluster of Burners he walked by, each of them wishing he'd stop and say hi so that they could genuflect and kiss the ring, thanking him for creating this thing that changed them forever. "Swordfish!" they'd say, nearing hero-worship orgasm. "That's Swordfish!" Yes, even Larry Harvey had a playa name. As soon as he stood, the Man started to burn. He was right in front of us and we couldn't resist. "Sit down, buddy! You're right in our way!" Low Rent screamed. Larry cocked an annoyed look at us and ignored the entreaty entirely, turning back toward the burn. "Fucking old guys at music festivals, I swear to god!" someone screamed. "Hey, pal, just 'cause you bought the VIP package doesn't mean you have the right to ruin the view for the rest of us! Sit down!" Suddenly all fifty of us started chanting, "Swordfish! Down in front! Down in front!" Larry was fully irritated at this point, no clue what was happening. This was supposed to be a group of Burning Man's hardest workers, rewarded after a job well done. They would never act this way. They would display an obsequious respect in their every interaction with the founder. But somehow, here in the closest thing to box seats that Burning Man had, he was getting heckled by a group of misfits who'd crashed the party.

Was this super obnoxious? Without question yes. If I'd been Larry, I'd have been pissed. The burn was his thing. His world. His Frankenstein's monster. Every year he got to enjoy a cigar and look back at the thing he created, tiny and nearly meaningless when he thought of it and set fire to a statue of a man for the first time, now huge, massive, saturated with meaning, and monumentally important to so many. But in a way there is almost nothing more "Burning Man" than the founder of the entire event having his burn ruined by a group of uninvited shitheads.

This was classic Cacophony Society. This was culture jamming, brought right to the sphincter at the center of the event.

Larry Harvey didn't deserve more than this. He was being force-fed participation, just another citizen of Black Rock City.

It was perfect.

Those were the people I gravitated toward at Burning Man, the clowns who still had a bit of the Cacophony in them.

After years of attendance, I once again became covetous of the kind of social and meager financial capital that comes with dancing over the line between participant and professional. I clearly hadn't learned my lesson from the rave scene of the curdling effect this has on the thing you love.

Burning Man operates on a labor model that is one part capitalism and one part *Wizard of Oz*. Knowing that attendees rejigger much of their lives around their connection to the event and that people's emotional relationship to Burning Man runs closer to "pilgrimage to Mecca" than "some event I attend," Burning Man figured out an ingenious way to solve an ever-expanding logistical need for labor: Pay your employees in vibes instead of money. While some of the help at Burning Man do get paid, that's a tiny fraction of their workforce (who earn a tiny fraction of what they *should* be paid). Much of the labor force at Black Rock City do forty-hour weeks of manual labor for the love and a free ticket to attend. And not always even a free ticket! That's right, people love this shit so hard, some of them *pay to attend an event they will spend the entire time working.*

All the drivers of the Void seemed to be volunteering at the Gate, so I agreed to turn my annual vacation into a work vacation just to squeeze a little more insanity out of my trip. In Black Rock City, the hippies and good-vibe warriors were taking over and, while I love a vibey hippie, that's not me. I'm looking for chaos and a good story. I found that up at the Gate.

These people sucked nitrous oxide like the dentist in *Little Shop of Horrors* and then went to work for twelve hours straight. These people brought a shop vac with its filter removed and pretended to be hard at work "vacuuming" the playa to clean out their work-space while "accidentally" blowing a 10 psi stream of dust into the vehicle of whatever idiot decided to arrive in a brand-new Lexus. These were my people.

Working at the Gate is hard and boring work, filled with endless searches and acrobatic climbs into box trucks and moving vans stuffed to the gills. It's sucking down exhaust for six hours at a time. It's standing still in a dust storm, totally blind while you know ve-hicles are moving by you on every side. It's dealing with people at their grumpiest, after a ten-hour wait in traffic. Back home I was getting successful at comedy (more on that scene later) and my agents and peers had a hard time understanding why for a month each year I went off the grid to go be a psychedelic mall cop outside of Reno.

Because I loved it.

I loved something about the in-between space of the Gate, the spot where cars are searched for stowaways and tickets checked and ripped, something about the fact that that space is neither toxic like the real world nor magic like the Burning Man world, something about its inherent "neither-here-nor-thereness" creates the strangest energy and decision making. Or maybe it's just the combo of lots of driving and lots of drugs.

The Gate became a family to me, a gang, a tribe. Burning Man was the last holdout of the raver in me and it had become, in some ways, even more important to me than raves ever were. Here in Black Rock City was a community I did not need to outgrow, I did not need to have my ego validated in order to feel like I belonged. And in an even more concentrated way, the Gate became the center of that belonging. Working at what is more or less a grunt job at Burning Man gave me a tiny feeling of ownership of the entire expe-rience. I was a small part of what made this massive, brain-boiling carnival possible. It was summer camp, but more than that, it was my temporary home. When I stepped across the line into the Tem-porary Autonomous Zone, that's where I landed.

I worked the Gate for fifteen years.

I started with searching cars and slowly moved my way up the department until my job was to mitigate all the strange things those searches turned up.

Then, in 2011, the event started selling out before it began, and ticket scarcity became an issue.

Things got even stranger.

Prior to the sellout years, tickets could be purchased on-site at the box office, and that fact made the energy at the Gate much more playful and fun. If we found a stowaway in a car, for example, stuffing our hands under couches in an RV only to feel the stubbly arm of a partially asphyxiated hippie who'd been riding inside of a fold-up couch for hours, we could assess what his penance should be. If he was cool and friendly and adopted a "You got me, I'm a moron" approach, we might just sell him a ticket and send him in, admonishing him to tell his friends in the didgeridoo community that we'd caught him and if they ever tried anything like that, we'd catch them, too.

But if he was a dick? If he was cocky or obnoxious in any way? We'd assess an "asshole tax" where the price of a ticket became directly commensurate with how much of a prick the person was. Some tickets sold for thousands.

Like with raves before it, my life at Burning Man became all about work. I'd go up to the playa for a month at a time and work every day. It was the only hard labor I'd do all year, and my soft burgeoning-comedian hands loved feeling useful. And, as labor went, it was pretty fucking fun. It all felt like a game, like theater.

If we caught someone trying to sneak in and they stormed off saying "Forget it! I'm not going to Burning Man!" and headed back to Reno, it was usually a bluff and as soon as they were out of our sight, they'd double back and try to sneak in again. If we ever saw that person in Black Rock City after we'd clocked off, we'd smile at them and wave hello. They'd won the game.

There were many ways to sneak into Burning Man and many ways to get caught. Stuffing yourself into a crevice in an RV was pretty rudimentary. People have gone to much greater lengths. Famously a contortionist was rumored to sneak in every year by stuffing himself in a tiny box, too small to bother checking, that sat on the passenger seat of his friend's car. We caught people in desert khakis painted with playa dust, military crawling toward the entrance. People fully rolled into oriental rugs. We once stopped a vehicle that had been reported as carrying stowaways from the side of the road near Reno. We searched for hours as the extremely polite driver of the truck swore he would never do anything like that. Four hours into our search someone found a switch and flipped it and a door swung open revealing a fully hidden inner chamber that seemed, if you'd looked at it a thousand times, like it was a part of the body of the truck itself. Inside were a bunch of scared, broke Burners. The driver smiled and just said, "Sorry." He was cool as a cucumber, and we asked him why he wasn't nervous to be caught. "This is nothing!" he explained, "I'm a coyote at the U.S. border. Usually if I get caught it's a federal offense! I just had some downtime and thought I'd make some money on these freaks!"

Once, a guy pulled up in an armored car, elaborately built and remarkably official-looking, claiming to be a U.S. marshal with a warrant to deliver. Security cameras were affixed to multiple points of contact in the vehicle. When we asked him to open up the locked security door to the back of his vehicle, he started talking about chain of custody and federal law inhibiting his ability to allow access to the sensitive documents back there. All of the senior leadership in my department believed him, but I insisted. "You can't just say the words *chain of custody* and get into Burning Man without a ticket." He started yelling at me, making threats of indictment from the attorney general. I sent him on his way. A half hour later I was running an errand that took me up to the highway. I drove up to see the guy, pulled over in an embankment, the "security door" wide open and what looked to be a Cirque du Soleil fire dancer emerging from the back. Peering in I could see a bedroll and pots and pans hanging from above a camp stove. I smiled and waved from the truck, yelling, "Chain of custody!" The marshal smiled back. Busted. Clearly he had a van and some meth, a TIG welder and a plan.

The Gate was the closest you could get to Burning Man without needing a ticket, so it became a magnet for the odd, desperate demographic of people who could not get a ticket but were not willing to let that stop them from attempting to attend. This is a very specific demographic; the mere idea of a festival occurring without you is enough to get you to pack up a car and drive six hours in the hope of procuring a miracle. This is God-level FOMO. I understood this on a molecular level, having felt precisely the same way about raves. With raves, I was going to get in, no matter how broke I was, no matter what I had to do. I put myself in the epicenter of this exact mentality at Burning Man.

Every year at about midweek, a critical mass of deadheads, ravers, druggies, and just general off-grid wizard types would congregate in the parking lot hoping for a ticket. It became our job to herd them. Left alone they would attempt to sneak in, wandering between cars, attempting to jump on the back of a vehicle that had already been searched or some such mischief.

One year, we encountered a huge ball of hundreds of plush Winnie-the-Pooh dolls that had been de-stuffed and sewn together to create a giant Pooh sphere about the size of a yoga ball. These kinds of objects are not unusual finds at Burning Man. We walked it in, past all the gathered unticketed folk, who started to follow it like the Pied Piper. They were drawn to the Pooh. Setting the sphere down in a lot where we could keep our eyes on them, we surrounded the delighted hippies with a plastic chicken-wire fence and created a kind of playpen/internment cage. After a few hours of their delightedly tossing the ball back and forth, I approached the pen and informed the kids there that they'd have to leave eventually. They'd need tickets to attend. One of them confidently produced a vehicle pass, essentially a parking permit for the event. "Here's my ticket!" He smiled. I tried to be kind and explain that what he was holding was not a ticket but a vehicle pass, and since he clearly did not have a vehicle, it wouldn't help him much even if he had a ticket. I walked away after giving them a warning to clear out. An hour later I went to check on my pen kids and they were gone. I was satisfied I'd done my duty. Then someone started screaming for me from the lanes. In traffic, in line with the cars, were about twenty of the Pooh kids, holding one another's shoulders like a conga line. The guy in front was the kid who'd shown me his vehicle pass which was now stuck on his sunglasses. I approached them and asked what the fuck was happening. They all looked at me like I was stupid and chanted, as one, "*Spiritual vehicle!*" and pulled up as the car in front of them was granted entry to the city. This was all too much for me to deal with, and I laughed for about an hour before I finally explained that while I loved their engineering spirit, they still needed tickets for entry.

People were desperate to get in. And that desperation only got worse when the event started selling out. Once that happened there was nothing we could do to help. Well, almost nothing. I remember a car full of hippie kids in a Buick arriving fresh from a twenty-hour drive from Oklahoma. They explained that they didn't have tickets but that they really wanted to come in. They'd driven halfway across the country to a sold-out event just hoping things would work out. We explained that it was impossible. There were no tickets for sale. There was nothing we could do to get them in, even if they did have money. They would have to turn around and head home. Understandably they were reluctant to go back to Oklahoma. They were so close. They pleaded with us. Wasn't there anything we could do?! "Nothing. There is absolutely nothing we can do for you."

There was a pause I knew well. It's the pause where someone is out of options but the reality at which they have arrived is unacceptable. I'd seen this pause countless times over the years; it happened constantly right here, mere yards away from entry into a dream. It was always hard to watch. It always ended the same way. With a deep exhale and a U-turn back to the highway. Not that day, though. I guess they make their hippies a little different down in Oklahoma.

Someone repeated, "There is nothing we can do for you. You'll have to go now."

The driver of the Buick leaned in. "We will give you our car."

"I'm sorry, what?" I asked, not sure I'd heard him.

"The car," he repeated, with more conviction now. "I got the pink slip here. It's yours if you let us in."

Within ten minutes they had signed the Buick over to us and were walking into Burning Man holding their luggage as we celebrated the acquisition of a new vehicle to drive around with. Oh, it would have to be modified to be approved to drive, wouldn't it? Minutes later our department's new Buick was flipped over, fully upside down with a javelin poking through its windshield. It was the quintessential "This is why we can't have nice things" moment. Eventually we flipped the car right side up again and it became like a mascot, a clown car for the last clowns left at Burning Man.

Not everyone was so desperate. Once I checked in a school bus that had driven all the way from North Carolina, a thirty-five-hour drive. When I climbed on the bus I saw that the driver had, at the back of the bus, an entire living pine tree. Due to the strict "Leave no trace" rules of Burning Man, plants were not allowed inside for fear their detritus would dry up, fall off, and be blown into the ecosystem. I gave him the bad news. He was ashen. He told me he'd driven the tree all the way from North Carolina. An unspoken "WHY?" floated in the air. I suggested he go back to Reno and get the tree a hotel room for the week. He looked at me like I was crazy. "I can't leave her alone like that!"

"Okay," I said. "Well, I can't let *her* in. So you'll have to turn around and leave."

He started up the bus, looked at me, and said, "Fine."

As he made a U-turn and headed out, with his ticket in his hand, I said, "You might want to look into your relationship with that tree."

He frowned at me. "You know, that's really none of your business." And he was right, it really wasn't.

The longer the event went on selling out instantly, the less fun my work up there became. Over and over again it just became telling heartbroken people who'd been ripped off buying fake tickets from a scammer that they had to go home. More and more it became yelling at angry rich people to get back in their Teslas. One day I stopped a sixty-year-old deadhead running into the event during a dust storm, and we sat there as he begged me to let him in without a ticket.

As we sat and the guy looked at me, ashamed and near tears, I realized that I could give a shit about whether this guy had a ticket or not. Hell, I wanted him to sneak in. When it was a game, it was fun, but now that there were no tickets for anyone, and in particular for anyone poor, it wasn't fun to stop people. I felt like a counterculture TSA agent.

I quit.

It wasn't just the work that felt unfulfilling, Burning Man had become entirely work for me and thus the entire event was becoming unfulfilling to me. The workforce at Burning Man is loyal, nearly religious in its devotion to the ideal it is trying to create. The problem is that the people who run the place seem to care a lot more about the seventy thousand attendees of the event and the money they bring in than the two thousand or so barely paid or unpaid workers who make the event possible. It makes sense in a way; every worker is replaceable, and the event itself is one of a kind. But it's sad. Sad to watch as this cycle repeats itself over and over again: Person attends Burning Man. Person finds community, vitality, inspiration, identity at Burning Man. Person falls in love with Burning Man. Person wants to become a part of Burning Man. More than an attendee, Person wants to become a part of the apparatus itself. Person gets a job at Burning Man. Person works at Burning Man, giving their life to it for little more than the love of the game. Fifteen years go by. Fifteen of the prime years of Person's working years dedicated to this thing that happens only for a month a year. Life events are put on hold. Default world career advancements are stymied. When it comes to Burning Man employees, don't think hippie, think carny. The season stretches from June to October. There for setup. There for event week. There for teardown. There until the bitter end. Drugs fuel the whole experience. Then suddenly, Person is forty. All that Person has done is burn. Person hurt their back, wants more money, expresses dissatisfaction with working conditions with being asked to work eighty-hour weeks for less than minimum wage, anything really, and Person is let go. Fired. Or, more accurately according to labor laws, Person is not invited back to participate in temporary, at-will employment. Person's world is over. And the people who fired Person never even learned Person's name. Person loses community, vitality, inspiration, identity. Person can't turn back to the other fulfilling parts of their life because they don't have any of those. Sadly, much too often, Person takes their own life. This is not hyperbole. In the years I worked at Burning Man and since, I lost count of how many people I used to see around who are now gone, dead from overdose or deliberate suicide. It's a grim tally.

Luckily for me I had comedy and was never willing to permanently cede my identity to a temporary community. I wasn't looking at existential angst when I quit working there. But I was looking at something that had once brought me more satisfaction and inspiration than anything else and was now starting to feel just not worth the trouble. I didn't get much out of it anymore, but I also didn't want to stop going. Why? Maybe I'd just formed a habit.

So I did something I hadn't done before, at least not successfully. I attempted to change my spiritual state. I downgraded myself from professional back to participant. I stripped myself of privilege and power and slipped back into the masses. To get back to the heart of the thing. No mastery. No authority. Just the thing itself. Let's be honest, when I worked at Burning Man I got paid to be there, and something about that and the two decades of attendance made the event feel repetitious and almost boring. Burning Man should not be boring! You should never be staring at a conclave of five hundred fire dancers as an acrobat falls forty feet on a set of silks, catching himself at the last second before hitting the ground, and find yourself yawning, "Fire silks again, eh?"

Burning Man had become rote to me, sure, but it also had fused to the rhythm of my life. It became like New Year's Eve, a chance to assess where I'd been in the year past and where I wanted to get to in the year to come. Burning Man being on Labor Day means it's right next to the Jewish High Holidays on the calendar, those holidays called the Days of Awe, where you take stock of yourself, where you've been, and where you want to be. So I roped Burning Man into that introspection. Burning Man, Rosh Hashanah, Yom Kippur. I made the High Holidays a little higher. Anyway, what's more Jewish than dancing around an idol in the desert?

Also, I literally don't have anything better to do. What am I going to do instead? Hang out with my family more?! BO-RING! It still feels like I have lessons to learn from it. I still want to go back.

And so, after the year we all took off, I headed back in 2021, even though there was no official event happening. I went back to what they called the renegade burn. No cops, no rules, just the people and the desert. Cars zipped past me at sixty miles per hour. It felt like 1996 again. Only, now I had a daughter and a wife waiting at home. I begged my younger friends with more expendable lives to park in front of my camper. Please die so I can live.

The whole affair was rather benign. It was sweet. Bittersweet maybe. It was like partying in an echo. Out there I realized once again what I love about Burning Man: people ripping themselves from their lives to do something different. It didn't feel as vital, as urgent as it used to, but it didn't have to. Because it was still a shift from real life. It was still past the line that was drawn in the dirt decades ago. Burning Man still has that ability, sometimes, to make your jaw drop, to make you feel like "What did I just see?" The trip is worth it just for that. I don't ever want to lose that. And someday, if it still exists, I think I'll take my kid to see it, too. Maybe she'll find something there that makes her feel alive like I did. Or maybe she'll just stare at the pretty lights. That can be enough, too. I'm not a sixteen-year-old raver anymore, but I still like to stare at them. Stare at them and remember who I was, what drew me here and what keeps dragging me back.

Shit, I realize I forgot to describe the main event: the burn. Everything is centered around that. The Man, glowing in neon, standing watch as the twelve on the clock, is the focal point of the entire thing. He's the north star and the navigation point. Literally and energetically.* The closer Saturday gets, the taller he stands. We

---

* In 2007 a man named Paul Addis couldn't wait for him to burn and set the Man on fire four days early during a lunar eclipse. We all shook our heads in horror and jealousy that we hadn't done it first. In 2017, a man named Aaron Mitchell couldn't wait for him to fall and ran into the flames to his death. That was just pure horror.

know he's a dead man walking and what a pleasure it will be to see him burn. Finally, as the pressure hits its apex, his body explodes for the body impolitic of Black Rock City. On Saturday night every participant in the city gathers around the Man to watch him immolate.

The burn itself is wild and savage. His arms, which have been at his sides all week long, are raised into a dual salute to the city that has formed around him. Fire dancers spin flames at his feet, a thousand of them. Then, suddenly, from inside his body, a bright orange flame. It builds and licks his body, growing, fireworks shooting from every part of him. A display more dizzying and pyrotechnically overwhelming than you'll ever see on the Fourth of July. Then massive gas bombs explode again and again, engulfing his body in black-and-orange fire as everyone, all seventy thousand of us, scream in a frenzy.

Then, quiet.

The show is over and now it's time to watch our north star disappear. A hush takes the crowd as we wait for him to fall, that man on fire.

Guy Lombardo sang, "Enjoy yourself, it's later than you think."

We are impermanent. We die. We immolate. All of us is a person about to catch fire. Before the flames come, we try to live a comfortable life. But with that comfort, it's easy to miss doing much of anything. Life promises nothing but death. While we are here, I want to live a life that's filled with oddness and wonder. I want to see things that make me feel excited and scared. I want to meet people that do things differently. I want to stare at the lights.

I want to participate.

The Jews, or a Drop in the River

I was twenty when my father died. I'll get into the parts that will make you cry later, but I'd like to tell you a little about the Kaddish first.

After he died, every day, three times a day, ten men would gather at the house my father used to live in and say a prayer for his soul. The idea is that for the first week, the days of shiva, the soul is hovering, floating in the in-between space, neither in a body nor ascending to the heavens. The fact that we don't quite believe in "the heavens" is not to be discussed.

I was grief drunk at the time, barely conscious. Three times a day, I'd stumble up and say "Amen" as a group of Hasidim muttered the prayer for the dead. I remember looking around at them, laughing to myself, wishing I could offer a live feed to my friends back home. They just wouldn't have been able to believe it. Surrounding me were men from the old country, wizard-like, with long flowing beards that reached down to their bellies. When I was younger, I spent the summers with my father in New York, and I'd sit in synagogue and watch these men, their deft fingers rolling their beards up into little curls that they'd tuck into the body of the beard like a pig in a blanket. Their socks were ribbed and high, pulled up to their knees with pant legs tucked in like jodhpurs. Their shoes were ancient, massive black leather clogs that just screamed, "I've only ever had sex with my wife!" They were cloaked in gowns that reached to their ankles, some with designs embossed on them, little bouquets of flowers or golden stripes. They looked like creatures from another world, another time. And in many ways they were.

The unfortunate side effect of being in New York only in the summer was that all the fun Jewish holidays were already done by the time I'd arrive. No Hanukkah, no presents, no Passover, no seders, no apples and honey, just Tisha B'Av. Tisha B'Av is a commemoration of the destruction of the Great Temple in Jerusalem. This happened twice, by the way, once in 586 B.C.E. by the Babylonian king Nebuchadnezzar, after which the Jews rebuilt it only to see it toppled on the same date five hundred years later by the Romans. Tisha B'Av commemorates the destruction of both on the same day. A grief twofer.

It's a mitzvah on Tisha B'Av to weep in honor of the temples so I'd sit next to these old men as they scrunched their faces and forced tears to fall like the final exam at a Stella Adler acting workshop. I had no idea what the First Temple or the Second Temple were or why I should care that they'd been toppled a thousand years ago. But I wanted to fit in with these guys, so I'd think of sad movies I'd seen or times when kids made fun of me for being white in class back home in Oakland and I'd grimace and moan, shucking back and forth wailing, "I miss those two buildings so much, fellas!"

Try as I might, I never quite managed to drop a tear.

But after my father died, I was finding my tears flowed quite easily. I wanted so badly for my friends to see this image of me, standing with these time travelers. It felt like it would do all the work of explaining who I was, where I'd come from, why I was the way I was. Just the image of me, nose pierced, in raver gear, standing next to a man who looked like he'd climbed out of a Chaim Potok novel; it would contextualize me. This is my family! This is my father's community! This is where I spend my summer vacations. This, in some strange way that was not clear even to me, is a part of who I am. I'm one of these guys, even though they'd never, ever accept me. We are bound together. But who are these guys? Literally and figuratively. I didn't know most of these men, but also, who are the Hasidim? Who are the Jews? How did they come to look like this, act like this, how did they come to be in my living room? Let me try to explain. But in so doing, I'm going to have to go back. I will now recount the six-thousand-year history of the Jews in about six pages while trying to make it fun!

In ancient Ur, way back when countries could have super-short names and people would still know where you were talking about, lived a man named Abram. Abram was the first guy to tell his local community the whole "I just heard God speak to me" thing. People listened.

"Few things! First, there's only one God!"

"Interesting! New concept! We like it!" the people called back.

"Also, my name is not Abram anymore! God gave me a new name! A powerful God name!"

"What is it?!" screamed the people. "Tell us the God name!"

"He added an H-A! I am now Abra . . . Ham!"

"Oh yeah. That's very different sounding. Our God is an awesome God!"

Abraham continued his stump speech. "There are two things he told us to do! First! We must move to Tel Aviv!"

"Cool!" the people cheered.

"And second! All the men have to cut their foreskins off!"

"Much less cool!" half of the people screamed.

Dicks cut, they jaunted off to ancient Canaan aka Israel aka Palestine aka the world's most chill landmass, where God told Abraham, in thanks for the foreskins, "I just got your eighty-nine-year-old wife pregnant!" Abraham, assuming God was cracking one of those classic "God jokes," gave a little chuckle and looked over at his wife, Sarah, who was heavy with child.

"Yikes," said Abraham, glancing guiltily at his housekeeper, Hagar, whom Abraham had also gotten pregnant, Schwarzenegger-style.

By way of apology, Abraham made an offer: "Look, Hagar, I'll tell you what. To make it up to you, why don't I . . . banish you to the desert?"

With that, Hagar stole off to create all the Arab peoples and

Abraham comforted himself at having nipped the whole "Jews and Arabs" thing in the bud. He had a new family to focus on. He named his new son Isaac, which means "Good one, God!"

Abraham was grateful to God for the blessing of his new son, and God was like, "No worries at all dude. Now kill him."

"K," Abraham nodded, and grabbed a knife and his son. He was ready, like a capo in the Genovese crime family, to whack anyone the God/Father commanded, no questions asked. Abraham raised the knife over Isaac and then God stopped him: "Damn, dude, I was just kidding! Kill a ram instead. Psycho."

Abraham nodded, laughed nervously, and killed a ram.

Thus began the Jewish people. Things went on that way for a while. Animal sacrifice was the religion. Canaan was the region. Isaac was the new patriarch. He had a son, Jacob, who had a bunch of sons, one of whom, Joseph, was gay* (rainbow coat, very dramatic). Being jealous of his fashion sense, his straight brothers sold him into slavery in Egypt.

As luck would have it, the Pharaoh had a position open for a vizier who could interpret dreams, and Joseph got the job and rose to prominence. When famine hit Canaan, Joseph welcomed the Hebrews to his new home, much like when a modern gay person invites his Evangelical family who lost it all in multilevel-marketing schemes to leave Tallahassee and move into his guesthouse in West Hollywood. Upon arrival they're like, "Dang. It's nice here. You might have been the smartest member of the family. Sorry about the whole condemning you thing!"

Years passed. Joseph died. At his funeral, the ancient Egyptian equivalent of Elton John performed a proto "Candle in the Wind" homage on the lyre. Pharaoh looked down at Joseph's rhinestone-covered sarcophagus and through tears cried, "This was a good Jew." Then *he* died.

---

* This observation was given to me by a gay Jew, the comedic genius Guy Branum, and I stole it for this book. He gave me official permission to do so, as all Jews communally share intellectual property so as to further our eventual goal of controlling the entire thought-world.

With a new Pharaoh installed, as was to become a repeating motif in the history of the Jews, the nation that had welcomed them became resentful toward them and started making them wear funny hats that said "Jew."

They were taken into slavery in an episode so shameful to the Egyptians that they erased any record of the story being true from their historical records.

The man who led them from slavery was the Charlton Heston of the ancient Hebrews, the most awesomely named . . . Moshe!*

After accidentally inventing the cracker, Moshe led the Jews across the desert from Egypt back to Canaan where, on the way, he climbed up a mountain and received two tablets which were really a scroll which was really five books which was, of course, the Bible. Moses yelled to the people, "If you thought that whole foreskin thing was bad, get a load of this: We can't eat pork anymore!"

"No!" said the people. "We love Egyptian bacon! Is that the only thing we can't do?"

Moses chuckled to himself. "No, my friends, it is not. There are so, so many things we can't do! You're gonna love it!"

They marched to Canaan and reestablished a kingdom that eventually became Israel and a national homage to ritual slaughter. Cows, birds, and grain were constantly destroyed to feed the hungry God.

If you've seen *Apocalypse Now*, you know how beautiful the religious ritual of hacking the head off a cow can be, especially when scored to the Doors, but all good things come to an end, and they ended as all things did back then: at the heel of a Roman centurion's boot. The Jews proved stiff-necked and annoying, and Rome lost legions of soldiers trying to occupy the various delicatessens of ancient Israel. But Rome, not to be deterred, kept hacking away and

---

* Also known as Moses, but actually not known as Moses at all. All of the biblical names we know are the Greek translations of the actual names in the Bible. No one ever called Moses "Moses," nor Jesus "Jesus." Moses was Moshe and Jesus was Yeshua. And as hard as this is to believe, King Solomon, the wisest and coolest-sounding king in the Bible, was . . . King Shlomo. *King Shlomo*. Sounds like the zany founder of a smoked salmon empire.

took Jerusalem in 70 C.E. They kicked the Jews out of Israel for good and said, "Don't even think about coming back until 1948." Thus began the diaspora.

Jews started moving everywhere that sold pastrami and ingratiating themselves quite unsuccessfully into the societies of Europe and the Middle East.

Here are the some of the various troubles the Jews encountered on their wanderings:

Accused of killing God (who they thought was just a local guy named Jesus).

Accused of starting the Black Plague. (Pranks go wrong sometimes.)

Accused of Gentile baby blood-drinking. (Could explain their tolerance to the taste of gefilte fish.)

Accused of dual loyalty. (Who wouldn't be loyal to people who accuse you of eating babies?)

Expelled from England. (Incidentally created the blueprint for Brexit.)

Expelled from Spain. (Too much ham anyway.)

Expelled from France. (And you thought the French were rude *now*.)

Pogroms, crusades, expulsion, pogroms, crusades, expulsion, pogroms . . .

Massacre after massacre befell the Jewish people. Disaster and distrust everywhere we went. And then, finally, a light among the nations illuminated itself. A placid island in a sea of European agitation. A place where the Jews could settle and be safe for good. The olly olly oxen free of eastern Europe. Our safe space. Beautiful, sunny . . . Poland.

For a time, Poland was, in fact, a place that welcomed Jews and promised they would be safe there. In the eleventh century, the king of Poland, King Casimir, inventor of the overpriced sweater, opened the gates of Poland to all Jews. Some say he did it because he had a Jewish mistress, and one must never underestimate the power of that sweet Jew tuchus. Some say he did it because he saw an economic opportunity to exploit Jewish wealth.

Regardless of the reason, the Jews came.

By 1939, there were three million Jews living in Poland. In the city of Lublin lived 250,000 Jews, a concentration so heavy that the city was nicknamed "Little Jerusalem."

In 1999, my aunt Breindie Kasher, a Holocaust historian and filmmaker, made a documentary called *The Last Jew in Lublin.* They were down to one. One Jew born in Lublin. His job was to tend the Jewish cemetery, the only one left to say the mourner's prayer for the Jews of Little Jerusalem. When he died, who said it for him? Who mourned him? There was no one left.

After World War II, after the Allies liberated Poland, some Jews rejoiced and returned to their villages. To their homes. But they returned to find their homes occupied. New families sitting on their furniture. Using their things. Creating new memories.

Thousands of the returning Jews were murdered.

After they'd survived the war, the Holocaust, massacre after massacre, after they'd finally made it to liberation, to freedom, to a place beyond fear, they were killed by regular people for their homes.

Can you imagine?

Returning home after surviving one of history's greatest evils, fighting your way through death camps staffed by your countrymen, your neighbors. Marching the long march. Seeing your loved ones die all around you.

But you don't give up! You don't give up hope! You are freed. The war is over. You make your way home. Only to be killed on your front porch. Killed looking in your front door. Looking at your life. Your memories. Your challenges and triumphs. The place your children took their first steps.

Your dead children.

Smokestack smoke.

Teeth in the dirt at Auschwitz.

You survived to die. Right on your front porch.

Today, fewer than ten thousand Jews live in Poland. Fewer than ten thousand left from three million. That was the haven for Jews. That was the safe place. Gone.

Now, I'm not saying Poland was complicit in the Holocaust, because a 2017 law passed by Polish parliament made saying that a crime. What I am saying is that even what seemed like a place of refuge became the seat of our destruction. After the war, the entire Jewish people had multigenerational PTSD. It was with this trauma that the remaining Jews attempted to find another place to wander to. We wandered to America, to England again, who'd allowed us back in 1605. We wandered to France and, of course, we wandered back to Israel where, despite our best attempts at cognitive dissonance, people were living who didn't appreciate our return. War ensued and in 1947, the State of Israel declared its independence.

And everyone there lived happily ever after.

The end. (I told you it would be fun!)

Okay, that wasn't the end.

Let's go back again. I forgot about the rabbis.

When the Jews were exiled from Jerusalem and their holy temple burned down (Tisha B'Av, baby!), they faced a conundrum:

How does a religion centered around ritual slaughter at a specific temple continue to function when the temple is ash, and they are barred from the city where its cindered foundations lie?

Enter the age of the rabbis.

The ancient lay leadership ascended into the true champions of the religion and took over control from the priestly class. The priests were the ox killers, the divinely ordained ruling class that, once their slaughter ground ceased to exist, had little to do or say. "We always just killed a bird in times of trouble," they'd say. "Not really sure what to do now." The priests were finding livestock difficult to wander around exile with.

So the thinkers took over. The rabbis, who had no authority other than popular support and an understanding of the Torah, filled the power vacuum left in the wake of the sack of Jerusalem and became like parliament to the priestly monarchy. The priests could have their gowns and breastplates and their bloodline. The rabbis would rule the religion.

But how? What even *was* the religion of Judaism now that there was no central religious ritual? The foundations of the religion were outlawed and, thus, there was no Judaism. The rabbis would have to create a brand-new religion from the ashes of the old one. They would have to construct a temple of the mind, one centered around what was available. The Five Books of Moses. The Torah. They'd read it and study it until they knew exactly what God meant in those books.

Of course, like every important document, the meaning is up to interpretation. So they wrote more documents. The Talmud, the main object of study in Jewish intellectual tradition, is a transcription of the struggle to figure out just what is meant in the Bible or what doesn't even appear in the Bible but really ought to be in there! They wrote books to figure out what books meant! These people loved books!

The Talmud is an unfathomably complex document. Sixty-three books make up 517 chapters that total 5,894 pages. Each page is a map of intellectual mazes about which I'm reluctant to even describe the format of, lest you lose interest, stop reading, and go watch unrelated YouTube videos.*

But here I go.

MISHNAH: This segment is the collected oral law, a compendium of the various discussions and expansions of the text in the Old Testament. It was eventually written down when people realized the Jews weren't so good at oral.

GEMARA: This is where it starts to get weird. The Gemara is the discussion *about* the Mishnah, which is itself a discussion *about* the Bible. It's a metatext, kind of like when R. Kelly did commentary on "Trapped in the Closet" by sitting in a director's chair on the right

---

* If you're considering that, fuck you, don't! I once read an article in *The Atlantic* that was all about how the internet has fried our attention spans and made us intellectually incapable of staying focused on long reads. This article was, of course, very long. That's a neat trick. Baked into the thesis of the article was the proposition that if you *didn't finish* reading, it was because the internet had made you too stupid to do so. So I propose that same idea. Should you lose interest in any section of this book, in particular the above description of Talmudic structure, it is because you are dumb and also an anti-Semite.

side of the frame and turning to the camera every so often to explain his filmmaking choices and why "Twan opened the door and it's Rose the nosy neighbor . . . Ooh, with a spatula in her hand, like that's gonna do something against them guns!" was the most exciting and compelling lyric in a particular segment of a song. "I just thought it would be funny if she brought a spatula," he said. By the way, years later, the comedian Paul F. Tompkins did a live show at Upright Citizens Brigade Theatre, setting up a director's chair onstage, just to the right of a projector screen showing R. Kelly's director's commentary. Every time R. Kelly would turn and say something like, "She brought a spatula!" Paul would turn to the audience and explain, "He's saying she brought a spatula. Rose brought a spatula." This is essentially what Gemara is.

RASHI: The rest of these segments are commentary on the commentary on the commentary. This long one is dedicated to the analysis of the giant of Torah commentary, the Shakespeare of biblical analysis, the **Rabbi Shlomo Yitzchaki** (known mostly by the acronym of his name, Rashi). Rashi is the gold standard when it comes to Talmudic thought and really the ultimate authority. Rashi is a legend in Jewish studies circles, a kind of brainiac superhero, his life is steeped in legend. He even has a cool origin story.

One night in France, Rashi's father was at a wild medieval Jewish rave. Wine was flowing, people were getting trashed, tossing their yarmulkes into wine goblets in an ancient form of beer pong. Shit was going off. Everybody at the party was drunk except Rashi's dad. He was stone sober and disgusted by the drunkards. He slipped into the library to study a little Torah, and in that moment, for some cosmic reason, he was the only person on Earth doing it. There is a folk belief that studying the Torah is so important that it is literally the force that keeps the world from ending. Should there ever be a moment when everyone stopped studying, the world would crash into end times. So there he was, a lone French rabbi, saving the world without even knowing it. For that deed, it is said, he merited a son like Rashi. Cool story, right? Until you think about what an absolute fucking nerd he must have been to be at a rager and be like, you know what, forget this, I'm going to . . . the library?

But my favorite Rashi story is about his mother. One night, while pregnant with Rashi, she got trapped between a fast-approaching carriage and the walls of the synagogue of Worms, Germany (known as the "Worms Synagogue," which, out of context, does sound vaguely anti-Semitic and, if you picture it correctly, vaguely adorable). The carriage was barreling right for Rashi's mama and as she turned to the wall of the synagogue, the bricks indented themselves, making a space just big enough for a fetal rabbinical genius to fit. The carriage rode past, unborn Rashi and his mother were unharmed, and you can see an indentation in the walls of the Worms Synagogue to this day.

TOSAFOT: Tosafot, or "additions," is a collection of the medieval commentators that weren't Rashi. It's a roundup of all the lesser commentators, like when you get an album of reggae hits with no Bob Marley. During the time of the tosafists, France outlawed the text of the Talmud. The idea was that if the book was illegal, the study would cease and, I guess, every Jew in France would start eating croque monsieurs. It didn't work. In a heroic act of intellectual resistance, the tosafists were assigned a segment of the Talmud to memorize, to commit so deeply to memory that they could teach every word of their segment without looking at the page. So they took a commentary that started as an oral tradition, was then codified into a text, re-deconstructed it, and brought it back to its oral roots. All to preserve the ability to study.

In the end the French ban didn't take, so we have the text. Tosafot consists mainly of intellectual problems posed by the Jewish law and a record of rabbis finding the solution. How did they figure out the solution? They did it the Jewish way. They argued.

The Talmud is essentially a super-document of the most long-winded argument in history. Each tractate in the Talmud is a text history of a group of old Jews yelling at one another. It worked much like this:

"Okay, so the Torah says don't cook a kid in its mother's milk. But what does that *really* mean?" Rabbi One says.

"Well, it's obvious, you fucking moron," replies Rabbi Two. "Don't cook a baby goat in the milk of its mother. It says it right there."

"Sure, if you're unable to read or think," replies Rabbi One. "But if God didn't want that, don't you think He also wouldn't want a kid cooked in *another* goat's milk? And what if there was some kind of mix-up and you went to cook a kid in its cousin's milk, but you accidentally did the whole mother-cooking thing?"

"Okay, legit," says Rabbi Two. "How about: Don't cook a kid in goat's milk at all? Like, does that even taste good?"

"I don't know," says Rabbi Three, wandering into the conversation. "Goat chefs are notoriously stupid and have bad eyesight. What if they went to cook a kid in cow's milk and mistook a goat for a small fuzzy cow?"

"Great point!" murmured the assembled minds of Israel. "No cooking a kid in milk of any kind!"

Somehow this argument went on and on until, finally, Jews couldn't have cheeseburgers. Judaism had become a religion of laws.

These laws ruled Jewish life for two thousand years and were a kind of accidental genius. By supplanting the arm's-length religion of a priestly interlocutor slaughtering an animal in your name with the study of the law as the primary function of Jewish ritual life, each adherent forged a personal relationship with the religion, each household became a tabernacle, each family became a priesthood, each town a Jerusalem.

This pivot, from an ancient religion of the spectacle of ritual sacrifice to a more modern and intimate one of the book and the mind, is, in my opinion, one of the reasons this tiny religion has found a way to stand the test of time. While the great pagan cosmologies of Greece and ancient Rome have crumbled into absurd fairy tales, as we inexplicably tell our children about horny Zeus's quest for Earth pussy and the dogheaded gods of Egypt bark no more, the Jews somehow are just still there.

Also, in a strange way, being exiled from our homeland was a trick of longevity no one could have foreseen. Scattering us to the far corners of the world crystallized our identity in ways that staying put would have compromised. In whatever community we wandered to, we were always an outsider people, always an other. This forced the Jews to look to one another for community and to pre-

serve identity as a means of survival. Had we just stayed in Jerusalem, eventually the Romans would have breached the walls of our
identity, spilling into the streets and overwhelming us with the
temptations of aqueducts and orgies.

Assimilation on the timeline of millennia does not result in fitting
in; it results in rubbing out. Erasure. No one could withstand the
pressure of Rome from within, not even the stiff-necked Jews. Our
only hope for survival as a people was to be isolated on the outside.
Never welcome. Until finally the "Fuck you" from culture at large
turned into a hearty "Hey, fuck you, too!" Through this "Fuck
you," we last. Through the rejection we persevered. We didn't need
them if they didn't want us. Giving up on trying to assimilate us, the
world eventually turned to trying to obliterate us. And this, too,
didn't work. But, hey, kudos for trying.

Looking to Jerusalem every Friday night in prayer, Jews in Warsaw and Leeds, in Shanghai and Tunis, and all around the world
faced a city they'd never visited and said, "Someday, I'll go home. In
the meantime, I'll study the law."

This isn't to say the study of law was all there was to Judaism, but
Jews study like Buddhists meditate. All day, every day, reading, arguing, diving into tomes that would be criticized by a geology graduate student for lacking pizzazz. For the Jews, to study was to
worship. Learning was divine action. And it stayed that way for a
thousand years until the Hasidim came along, flipped learning upside down, and pulled a mystic rabbit out of a fur hat.

At this point I ought to mention that, as I move into the parts of
this story that concern my own exposure to Judaism, this chapter
will now largely concern itself with my people: the pale Jews, both
literally and literally. As in, I'll be talking about Jews of European
descent (pale face), who mostly lived on the "Pale of Settlement," a
Russian reservation that sliced through various nations and was the
only place in those nations that Jews were allowed to live from 1739
to 1917 (pale place). These Jews are called Ashkenazi and are the
ones that Whoopi Goldberg was thinking of when she called the
Holocaust "white on white crime."

The "Are Jews white people?" question is a fraught and annoying one, usually belying an unconscious desire to minimize the degree of Jewish suffering by pointing to the maximized Jewish privilege some Jews currently enjoy. This dichotomy is steeped in American bias and contextual ignorance. It is a historical argument with a very short memory and rather little information extending beyond the borders of the continental United States and prior to 1776. It is, in short, an intellectual argument born of the kind of myopia that American exceptionalism engenders. (The only Jews that exist are the ones in the greatest nation on Earth! Greatest Jews on Earth, baby!)

If you want to know if Jews are white people, just ask people who *really really like white people*. To those people, those who hold whiteness as the über-race, the ultimate in racial purity, Jews are not only *not* white, they are the anti-white. They are the demon race agitating against the front lines of the holy war with whiteness. They are the masterminds of some plot to subvert, disempower, and eliminate whiteness. I would guess that part of the reason those white-lovin' good ol' boys hate Jews so particularly is the very same reason that some well-meaning people think Jews are just another group of white folks: We look white! I mean, I certainly do. I need SPF 700 to avoid turning into a human slice of (corned) beef jerky. If a cop sees me driving through a fancy neighborhood, one where he'd be likely to pull over a Black dude just to "check out what he's doing in the neighborhood," he's never going to pull me over because he suspects I might have a "touch of the Hebrew" in me. So in that way, we *are* white. In terms of whiteness being understood solely as a physical characteristic that allows you to travel unmolested through the parts of a society that discriminate based on color, we are the right color.

But this is really an American idea of race and "white." For thousands of years, the various flavors of white were very specific. Walking through the streets of Luxembourg with a pronounced nose, hairy arms, and brown tightly curled hair, you could easily be identified as, if not Jewish, at least not Luxembourgian—at least not quite right. Here in the States, there is no über-Luxembourger; there is only the binary of white/not white. So Jews walk around America enjoying the benefits of white privilege while still needing to protect themselves from terrorist attacks by white supremacists bent on our destruction. It's complicated.

Judaism is an ethno-religion, one that encompasses both ethnic identity *and* religious belief. It fucks people up trying to understand that, because we lack historical context for it. But it used to be common. Six thousand years ago there was little difference between a Greek person and a worshipper of the Greek gods. If you asked an ancient Egyptian, "What gods do you worship?" they would reply "I am Egyptian. I worship the gods who attacked Kurt Russell in *Stargate*." The word *Hindu* in Sanskrit more or less means "person from the Indus Valley," aka, a dude from India.

Back then, religion and ethnicity were not two things. Judaism is not unique in this, but it is unique in that it stuck around long enough to confuse people's ideas of what religion means. In this country we are used to thinking of religion as a consumer choice, a set of beliefs that suits our disposition and that we therefore signed up for. Judaism is more than that.

People point to conversion as a proof that Judaism is no ethnicity; after all, how can you convert to an ethnicity? But this argument actually proves the point. People convert to the belief system but never to the ethnicity. No one ever says, "A by-product of my conversion was the development of hay fever and coarse body hair." You can therefore convert *into* Judaism the religion, but you can never convert *out of* Judaism the ethnicity. That's why there are Jewish atheists and Jewish Buddhists: people who have long since abandoned any semblance of connection to the religious beliefs of Judaism and remain, nonetheless, fully Jewish.

Regardless of *all* this explanation, the entire conversation around Jews and whiteness has a wildly racist unintended consequence: the erasure of the substantial number of Jews who are not white no matter how you define whiteness. There are Iraqi Jews and Yemenite Jews, Turkish Jews and Kurds, Moroccan Jews and Persians, Ethiopian Jews, and more.

The Jew, as he wandered from place to place, slowly matriculating into various societies, was, regardless of color, subjected to oppression visited upon them by the dominant culture—often distrusting the "looks just like us" stranger within their midst. And no stranger was stranger than the Hasid. The Hasidim would, somehow, become family to me. These were the men who showed up at my father's house to pray with me.

Hasidic Judaism was an upstart movement. Its thrust (and it was a thrust) was to shock Judaism awake. To comfort the discomforted and discomfort the comfortable. It sought to jump-start Judaism's prosaic battery with a charge of spiritualism.

It sprang up from the bosom of the Polish safe space. Their founder was Rabbi Israel ben Eliezer, better known by his spiritual nickname, the Ba'al Shem Tov, or "Master of the Good Name." This guy was the Besht. No really, people called him "the Besht." That was his secondary nickname. When people got tired of the labor involved in saying "the Ba'al Shem Tov," they gave him a Biggie-Smalls-to-Biggie-style conversion and just started saying "Besht."

He was an itinerant rabbi and mystic, wandering from town to town supplying rabbinical services and selling the occasional trinket or amulet. His message sounded more forged in the fires of Tsfat, the mystical city of the Kabbalists, than in the study halls of the great seminaries of Europe. The message was simple: God is everywhere. He's in you, too. Within each person lives a spark of divinity. A little George Bush, Sr.–esque point of light glowing within them. Your job on Earth was to return that spark back to the divinity mother ship that is God. In so doing, I guess you'd be spiritually sucked up, *Close Encounters* style, into the divine. The path to finding your spark's way back? Joy. Find a way to joy and you'll find a way to God. Doesn't exactly sound legalistic, does it? This was a simple reformation, not so much a Bible nailed to the door of the synagogue but rather an unadorned whisper of "Find a way to connect." After a millennium of arguing about dairy practices and the proper weight of incense for an offering meant to be burned in a temple that had been destroyed a thousand years ago, this message was radical in its simplicity. Find joy. Even if it meant being weird.

Hasidim sang and danced looking for joy. They dressed like men shot out of cannons in a Russian bear-wrestling circus looking for joy. They had their wives shave their heads and wear wigs, looking for joy.

Okay, fine, that last one wasn't for joy. It's a much weirder story.*

---

* The "married women wear wigs" thing is a fairly tough sell to non-Jewish observers. The shaved-head thing even more so. It all starts with biblical-mandated female modesty. I think we can all agree that, if there is a God, he for sure cares how much leg the ladies are showing. At least we can *understand* modesty clauses. Every big religion except the *Wild Wild Country* one seems to be concerned with modest dress, and mostly for women. It's a method of controlling women's bodily autonomy, sure, but it's *our* method. For some reason, in the Middle Eastern religions the main concern is women's hair. A thick mane of hair drives desert men wild with erotic desire. So Muslims and Jews have their ladies cover that irresistible head muff. It's an old Jewish practice. The Mishnah (which we discussed above, don't make me repeat it, neither of us wants that) lists as grounds for divorce "appearing in public with loose hair, weaving in the market-place, and talking to any man" (Ketuboth 7:6). Who among us would not cry out for the end of our marriage if we walked into a town square and saw our wife, hair all loose, crochet-chatting with some man?

So it was that Jewish married women kept their hair tied up in a bandanna, 1990s gangbanger style. The idea was that the glimpse of the unbridled eroticism of a full head of hair was a treat reserved for the husband only. Only he could take in his wife's full beauty. Then one day, a prominent rabbi's wife, having found a loophole, went to the opera in a wig. "It's not *my* hair I'm showing." From that night on, European Jewish women started wearing wigs. Confounded, the rabbis huddled. "Okay, we seem to have lost the beat on the whole head-covering thing. That damn rabbi's wife is going to put us out of a job if we aren't careful!" The fellas came up with a counterproposal. They would let women wear the wig but only a special, semi-ugly wig. Literally. The sheitel is a wig made specifically for the ultra-Orthodox, one that allows women to feel and look natural but also manages to make their hair look slightly off. Just off enough that it is ensured not to arouse any Hasidic boners. It's the uncanny valley of hair adornment. Problem solved.

A more mystifying tradition is that of head shaving. To ensure even more modesty and to offset the possibility of an errant hair bursting up from beneath a troubling-looking sheitel, some groups demand married women shave their heads *under* the wig. To recap, men love a hot head of hair, that kind of overwhelming hirsute hotness should be reserved ONLY for the husband, and, to ensure this ordinance isn't violated, the women must shave their heads ensuring no one, including the husband, ever sees that beauty. It would seem in this case the rabbis talked themselves out of something good. They legislated bodily control over women so severely that the sexist power system couldn't even take advantage of it. Talk about taking one for the team!

Hasidism was a populist movement, too. It rejected as elitist the notion that holiness and learnedness were one and the same. The Hasidim loved learning, too, but they were not convinced that learning was the sole road to connection to the divine. Some smart Jews were scoundrels, some simple Jews saints. And some scoundrels were saints in disguise. Hasidic stories are filled with drunkards and louses who have some spiritual power that their circumstances obfuscate. If everyone was born with a divine spark, the pious and learned had no more inherent holiness than anyone else. Each being was a spark that shone in the dark of the world. In this way Hasidic Judaism turned Rabbinic Judaism on its ear. It upended the hierarchy of holiness and handed the keys to the kingdom back to the people.

This radical notion of an egalitarian divinity, a divinity that could not be added to or reduced by pious acts, intellectual rigor, or even committing misdeeds made the Hasidim quick foes of the religious status quo but, predictably, the people loved it. Not much of a competition, really; one school of thought made you essentially get a PhD in Talmud to become a holy person, the other was like, "It's all good! It's in you already! Drink some shtetl rum and be holy!"

The Ba'al Shem Tov was a singular spiritual revolutionary, an iconoclast grinding against the religious power machine. But as Paul figured out shortly after he fell off his horse on the road to Damascus, the difference between an inspirational religious figure and a new religious movement is an army.

Hasidism found its Saint Paul in Rabbi Dov Ber, the Maggid of Mezeritch. Dov Ber was the successor to the Ba'al Shem Tov and is largely responsible for Hasidic Judaism's remarkable spread.

Rather than wander from town to town, preaching the new, gooder word, the Maggid stayed put in one town and established a court of disciples to whom he could teach Hasidism. He franchised, essentially. Each of these disciples turned into great and powerful rabbis who, in turn, dispersed themselves throughout Europe, settled in Jewish communities, and established similar courts. Within three generations of the Ba'al Shem Tov's death, Hasidism had spread all over Europe and had hundreds of thousands of adherents.

Each town in Europe became a dynasty, a mini empire of tradition. The head of the empire went from rabbi (my teacher) to rebbe (my master). In truth they're essentially the same word, but they don't occupy the same world. The rebbe would become master of a kingdom, a charismatic leader with absolute authority over his followers. A rabbi might ask you to donate to the soccer team. A rebbe could demand you start playing. Almost every town in Europe where there were Jews, there was a rebbe and a Hasidic dynasty named after that town.

There were Belzers and Bobovers, Lubavichers and Gerrers, Vizhnitzers and Karlin-Stoliners and then, of course, there were the two dynasties that were to play their part in my life, two of most severe Hasidic sects of them all: the Skveres and the Satmars.

Before I jump into how I met them, let me tell you a little story to illustrate the effect they had on my life. When my brother (who is now a rabbi himself but was not one at the time) was in college, he took a semester abroad at the Hebrew University in Jerusalem. In his program, a Hasidic Jew who did awareness outreach about his community for a living came to give a talk to the secular kids from America about Hasidic life. Oh, the joy he claimed it was. A celebration of life and wonder, of divinity in everything, a dancing, eating, loving party of a spiritual experience. In the back of the room, my brother fumed, getting angrier and angrier with each fantastic claim.

"It's not true!" my brother shouted, finally able to take no more. "You keep saying how joyful and fantastic Hasidic Judaism is, but I grew up with it and it just isn't true! The summers I spent with my family in New York were filled with judgment and rejection and sometimes even cruelty!"

When the Hasid spoke, he asked softly, "Do you think you could tell me *which* Hasidic sects your family is from?"

Unsure why that mattered, my brother told him, "Skver and Satmar, why?"

Now the Hasid winced. "My friend, I don't know how to tell you this but . . . well, you just named the two most judgmental, rejection-prone, and occasionally even cruel sects of Hasidism there are. I hate to say it, but you just had really bad luck."

If my brother and I thought *we* had bad luck, just wait till you hear why those sects became that way in the first place. To illustrate, allow me to break the fourth wall for a minute.

Hi, it's me, Moshe. Funny stuff so far, right? Interesting too, I hope? Anyway, when I was writing the paragraph above, where I listed names of Hasidic sects, I looked them up on Wikipedia, because I'm a comedian; it's good enough. Wiki listed all the great houses of Hasidic Judaism, and then below those were the minor sects, my favorite being the Boston Hasidis, a sect of Hasidic Judaism founded in Boston, Massachusetts. Something really tickles me about all these grand dynasties of European Hasidim, moving to the United States and Israel after the war and carrying on the namesakes of the bombed-out towns they came from; the mysticism of Old Europe with its golems and Draculas still wrapping them like an Eastern European fog, and then, in the middle of the list: the Boston Hasidis. Sitting in that list like a sports team. Or a group of no-nonsense, thick-necked goons in fur hats who drink Guinness out of kiddush cups and will kick the shit out of you if you disrespect the memory of Paul Revere. Anyway that was segment two.

Segment three broke my heart. It was a list of the dead dynasties. The houses that had no one left or so few that they couldn't even be called a dynasty anymore. Burned in the ash of the Holocaust, melted under Nazi fire. They crumbled and remained only as a list of what is no longer there. The great houses had 10 dynasties. The minors had 27. The dead list was 167 sects long. 167. All representing a community. A congregation. A village. A Jerusalem. Sacked once again by a New Rome holding the same outstretched salute of victory and destruction. So when you encounter a Hasid in the wild, a man looking like he wandered off the set of *Yentl* straight onto Fifth Avenue in Manhattan, when you feel him looking past you, when you notice how walled off his community can be, how unfriendly, remember the man you are seeing now is not simply a product of Hasidic Judaism. The man you are encountering is a product of Hasidic Judaism's own encounter with the destruction of most of their brethren, with their way of life. Hasidic Judaism is permanently, inexorably, profoundly altered by the insertion of mass genocide into their history and community. They will *never* be the same community they would have been had they been allowed to find joy and peace.

Joy and peace were also not to be the order of my family. Like almost every path of European Jewish families, the cobblestones of mine are made of bone. Just about every American Jew you know (if you don't know any Jews, that means this book is selling really well!), is alive due to some chance decision made, some pinball bounce that sent the trajectory of that person's family into safety rather than destruction. These usually weren't the geniuses of their community, seeing the writing on the walls and pulling themselves out of harm's way. These were random choices made in response to circumstances that made one part of a family move to America and another to stay behind. One family gets the lucky card, one steps on the trapdoor and rides the chute to the incinerator.

My family, the Sterns, got a lucky card.

Aaron Stern, my great-grandfather, was a Kabbalist and a butcher and a follower of no particular rebbe when he boarded a boat for the United States in 1922. By the time he called for the rest of his family in 1932, he imported a family in crisis. Particularly, a crisis of faith. His daughter, my grandmother, Hinda Stern, having lived with a mere memory of a father for ten years, was now twenty-two and absolutely not having it. Upon arrival in the United States, she became Helen Stern, left the fold, and went searching for adventure in New York City. When she joined the American Communist party, she was disowned by her father.

But it was a short-lived disowning. When her son, my father, was born a deaf kid in Brooklyn, Helen was welcomed back for Sunday gatherings, and Helen and her father would sit and eat cake and talk about better times.

Her husband, my grandfather Duvid Kasher, was a novelist and apparently a very funny guy before he lost his health, whether mental or physical or both is unclear, and spent the rest of his life, which was not long, in and out of hospitals. His father, my other great-

grandfather, was an actor in the Yiddish theater, which allowed
Duvid to not be weighed down by Old World traumas of religiosity.
Duvid loved the weekly family visits with their dry cake and tut-tuts
lobbed at him for abandoning Mosaic law. For him it was probably
a gold mine of material. For my grandmother it was a mine shaft
into hell. She hated anything religious. She, like all good commies,
thought it the opiate of the masses, and the masses seemed to be
gathered in Brooklyn.

In that time, Brooklyn looked like the shtetl, religious nuts mixed
with Communist nuts on the same blocks. The lines hadn't been
drawn. Duvid cobbled together a living tutoring Yiddish and
scratching out freelance gigs with *The Forward* and the Yiddish
Communist paper, the *Morgen Freiheit*. How could he have known,
typing on his Yiddish typewriter, that he was among those writing
the last gasps of a dying language: secular Yiddish. Yes, Yiddish,
the language that brought you the schmuck and the schmeckle, the
bagel and the boychik, was dying an unusual death: the death of
the most vibrant of its users. Secular Jews slowly scattered into the
seductive, irresistible stew of meltwater that was American culture
and its flag bearer: the English language.

While the Zionists in Palestine were forging a new language from
an ancient one by reinventing Hebrew as a spoken tongue for the
first time in two thousand years, a kind of reverse polarity was occurring with Yiddish in America. The early Zionists took Hebrew
out of prayer books and hammered out a language in which a young
sabra could order a falafel or a prostitute. But Yiddish slowly trick-
led into the mouths of only the very old or the very pious.

Gone soon would be the foul-tongued Yiddish of vaudeville, sup-
planted by the burgeoning art form that would someday pay my
bills, stand-up comedy. Gone soon would be the giants of Yiddish
theater, supplanted by the Jewish giants of Broadway: Irving Berlin,
Gershwin, Bernstein, and Sondheim. Gone soon were the greats of
Yiddish literature—Isaac Bashevis Singer, Sholem Aleichem, and
I. L. Peretz—supplanted by Ginsberg, Wouk, Bellow, Roth, and
Mailer.

The era of artsy Yiddish was coming to an anticlimactic close as the era of European Judaism came to a catastrophic one.

And there was my grandfather, bent over his typewriter, hammering out prose no one would read in a country he barely knew, which itself is like a Yiddish story: the little Jew, across the sea from his shtetl, mashing keys into the void of history.

Meanwhile, religious Yiddish speakers were thriving. It was the perfect language for a nearly broken people who were determined to hide in plain sight; the perfect thing to hold on to to keep them intact as a unit, whole and insulated from the world around them. That was the goal: Save the culture that had been set on fire. Save the pious ones. Save the world by hiding within it. Remember, if no one studies the Torah, the world will end. Those who came out of Europe had looked into the fanged mouth of that end and were determined to fight it off. Jews generally were determined to live and thrive in spite of the bastards across the sea, but the approach was so different. The secularists would thrive by eschewing what they saw as Jewish weakness and odd isolationism. They would dive into Americanness. They would out-America America.

The Hasidim, those who were left, would retreat further inward. They would use the freedom of religion promised here to build societies inside of societies, like little Jewish Wakandas. They wouldn't out-America America; they would *Europe* America, right there in Brooklyn.

That Yiddish crossroads, the meeting of secular Yids and religious Yids, was the corner my father was born on. When he was born, the lives of my grandparents changed. He became the nucleus that my family spun around.

He was a firecracker, a bold boy, born to the stickball-playing alleys of Brooklyn. Deaf and addled with Gaucher disease, he lived beyond the doctors' prognosis and began to thrive. Though maybe not socially. He was repeatedly picked on by a local mafia don's son, mocked and teased for his voice and his deafness. Until one day he snapped. He beat that kid's ass. The local boys, Jewish and Italian, stood around, mouths agape. You simply did not touch the son of the don. Across the street, in some kind of numbers-running bar or some kind of garment-stealing bar or whatever kind of bar mafia guys liked to hang out at, the don noticed the commotion. Storming across the street came this mafioso, rage in his eyes. My father stopped punching, stared at him. Terror struck. This was it, the end. Certain to be mowed down by a tommy gun in a trumpet case, my dad quickly made peace with his maker. The don came right up to the scuffle and reached a fist down, grabbed his son, shook him. "You fucking lousy wimp! You let a deaf Jew beat you up?! I'm ashamed! A deaf Jew?!" Picking my dad up off the ground, the mobster patted him on the back. "Good job, son. Run along." He flipped him a dollar coin in congratulations and dragged his son to the bar in shame.

The number of times I heard this story sapped it of any excitement. But it illustrated my father's view of the world. Fight your way into spaces where you aren't welcome.

My father attended those Sunday cake gatherings with his family and, though doubtlessly left out of the conversation, picked up what could be described as an aesthetic love for Hasidism. The white tablecloths. The plain wool suits. The mink-fur-lined shtreimel hats, reserved for special occasions, that sit atop Hasidic men's heads like a Russian folk dancer ready to do the splits. He loved the chests of silver curio that every Hasidic family has on display for all visitors to admire. He loved the neat lines of Hasidism. The black-and-white. The order.

His own life was totally out of order.

By the time he was thirty and met my mother, my father was an irreligious beatnik painter living in a brick co-op on the Lower East Side. He was also a filmmaker and a mime. So good of a mime that, according to family legend, the world's only famous mime, Marcel Marceau, once saw him perform and invited my father to join him as an understudy.*

---

* Let's all take a moment to appreciate how great Marcel Marceau must have been at miming to have taken a performance form that literally no one enjoys watching or doing and actually make it big. Hacky sack, for instance, has no Marcel Marceau of its own.

My father didn't run away with the silent circus. He stayed put and had a family. My brother, then me, born hearing to two deaf parents, the only two able to hear the screams of a family set to implode.

By the time I was nine months old, the marriage was over and I was shuttled out of New York, literally stolen in the night back to my mother's hometown of Oakland.

My father, in the detonated absence of his family, with chaos brought to his threshold, sought order and stability. The source of that order was obvious. Go back to the old country. Find the ancient order of the Ancient Order. My father was reborn. He was no longer a mime or a painter but an Orthodox Jew. No, scratch that, an *ultra*-Orthodox Jew. He donned a black fedora, grew out his beard, and never looked back.

And then there was me.

I was raised with my mother as a tremendously secular kid, in Oakland public schools, with little experience of Judaism except the occasional holiday and Sunday school at the local Reform temple, where my teacher admitted she didn't believe in God. I didn't mind her atheism, but it did strike me as slightly odd that a religious schoolteacher didn't believe in religion.

Judaism loomed little on who I was.

Until the courts got involved.

My father was granted visitation rights when I turned four, and I began flying back to New York on a kind of cultural exchange program. I'd fly back in time and my father would pick me up at the airport and shuttle me to the old country. We'd do a costume change in the car, and my acid-washed jeans would be traded in for a pair of slacks. My A's cap got tossed and replaced by a velvet yarmulke. We'd drive to his new community, Seagate, a Hasidic enclave in South Brooklyn, and I'd live the life of Tevye the Milkman for a few weeks a year.

Most of the family on his side left Williamsburg for the ultra-orthodox hamlet of Monsey, New York, a ten-minute drive from the village of New Square, New York, where the powerful Skverer rebbe reigned supreme. In 2000, everyone in New Square voted for

Hillary Clinton for Senate. I mean every single person. Literally. In a totally unrelated story, in 2001 Bill Clinton commuted the sentences of a bunch of town officials who had been convicted in a Pell Grant scandal.

In New Square, women did not drive. Let's just say that again. In a town in upstate New York, women were not allowed to drive. Men and women walked on different sides of the street. Young men were not allowed to leave the town without permission from their seminary schools. My father used to take us to New Square to visit family and to receive a blessing from the rebbe. You know, classic summer vacation stuff.

Back in Seagate things were way (?) more normal (??). My stepmother and her entire family belonged to the Satmar sect of Hasidic Judaism, and they totally let women drive. On the other hand . . . that's the sect that does the whole "make married women shave their heads" thing, so it's not *exactly* a feminist hot spot.

I strangely had both a profoundly *more* and *less* Jewish experience than most of my Jewish friends. I never got the summer camp experience, an annual ritual for most young American Jews: sleepaway camps in the forests surrounding the big northeast cities of America, little Zionist training camps where boys learn to stare at flat-chested Jewesses and dream of a future together spent threshing corn in a desert they'll terraform using donkey piss and Talmudic incantations. Jews really love summer camps, and I've barely met any who didn't spend their summers making lifelong friends, weaving Jewish dreams into lanyards.

My mother was broke, on welfare, and probably wouldn't have bothered sending me to camp if we'd been rich.

I didn't learn Hebrew at all. Most American Jews are force-fed Hebrew lessons starting at age ten, drills of transliterated memorization banged into their brains to prepare them for the Bar or Bat Mitzvah. By the time they turn thirteen, they are prepped and ready to recite, nearly from memory, an entire chapter of the Hebrew bible before the congregation. It's much like a marriage ceremony in its declarative ritual. Here we are, consecrated together before the body of the congregation. Only this marriage is solitary. In a religion of the book like Judaism, the rite of ascension to adulthood is to declare fidelity to the book itself. To declare your allegiance to the text and become a fully vested, fully naturalized citizen of the people of the book. It's a communal performance in which the sheer volume of memorization declares to the community: This child is one of us now.

After this performance, they generally immediately forget all they have learned, abandon Judaism altogether, and do not revisit it until they get married and start feeling anxious about the legacy they are leaving their children. This guilt reaches a fever pitch at about nine years in, just in time for them to have a major awakening about how they will carry on the tradition. The answer is obvious. Throw their kid into Bar Mitzvah prep courses! This cycle of legacy torture will continue until the messiah arrives and grants us a reprieve. The world to come will have no Bar Mitzvahs, and everyone will finally be happy.

That's not to say the Bar Mitzvah is pure hell. After the performative religious ceremony, there's the bash, a huge party where an LMFAO parody band is hired and thirteen-year-olds can floss dance for one another.

My Bar Mitzvah was so different. I didn't even know the Hebrew alphabet going into my twelfth year. My father, knowing this was an issue, couldn't help. Despite his religiosity, he didn't know Hebrew either. Like I said, my father's relationship with Judaism was mainly aesthetic, and that included admiring the Semitic script but not deciphering it. As a result, I was raised a summertime ultra-Orthodox Jew who didn't even know the Hebrew alphabet.

My extended family in Seagate, my cousins Leybe and Shner, both spoke with eastern European accents despite the fact that their parents did not. This phenomenon is a bizarre facet of the American Hasidic community. The boomer Hasidim were first-generation American and, as such, had the "early arriver" pressure to fit in that made them speak like the community surrounding them. By the time they had kids of their own, the community was comfortable with their place in society and could indulge in a more insular language acquisition. As a result, my uncle sounds like a New Yorker and my cousins sound like characters in *Doctor Zhivago*.

And then there was me. I knew the word *bagel* and that was pretty much it.

I clung to my English prayer book in temple, desperately embarrassed to be exposed as the cultural interloper I was. The English script glowed brightly like a scarlet neon sign, "Look here, this boy comes from California! He is not one of us!" Simply holding the Hebrew prayer book and pretending I was reading it was not an option as I'd never know what page everyone was on and inevitably someone would look over and, pointing and laughing, tease me for being on the page for the counting of the Omer rather than the blessing of the new moon.

A local rabbi took pity on me and maybe my father, too, and offered to give me Hebrew lessons in his home. I know this sounds sketchy, but it was the eighties and at that time any authority figure could ask for some alone time with a child and they would be handed over, no questions asked.

Luckily the rabbi was a good man and all he taught me was Hebrew. Truly elemental Hebrew. The alphabet. Day after day. This was a Talmudic scholar teaching me the A-B-Cs. This would be like Alan Turing teaching me my times tables.

To say I didn't have a gift for the language would be like saying Helen Keller didn't have much of a singing voice. One day, noticing I was frustrated by how little progress I was making, stumbling and stammering over the alphabet, the rabbi called his son, Shmuel, into the room. A tall nine-year-old boy who looked strangely like Dr. Zaius from *Planet of the Apes* appeared in the foyer. "Yes, Tati?" he said, in a thickly accented English. "Say the American alphabet," the rabbi commanded. Shmuel gulped and began, "A . . . B . . . D . . . G . . . Z . . . F . . . X."

The rabbi turned to me and laughed. "See?! It's not so bad. You know English good, he knows Hebrew and Yiddish! Don't be discouraged!" This was an extremely touching move. A religious leader of the community was willing to publicly humiliate his oldest son in the hopes of helping me love to learn. This is also vaguely the plot of *Dangerous Minds*.

It didn't take. I didn't learn Hebrew. Eventually I turned thirteen and had my Bar Mitzvah. It was a solemn affair at a synagogue I'd never visited in front of an ancient rabbi I'd never met, ten strangers, and my dad. I didn't memorize anything but a single line, the blessing for the reading of the Torah. Someone else read the chapter in my name. Someone else made me a man. I just sat there like a cuck and watched him do it.

The party that night was a big bash but, strangely, aside from family members, I didn't know anyone there. My father had decided that my mother attending the party would be totally inappropriate, so she was not invited. How anyone would know she was there, sitting behind a partition in the women's section, was beyond me. Every friend I'd ever had was back in Oakland, so the party was basically just me, my brother, my dad's new family, and two hundred extras from *Fiddler on the Roof*, who all seemed to be having the time of their fucking lives.

American Hasidim don't really do much fun stuff like birthday parties and haunted houses on Halloween. New Year's Eve was out, too, because you don't generally center your year around the calendar commemorating the majesty of the God you don't believe in and also are accused of killing. Thanksgiving *might* merit a cold turkey sandwich and a single cranberry but probably not. Living outside the stream of society means living without its celebratory perks. As such, the main opportunities for Hasidim to let loose and party hard were weddings and Bar Mitzvahs, cheesy halls with a ruffled curtain partition slicing down the middle as a way to keep men and women both physically and visually separate the entire time.

The catering was catastrophic, always.

After dinner was dancing, which was the only real fun part and one of the only nonliturgical holdovers from the original Hasidism. Dancing in a circle, running round and round, faster and faster, like a dervish trying to spin yourself back in time to the Ba'al Shem Tov dancing in a town square in Ukraine. You could feel the blur between generations, and if you spun hard enough, you could almost grab one of those points of light hiding in between what Hasidism was and what it's become.

But mostly these were screechingly boring affairs if you'd ever attended an actual party. I hated them so much because I knew exactly what I was missing: fun.

Once, at my stepsister's wedding, the family was getting portraits taken before the ceremony. All the cousins, distant cousins, yet more distant cousins, aunts and uncles were lined up. My father and his new wife and their kids were gathered in the center, in the position of honor as the parents of the bride. They snapped a few, and then my stepmother's mom, I guess my step-grandmother, stepped out of formation and looked at the tableau of the portrait. She frowned. Something was bothering her. Then, her eyebrows cocked; she had it! She stepped forward "Okay, one more photo, this time, *just* family. Moshe, David, step out of the photo."

A little stunned, my older brother, David, and I shuffled out of the photo and stood there watching as just the twenty-seven closest members of the family took a *real* family portrait. My dad, firecracker though he had been, often had his fuse soaked in water when it came to religious affairs. He said nothing. No one said anything. They just smiled and took the photo. What a party.

So when I became an actual man by observing the secular rite of ascension in Oakland—smoking a blunt and drinking a forty-ouncer of malt liquor—I realized how little Judaism had to offer me. That's not to say I came to hate it. I don't know how, but I managed to never resent Judaism, despite all the weirdness I experienced, all the sideways looks and silent judgments. I never made the leap into blaming the religion itself. It always just seemed like it was the people I met. I think it had something to do with the relationship my dad had with his faith. It was ceremonial and external rather than dogmatic and personal. I never got the impression there was a God up there watching me and shaking his head at my horny thoughts or lack of faith. I just got told to keep the yarmulke on when in Brooklyn. Ultra-Orthodox Judaism never had the opportunity to wrap itself around my brain the way many fundamentalist Christians describe their religious upbringings, constantly worried that their every action, every thought, was a sinful slip, observed, tabulated, and recorded by a vengeful god. I slipped through the hole in the sheet* and managed to wear my religion like a loose garment. And while I didn't hate the garment, at some point, I slipped it off and said, "Maybe not for me."

Then my dad got lymphoma.

You never forget the call.

It's like a ripple in your timeline, a small utterance that you can feel in your skin is going to change your life. Dad's sick. A lump. Fine for now. Everything should be okay.

* The hole in the sheet is a fascinating Jewish phenomenon. It's everyone's favorite thing to cite about Hasidic Judaism: "You know, they have sex through a hole in a sheet?" And yes, this is definitely a fucking wild and insane detail about Hasidim. Except, it isn't true. They don't have sex through a hole in the sheet. Why would they? My favorite explanation of how this rumor started is this: Hasidim always lived in villages of people who had no fucking clue what they were like. They were odd, insular, and mysterious. Little Gentile kids would walk by Hasidic houses and stare, wondering what their sidelocked neighbors were up to. Staring into the backyards, they'd scan the laundry lines hung with Hasidic garb and try to suss out what they were looking at. Slacks. A jacket and . . . some weird cloth thing with a big ol' hole in it. These were the tzitzits, the four fringed garments that Orthodox Jews are commanded to wear. It's a big square of cloth with tassels hanging from each corner. In the middle is a large hole that you stick your head through like a bro's parka he bought on a trip to Cabo. Wearing it each day, Jewish men are reminded of their commitment to God's commandments. But the local Gentile kids knew none of this. All they knew was there was a big square of cloth with a hole in it that the weirdo neighbors had and clearly used for some purpose. So their imaginations went in the obvious direction. "I bet they drape it over their wives and fuck through the hole." Logical enough. What use is a hole in a cloth if you aren't going to stick your dick in it? So that's where the myth comes from. What's interesting about it to me is that over time, it became so pervasive a myth that Jews *themselves* began to believe it and cite it as a plain fact. The religiosity of the Orthodox Jew is so mysterious even to a secular Jew, he will believe just about anything. And so, my own people love to erroneously point out what weirdos Hasidim are and tell me, "They fuck through a sheet— did you know that?" I roll my eyes and reply, "I know, my dad isn't allowed within fifty feet of a Bed Bath & Beyond. Before he got there it was just called 'Bed & Bath.'"

A week later.

Maybe someone should come.

My brother and I had a meeting. Who should go? We decided he would fly back to Brooklyn without me and assess the situation.

When you go through this kind of crisis you often go back and replay moments missed, chance decisions made that, if reconsidered, could have been pivotal but at the time seemed like the right thing to do.

If I'd just said I'd go, too, I'd have had the walks around the block with my dad that my brother got. The sober talks they shared as my father's body deteriorated. My soul could have adjusted to his wasting form like eyes getting used to the dark.

But I didn't get that. I just got the second call that it was time to come now.

Come now means you really should have come before. *Come now* means come to the agony. Come to the end.

I came. I saw. I walked out of the room. I walked into my father's hospital room wholly unprepared for what I'd see. His body sucked up and lean. Frail in the bed. An eye pushed shut by some tumor growing somewhere in the back of his head. Cheeks sunk. Teeth exposed.

My heart started pounding. My body tingled. I had to get out of there. I flew three thousand miles to be by my father's bedside, got a ride to the hospital, took the elevator to the eleventh floor, walked into his room, looked at him, forced a hello smile, and immediately pretended I had somewhere else I had to go. It was an ugly, honest, human moment. Another moment I desperately want back. I don't want to have left the room. I want to have walked right in and taken his hand in mine. I didn't.

My dad smiled and asked my brother if I was scared of him.

I was.

I gathered myself and reentered the room. We all pretended not to know why I'd left. I sat down, signed, "How are you feeling?" and started the process of watching my father die.

Anyone who's been in a hospital for an extended stay knows the smell. Somehow it's different in your nose when the prognosis of your stay is grim. It sears your nostrils and camps in there, sort of like when you get food poisoning, and you can never really enjoy the food that made you sick again.

When a loved one goes in sick and leaves healthy, or goes in for a birth or something else hopeful, hospitals become memory palaces of great joy. The mastery of doctors. The wonders of medicine. The valiance of your loved one who fought and fought and vanquished their sickness. The arrival of a new human.

But when it's a losing battle, the hospital becomes a cathedral of pain, sickness, and dread. Thick dread. An ominous, sick basecamp of dwindling hope and time. You start with an hourglass filled with the sands of positivity and watch each day as the sand trickles out.

There are more memories. I'd been at my father's bedside for two weeks, leaving only for a quick shower and change of clothes before heading back to keep watch. We'd talk as much as my father was capable of, each day the conversation a little less active. He found it increasingly hard to sign, his hands weak with cancer.

But he was there. He was awake and alive.

It starts to grind on you, the endless, looping hours of care and despair. Finally I'd had enough. I needed to get out, to go to a meeting, something. Anything.

"I'll be fine," my father signed. "Go."

I took a train to New Jersey and went to a mediocre AA meeting with a friend. After the meeting she asked if I wanted to stay at her place and it sounded great to sleep in a bed, next to a woman. Better than trying to catch sleep in a hospital easy chair.

We went to bed and at some point in the night started hooking up. It felt rote, robotic, a mechanical proboscis extending, searching for emotional or physical pollen. I had an empty orgasm and passed out.

The next morning, I returned to the hospital and my father had slipped away from consciousness. He was in a coma. Alive but not, there but not. Machines were doing all the work.

I've never been an "ashamed of my sexuality" type, not with the mother I had growing up, but once I realized what had happened while I was having that sex in Jersey, it instantly became a memory hot with shame. How dare I attempt to enjoy carnality at a time like that? How could I be fucking while he was leaving? Why did I do that? What is wrong with me?

It's like that in grief. You're falling and you're grabbing at meaning, looking for some foothold to tether you to the world. Sometimes that tether is hope, false or not; sometimes it's control and you're yelling at a doctor, and sometimes, when it's all you have, it's punishing yourself for not doing it right, for not being there at the critical moment, for not helping, for going to Jersey, for being dirty, for being bad. Delusional self-flagellation is more grounding than what's actually in front of you.

A dying man.

Your dying father.

Another memory: The doctor pulled us aside a few days later and explained the situation in the most detail we'd gotten yet. The cancer was aggressive, and the chemo was worse. He needed more medicine to fight it off, but his body was so weak that any more medicine would kill him. If the cancer wasn't going to kill him, the cure was.

It was the end of the line. Submission time.

My half sister signed, "Isn't there any hope?!"

The answer was not what she wanted.

Time slowed. She turned away from the doctor with such agony.

The negotiations were over. Endgame.

Judaism is nothing if not a religion where the bureaucratic becomes spiritual. The moment we passed the threshold where hope gave way to planning as the operating principle, the rules of Judaism started being enforced.

As we've discussed, in a religion of laws, there are rules regulating every part of life. Its end is no exception. To ensure death came with purity, a phalanx of distant cousins began keeping watch over my father. They would switch shifts with military precision, one guard relieving the next. There's perhaps no place more intimate and emotionally vulnerable than the space around a deathbed. And yet, all of a sudden, there were near strangers there twenty-four hours a day, watching over my father with eagle eyes, making sure nothing impure happened to his body.

All of this led to me experiencing some of my deepest anguish next to people whom I'd felt intimidated by and embarrassed around my entire childhood. Next to my grief post were the guests to my Bar Mitzvah, the people whom I'd been pushed out of the picture to make room for, the people who used to make my blood run cold with shame.

But I was older now and more comfortable in my skin, plus I'd abandoned Judaism for the less arcane spirituality of the twelve steps. So while their presence was odd, it was not particularly intimidating anymore. I spent late nights debating spirituality with Hasidic cousins, adjusting my nose ring with pride.

One night, a younger cousin, Yanky, sat with me in a kind of nervous silence. Finally he spoke, "You're not . . . religious, are you?"

"Not particularly," I answered, wondering where this was going.

He exhaled. "Can I tell you a secret? Something I can't tell anyone around me?"

Oh boy. Here we go. Cousin Heretic is here from California and now he has to act as a confession booth to sinful Jews. "Sure. Lay it on me," I said, pretty sure I knew what was coming.

Yanky trembled, gathering his courage. "I've always wanted . . ."

"To fuck men?" I thought.

Yanky took a breath. "I've always wanted to be . . ."

"Gay? Yes. You've always wanted to be gay. Just say it," I thought, almost bored at this point, mainly focused on injecting sincerity into my forthcoming "It's okay, I accept you for who you are" response.

"I've always wanted to be a . . ." He steeled his eyes. This secret was killing him and he was ready to get it out. He gasped, "A . . . a lawyer!"

"A lawyer? Like, to practice law?"

"Yes!" he sighed, a weight off his shoulders. "It feels good to say it out loud. I feel better now."

I was a little stunned. "I mean . . . you can. Just, like, go to law school and become a lawyer."

He laughed. "Ach, no. My family would never let."

What a world this guy lived in. His shameful family secret would be another family's wet dream. In the world of Hasidic Jews, there is no value in much other than Torah. To waste one's time and life energies with such frivolousness as secular law would be to bring shame on the family. To my knowledge, Yanky never indulged in the sybaritic decadence of investigating the perpetuities issues in probate documents or land-use planning permitting, and remains, to this day, in a lifeless job, earning just enough to support his family and study the only laws that matter: the laws of the Talmud.

There's a difference between alive and not alive. Seems obvious, but you don't really know it until you watch someone die who's already close to death. My father had been in a coma for a week when it happened. We'd been waiting. The distant cousins and me. I was the only real family member there when he died. It just happened that way.

There was a difference. A there and then a not there. As the machines stopped working, a pigeon appeared on the windowsill of my father's hospital room. A pigeon is just a down-and-out dove, right? It was kind of like a miracle, I guess.

I ripped my T-shirt in the ancient Jewish tradition of rending one's garment in grief. I can hear the sound of that shirt ripping with such acuity, even now, twenty years later.

It was the sound of the end.

Then the Hasidim took over.

The speed of the Jewish death rite is whiplash inducing.

The funeral was that afternoon. A plain pine box containing the pound of flesh my father had become sat at the front of a drab hall. Rabbis spoke in Yiddish, a language my father didn't know, extolling the virtue of a man they'd never had a real conversation with. Everything wrapped up quickly and we were off to the cemetery.

The plain pine box is one of the hallmarks of the Jewish burial. There's beauty in its austerity. While Gentiles sink into Cadillac caskets, the Jews use nothing more than is necessary. Luxury is for life, pine is for pain. But even the pine is too much. The box is not for the body; it's for the bereaved. As the box is lowered into its grave, it gets broken apart, dismantled, and all that is put in the ground is a body, covered in a shroud, the earth an inch away, ready to do its work.

Grabbing a shovel, I heaved dirt onto my father. The universe felt bent.

One by one, we buried him, a shovelful at a time. My octogenarian Great-Uncle Shloime sobbed as he buried his nephew. My family turned to head to the car, and I realized the path back was now lined with men, standing in formation, a gauntlet of Hasidim that we had to walk through. They shuckled and bowed, incanted and prayed. Through the prayers we stumbled, dazed; shirts ripped, shoes off, minds blown. It felt like science fiction.

We drove home. The shiva had already been set up. Seats had been put down, low to the ground, mirrors covered. The death ritual had ended; the grief ritual had begun. My father had been alive less than twelve hours earlier.

There's a strange kind of perfection to the Jewish grief ritual. It divvies up your pain into digestible strata of action. Your first task is to do nothing. You have to sit, low to the ground, and receive visitors who regale you with tales of your loved one. The idea is to really dive in. To agitate memories and make you be with the remembrances of the person you loved. It's eight hours a day, all day, sit there and stew. You don't bathe, you don't work, you don't do shit. If you're hungry, an aunt whips you up a bowl of soup or a hamburger and shoos you back to the grief seat. If you go to the bathroom, the mirrors are covered, lest the beauty of your face distract you from the task at hand, which, again, is sinking into a thick, stinky tub of full-sobbing, agonizing grief. For one full week you do this. Nothing.

Then, on day seven, they figure you've had enough. The mirrors uncover, you get up from the floor, and you take a walk around the block, releasing the spirit of your loved one and releasing yourself as well. It's time to get back to life.

But not entirely.

You return to work, you return to your routine, but you stay off-kilter. The idea is not to get back to normal. It's not normal to lose a father at twenty. It shouldn't feel normal. For a full month, you don't shave. You don't listen to music. You don't attend parties or celebrations. Your body is back in the routine of your life, but your spirit is still encumbered with the weight of your grief.

Then at the month mark, you go pretty much back to normal. You spend the next ten months in a light phase of grief.

Three times a day, you say a prayer for the departed and for some reason you still can't go to concerts. (For as we all know, a My Morning Jacket concert is a crutch that holds us back from a natural healing.) You're back in the stream of life, but there's a shadow following you. You spend eleven months with that shadow and then, at the year mark, you rip it off like Peter Pan and the windowsill.

Now you're back.

You faced and processed your pain, and you emerge back into the world healed.

For most of us, agony is as far as we get. When someone is ripped from our lives, we submerge in our pain and try to doggy-paddle to the surface. Able to breathe again, we imagine we've healed ourselves, but really we just found a way to survive the pain. But we always risk drowning. The grief ritual felt like the laws of Judaism pulled me into a rescue boat, dried me off, and dropped me back at shore. I don't understand how other people grieve without rules like that.

That ritual of grieving in the wake of my father's death was what reignited my connection to Judaism. It made it personal; it made it mine. In that way, my father *had* given me a connection to the faith. But he never saw it.

Every Friday that year, I went to a Shabbat service to ensure that I said the Mourner's Kaddish in remembrance of my father at least once a week. Remember, there's the idea that, for eleven months,[*]

---

[*] That's right, eleven months. Not a year. Why? God forbid any Jew, much less one you're related to, be such a scoundrel they need a *full year* of prayers for their soul. Even in grief, we negotiate.

the soul of the dead is hovering in a limbo state, neither here nor there as far as heaven/hell goes.* Saying Kaddish for the dead pushes its spirit ever forward, and to abandon the prayer is to abandon your loved one to slipping into damnation. Or something. Going to Shabbat services every week began to terraform my spiritual connection to the faith of my father.

It helped that it was all in the Bay Area and that, for the first time, I got involved in a Jewish community that didn't see English prayer books as a scarlet letter. Growing up, I always saw Judaism as a vessel contained behind the gates of my father's Satmar community, but finding a group of Bay Area weirdos who ostensibly had their own connection to this thing that didn't seem burdened or encumbered by doubts of its legitimacy was freeing.

Prior to this period of my life, any time I'd walk into a temple in the Bay Area, I'd sneer at how watered down it seemed. Even the Orthodox experience there was laughable. Ponytails and colorful shirts, sacrilege shit like that. What's crazy is that I also didn't enjoy the Judaism I was negatively comparing it to. How could I? Satmar Judaism was so insular, it wasn't just inaccessible, it was invisible. I rejected it. But still, any time I'd go to a Reform temple and I'd see

---

* The notion that Jews don't believe in hell is a spurious one. It's something people love to say, much like "Jews encourage questioning the faith" and "You can't be buried in a Jewish cemetery with a tattoo." Sorta true, but not really. Jews have a strange notion of the afterlife. There's some kind of vague idea of a good place, the "world to come," and a bad place, a "river of boiling shit." It is fair to say that this dichotomy didn't get so stark until the Christians came along and formed an entire religion around it. Jews, feeling they had to compete in the new "Act good, win prizes" marketplace, started crystallizing their mythology around just what happens when you die. Prior to that there was only one really clear afterlife event: the resurrection of dead bodies when the messiah comes. This is a wild zombie fantasy that involves expatriated corpses literally rolling underground like in *Tremors*, to get to Israel to greet the redeemer of man. Ask fifty Jews what happens when you die and you will get fifty answers. So while the idea that Jews don't believe in an afterlife is false, what would be more accurate would be to say "Jews don't really care about the afterlife." They are much more concerned with how you act when you are alive. Also, if you've ever had a Jewish parent, you'll know Jews don't worry about hell in the world to come; they bring it home into the here and now. Hell on Earth, baby!

a woman in a yarmulke in the Bay Area, I'd roll my eyes, "*That's not real!*"

Every part of me was a Bay Area kid, progressive and egalitarian, but when it came to Judaism, I had some kind of holy of holies in my brain that wanted to preserve stodgy old-world traditionalism. I didn't wear a yarmulke at all, and I had the right to judge how someone else wore theirs?

What strikes me now about this is that my objections were all aesthetic. It was like a mirror image of my father. The things I objected to about the non-Hasidic Jewish communities were the things that didn't *look* right. The things that looked out of place. You know, things like me when I was in Seagate. I spent my whole childhood being sneered at, and I became driven to pay it forward. But, of course, how things look is by definition the most superficial part of a faith community. To view religion like that turns it into a cult of the cosmetic, an idolatrous denomination, worshipping conformity and homogeneity over the divine, obedience over all spiritual connection. And that's *exactly* the kind of religion that Hasidism was a response to in the first place.

Week after week, service after service, I began to learn the language of the ceremony, to bond with it directly and to make it my own. It gave my pain purpose and was a respite from grief. In this way Shabbat became for me what it had been for the Jewish people for six thousand years.

A spiritual oasis in a painful world.

Commandment Five: *Remember the Sabbath Day.*

When this little homage to the freakin' weekend was plopped into the Ten Commandments, there was no way to know it would save the Jewish people. Growing up, Shabbat (or Shabbos as my family and Walter in *The Big Lebowski* call it) was twenty-four hours of TV-free torture. No lights to be flickered, no Nintendo to be played. You'd sit, staring longingly at your tube television and whisper to its supple form, "Soon, my love." My entire adolescence, Shabbat was mainly about waiting for it to end.

But there's a deeper story to Shabbat, one not predicated on the belief that a sleepy God needed a Saturday nap after creating the heavens and the Earth. Jewish history, in case you haven't noticed, has been a slog. There's been an unrelenting parade of abuses hurled at Jews everywhere they've lived. Poverty, abuse, attacks, violence, and expulsion have been de rigueur for the Jewish people. It starts to feel like anti-Semitism has a nearly mystical quality to it. It transcends station, as rich Jews and poor Jews have been abused in kind. It transcends the degree to which Jews assimilate into a given society, too. Germany had among the most assimilated Jews in all of Europe, so much so that other Jews called them, with a roll of the eye, "more German than the Germans."

It didn't help. Anti-Semitism is as old as Semitism.

People hate us for *everything*. During the Russian Revolution, the Jews were blamed both for being the Bolsheviks agitating to slit the throats of the capitalists *and* for *being* the capitalists, using their money to crush the worker's revolution. This is what the Jew is in the imagination of the bigot: the ethnic boogeyman, the demon behind everything. No matter where we go, we are met with the most bizarre and obsessive hatred. Part of it is somewhat explicable: The idea of Jewish greed comes from the hundreds of years where Christian anti-usury laws banned the lending of money at interest to fellow Christians. Since there was not a large movement of interest-free loans popping up and filling the lending gap, and since people in Europe still needed money for opening bakeries and building ships and pouring smallpox onto blankets, someone non-Christian had to step in and lend that money!

Enter the Jewish moneylender, Shylock, he of the pound of flesh. So, sure, think about how much you hate your creditors when they bug you about unpaid debts, and now imagine that for a few hundred years there was a uniform creditor ethnicity. You see how some resentment grew.

But what of the Russian peasant? The potato muncher who lived in simple squalor, lending nothing, living in the liminal space between Shabbats. Why was he hated?

Through time, this commandment to rest on Saturday became a

respite from this hatred and the drudgery of Jewish life. It was a built-in breath of fresh air. Every family in every shtetl, besieged by pogroms or not, could look six or less days into their future to a respite. It made the toil possible; it broke the troubles apart with moments of joy. It provided rest.

I contend, with no proof, and no academic authority, that without Shabbat, life as a Jew would simply have been too much. We wouldn't have made it.

It was the tiny brightness of a chicken meal and a few songs that made getting through the week possible.

That's what it used to be anyway. By the time we hit the modern age, life for Jews was generally not a slog. Things changed after the war, and what once was a scraping together of pennies to get a chicken became piles of pastrami, gallons of chicken soup, and an annoying time-out to the week.

Then came the internet that shattered our attention, sinking its fiber-optic tentacles into our cerebellums and making it impossible to read past the headline of an article without clicking a pop-up link to a "fail compilation" on YouTube.

Shabbat now has a lesson for the modern age. A time-out is what we all want. In this way it's got this bizarre mystical quality to it, like the ancient hand of heaven is reaching out with a gift we'd almost forgotten we needed. Twenty-four hours of internet-free, work-ending rest? Who *doesn't* need that?

It was like that with me as well—the services, hours I'd loathed when I was young, became filled with more than meaning . . . they became filled with healing. Healing from the loss of my father. And slowly, healing from the community of my father. Judaism healed me from Judaism.

Each Shabbat, I'd go to temple and, through my pain, forge a new and personal connection with the spiritual tradition that was my unwanted birthright. Here then was something active I could do to put back the pieces that my father's death had shattered. Each Mourner's Kaddish drew me closer to the faith of my father. And maybe that's its point. Not so much to repair the loss but to replace it with something else. A connection to your spirit and your people, a people who reach back in time all the way to Ur, to Abraham, to Moses, to Jerusalem, to the Exile, to the Holocaust, to the Diaspora, to the Lower East Side, to Seagate, to my dad, to me, to now.

In this way I came to feel that nothing is over when it comes to death. It's simply another note in a six-thousand-year symphony; one that you're both playing and hearing and feeling and dancing, always dancing. Another melodic point of light in the grand web that has a beginning but no end.

My relationship with Judaism, unlike my relationship with the raves or AA or Burning Man, feels permanent. It feels residual. It feels like it's soaked into my bones, a twist in my DNA helix. And that's literally true in some sense. Every time I look at my insanely hairy arms I am reminded of the woolly desert people from whence I came. It's in me culturally, too. My identity is forged from my people. From their stories. From their suffering. From their triumph.

My relationship with Judaism now is one of skeptical affection. Unlike AA, I can take what I want and leave the rest. It's settled into me.

More than anything, that's what I've been left with. A skepticism pretty similar to the kind you have for family. You know how you roll your eyes at your mother when she sends you the eightieth text message in a day about crime stats in a city forty miles from you? Or an article on how forest fires are affecting asthma rates in mountain towns or a recipe for lemon halva cups from *The New York Times* even though you've told her so many times to stop sending you any texts that she didn't write herself? But still, when she invites you to lunch, you go.

Because she's your mom. And please substitute another close person in for your mom if your mom was wildly abusive. Just go with me here.

That's how I feel about Judaism now. It's my mom. I roll my eyes at all of its absurdity and keep it moving. What's more is after a lifetime of feeling Judaically inferior, I'm at the point now where I got what I always wanted: a stable and secure sense of smug superiority. I love my new position as "guy who gets it." Oh, you feel that way about Israel? Ah yes, I remember that feeling well. Lots of us felt that way. Talk to me in ten years, pal. Oh, you think *that* about the divine nature of the Bible? Sure, buddy, sounds good, whatever floats your beard.

I remember once, when I was at a Shabbat dinner at a Hasidic family's house, I engaged in this really epic and intense dialogue with a young Hasid about why I chose not to spend my life engrossed in Torah study. He was alight with all the profound gifts he got from a lifestyle spent engrossed in Jewish texts and rituals. His mind, he said, had become fine-tuned and his spirit felt stimulated like it was on a supercharger. I told him about my life and my path and why I was the way I was. About how Judaism was a vessel for me, but within that vessel there was room for other philosophies, other modalities. My vessel contained room for the world. Back and forth we went, debating and dialoguing in the traditions of our ancestors. It was a powerful, deep, and intimate conversation. He really got me, and I really got him. This man was my spiritual and intellectual brother. Then, about an hour into our conversation, he looked at me with wise eyes and said, "You see, these books are so powerful because when they were written, there were people, the people who wrote them, who had the power to actually *fly*."

"Sorry, what?" I said, not sure if he was speaking in metaphor. "To . . . fly, you said?"

"That's right!" he smiled. "They would say a secret name of God and literally fly into the air, like birds."

Never in my life have I had such a profound intellectual connection to a person come to such an abrupt and total stop. My eyes went wide, and I excused myself to the bathroom.

And that's basically my relationship with Judaism. I love it, it's endlessly stimulating, but there are parts of it that are the same as *Harry Potter* to me.

After six thousand years, I feel an awesome responsibility to carry on, in my small way, this legacy into which I was born. I don't do it well or all that respectfully, but I do it because it's so deeply and fundamentally interlaced with who I am that I couldn't stop if I tried.

· · ·

After the Tree of Life synagogue shooting in October 2018, I posted something on Twitter about how it feels to live in a world so infected with anti-Semitism. My wife begged me to delete it. She just didn't want my response to such violence to be, "Look at me! Jew here! Please don't hurt my family!" I get it. She's new to it, new to life as a Jew in the world, having recently converted. But the truth is, the option of being silent about who I am doesn't feel like an option at all. I have to declare who I am in order that the people who killed my ancestors for who they were do not succeed. I've received death threats and anti-Semitic hate mail my *entire* career. That's part of what it means to live in the public eye as a Jew.

Being a Jew means making peace with anti-Semitism. Sometimes that is in small humiliating ways. It can mean that you occasionally look at the news and realize, *damn,* another cool rapper or athlete or actor or comic I like is spouting off a weird, regurgitated theory about Jewish control, or about how Jews aren't really Jews but some kind of con-race who shape-shifted into an ethnic identity in order to wrap their fingers further around the puppet strings of society. Sigh . . . no more Ice Cube for me. Ah fuck, just read his Wikipedia and now no more Roald Fuckin' Dahl?! The *Willy Wonka* guy?! Shit, I loved Pink Floyd; damn, now Kanye, too? Not Kanye. Please not Kanye.

Then, compounding your frustrations, are the errant tweets and comments from people you are actually friends with, people you've known for years, yes-and-ing these foul ideas, throwing a devil's advocate over here, a "Where's the lie?" over there, or suggesting the backlash to this kind of hate speech is, itself, evidence of the very conspiracy theory espoused in the first place. Defending yourself against bigotry is used as proof that the bigotry is based on something real. That's gaslighting that you never quite get used to, which basically boils down to: "If you weren't guilty of being hateable, why do so many people hate you?"

It's a mindfuck.

It leaves you feeling like people in your life harbor a secret hatred or at least a soft subconscious bias against you. It makes you paranoid. It makes you have . . . well . . . a persecution complex. It makes you feel like other Jews are the only people you can actually count on to push back against it.

Are Jews the only minority that feel this way? Of course not. But I'm not another minority. I can only tell you what it can feel like to be a Jew.

When my wife converted, she took nineteen four-hour classes and suffered through the indignities of "Prayer-robics" in Rabbi Neal Weinberg's "Judaism by Choice" program.

The class was made up of my wife and me, a few other young couples, some single seekers, and ten Instagram thirst-trap-level hot South American women who were marrying seventy-five-year-old Israeli guys that drove Bentleys. Those guys *never* attended the classes. I came to every one, because I am an amazing husband and have no Bentleys. Actually, I was just grateful she was willing. It's an insane thing to ask a woman, "Hey, wanna leave your identity behind and join mine?" I never asked her to do that. When she volunteered, it was the biggest gift she'd given me to that point other than allowing me to park my RV on our property.

Jews don't usually get the chance to hear what Judaism sounds like to a neophyte. It's a tough sell. The laws, the rules, the hate, the struggle, the endless history . . . care to join?

At the end of the program, she sat before a tribunal of rabbis who asked her, "Are you certain you want to tether yourself to the fate of the Jewish people? There may be catastrophe. And you will be linked to that catastrophe."

And in that question was more of a lesson on being Jewish than the entire nineteen-week course. Even this moment of joy and celebration must be punctuated with the memory and the possibility of catastrophic pain.

When we got married, we smashed a glass underfoot to make the ritual official. Jews do this to remind every couple that even in your joy, you must never forget the pain of our people. Even as you consecrate the temple that is your home together, you recall the destruction of the temple in Jerusalem (Tisha B'av, baby!).

It's a dour worldview. Because ours is a dour history. But it is ours.

Through it all, through thousands of years of oppression, through endless wandering, through a hate so ancient it seems like a primordial force, through all attempts to end us: *We are still here.*

And that's what I tell my daughter, who I've now dropped into the timeless river that is our people, mightier than the Jordan: You are a part of this, too. If you choose to, you can dive in. If you choose to, you can dip a toe. If you choose to, you can leave the river altogether, but even then, it will flow with a little part of you in it. Your existence, your birth, your birthright is what keeps the river flowing. And though we may weep on the banks of that river when we remember Zion, we laugh, too, when we remember Abraham, Moses, King David, Rachel, Leah, Rabbi Hillel, the Rambam, Rashi, the Ba'al Shem Tov, Alfred Dreyfus, Einstein, the uprisers at the Warsaw Ghetto, the last Jew of Lublin, Golda, Koufax, Sammy Davis, Jr., Mel Brooks, Dylan, Drake, the Beastie Boys, Zeidi, Duvid Kasher, my father, your mother, me, you.

You're a drop in the river. But because of you, we are still here.

And then we light the Shabbat candles.

6 *Comedy, or Funny over Everything*

Stand-up comedy is an art form with a chip on its shoulder, mainly about its legitimacy as an art form in the first place. You can tell how insecure comics are about stand-up as art by how often and how fervently they refer to it *as* art. You're not hearing a lot of sculptors calling sculpture "art." It's like, yeah, Rodin, we know.

It always reminds me of those types of dudes who broadcast how tough they are and how much ass they can kick. Real ass kickers stay quiet until they have their boot in your butt.

I think it's because we spent *so long* in unartful spaces, doing canned, interchangeable jokes, being called vulgarians and rank provocateurs, that we became convinced of our own non-artfulness even as we evolved into, yes, an art form. This evolution was slow. It took more than a hundred years for people to finally begin to laud stand-up comics as more than shticky detergent salesmen, selling bits for Borax.

Of course, there was already comedy. Comedy is really old. Before vaudeville and burlesque you had Greeks flipping each other's togas up and ramming cucumbers up each other's asses and calling it political satire. Aristotle called comedy one of the four original forms of literature along with tragedy (sad shit), epic poetry (shit you write while on LSD), and lyrical poetry (Tupac shit).

In the king's court, there were jesters who wore bell hats and had secret clown sex with princesses. For the common people, there were roving bands of bawdy bards who would sing dirty songs for mead.

After that bullshit, you had, I guess, farce, which was essentially British and French titterings about adultery and how aristocrats fart, too. All of this stuff took place outside of the United States, mostly because it didn't exist yet.

But stand-up comedy is an American art form, and while it may have ridden on the back of European tradition, it is homegrown. It is one of the gifts given to the world by the American experiment alongside rock and roll and the folksy wisdom of the Huckabee family.

The earliest, proto-stand-ups toured in medicine shows and Wild West revues, exchanging stage time for an hour or two in front of a circus tent, barking to disinterested passersby that there was a tincture for sale inside that would cure their diphtheria.

As America settled down from an outwardly expanding territory to a developed piece of stolen land, the traveling road show made way for permanent theaters. These were not playhouses like their cousins in Europe; their owners realized they could eschew the plot and expensive set design of the theater and focus on what people wanted: spectacle and laughs.

In between variety acts like strong men and tap-dancing children held in indentured servitude, comedians would come onstage to reset the room by telling a few jokes. Thus began the era of vaudeville comedy and its filthy cousin, burlesque. From the stages of such theaters came the Marx Brothers, the Three Stooges, Abbott and Costello,* and Milton Berle.

---

* Abbott and Costello hit the big time when they recorded their famous "Who's on First?" routine. Except it wasn't their routine. At the time, material, particularly at the burlesque-theater level, was largely open source; if you could memorize it, you could perform it. Prior to radio and film, what did it matter if Abbott and Costello were doing it in Cleveland and another comic duo was doing it in Boston? But once Abbott and Costello recorded themselves doing it, it blew them into the big time, and the routine was forever associated with them, to the horror of everyone else who made a living from the same bit. This kind of foundational insecurity about whose routine belonged to whom led to, in my opinion, stand-up comedy's obsession with smoking out joke thieves. In our collective subconscious, we have the intergenerational memory of the entire art form being built on borrowed material, and we work like mad to make sure that never happens again.

In the early 1900s there was a vaudeville theater in every town in America, and in the seedy part of that same town were a group of dirty comics that the vaudeville comics looked down upon.

Vaudeville was, at least eventually, defined by its family friendliness, and if you wanted to "work blue," which at the time I think just meant making googly eyes at a ruffled butt on a dancing damsel, you'd have to head the burlesque show.

Vaudeville comedy was so antiseptically clean that one prominent owner of a string of theaters set the standards as "Don't say *slob*, or *son of a gun*, or *hully gee*." This is a pretty far cry from Patrice O'Neal's "I love pussy farts" bit. Performers received censorship notes in blue envelopes that would outline specific lines in a comic's act to avoid saying. The comic risked being blackballed if those notes were ignored. These blue envelopes are why we say dirty comics "work blue."

How did these performers avoid working blue? By focusing on much more wholesome forms of entertainment: unceasing ethnic stereotypes. The squeaky-clean shows of vaudeville leaned heavily on what was called a "dialect comedian," essentially an act where a comic dressed up as his favorite ethnicity and performed an act filled with the buffoonery of that group. America being an immigrant nation, audiences were delighted by watching what it was really like when a German tries to order a washing machine but cannot help but call it a "wiener washer."

There is much talk about the good old days of comedy, where you could get away with anything, but the insidious hand of PC culture had already infected comedy one hundred years before the term *PC culture* was even coined. As far back as the 1900s people were complaining about the racist lambasting of these groups by the dialect comics.

When Groucho Marx campaigned to end dialect comedy in vaudeville, arguing that it was hurtful, famous dialect comics pushed back by saying that the Scots and Swedes, often the target of such comedy, weren't complaining, so neither should Marx about the characterization of Black people and Jews. Marx's reply? That Scots and Swedes had the privilege not to be offended because they "were not a minority being subject to oppression, restriction, segregation or persecution." Does this argument from one hundred years ago sound familiar? That systemic oppression changes the context in which racial humor is received? That positions of power matter when talking about race? Apparently people were exhorting comedians to punch up even when the punches were delivered in that old-timey "clean your clock" boxing stance. We have been having the same conversations about comedy for a century, then forgetting we had them and pretending that the generation before us was not burdened by such concerns.

With the advent of radio and movies, people suddenly realized that they no longer needed to pay for a ticket to see their favorite acts; they could listen to them from the comfort of their living rooms. With that came the death of vaudeville.

Theaters closed. Only Milton Berle's legendarily gigantic penis survived. It was too big to fail.

Comics who hadn't made it as radio or film stars had significantly fewer stages to perform on and significantly less audience to watch them. Comics wallowed in prime beef huts and Jewish getaway camps for years before someone realized that comedy could be used as more than a distraction between jitterbug bands.

That someone was the mafia.

Once the vaudeville houses closed, the only places that still could draw crowds for nightlife were the speakeasies, serving drinks and entertainment through the years of Prohibition. Then Prohibition ended and those speakeasies turned into totally legal nightclubs owned and operated by friendly guys who would stuff dollar bills up your asshole after they murdered you. These guys were the first modern comedy bookers. As Kliph Nesteroff wrote in his expansive and riveting book about comedy's history, *The Comedians,* "If you were a stand-up comedian, you worked for the mob."

One night in 1927, a Chicago comic named Joe E. Lewis, having just gotten offstage at a club, made a fateful mistake. He decided to do a second set across town at a different nightclub. But every single nightclub was mob owned and, I'm not sure if you've heard about this, but sometimes mafia people have rivalries and seem to have a tendency to be territorial.

Joe did his second set, and afterward a group of goons paid him a visit, slicing his tongue almost entirely off. Was this the end of his comedy career? In fact no! Once Joe's tongue grew back together, the mob was so impressed that he hadn't snitched about the whole tongue-cutting thing, they took him back under their wing and turned him into a hugely successful comic with a now-pretty-strange speaking style and a really cool story to tell. Though I'm not sure why a comic with no tongue was lauded for not talking when he literally couldn't.

Comics were getting punched and cut left and right, but it was exciting (for me, now, to think about—probably less so if you were getting stabbed). For one thing, the prohibition on working blue was lifted. There was something about a club manager named Sammy "Tits" Galanti that made saying the word *tits* onstage seem a little more acceptable. In this violent underworld utopia, comics could work, drink, get high, have sex with the girls who worked the mob-affiliated strip clubs next door . . . life was good.

In this era an evolution began to take place: Stand-ups started to write their own material as a rule. Open-source acts and joke theft still happened all the time but slowly, as the years went by, people would begin to say, "Hey, that's a Jean Carroll joke," or "Hey, that's a Don Rickles joke."

Then, as often happens when you work with the mafia, the feds came along and ruined everything. In the late fifties, the federal government started to come after the mob and, slowly but surely, the nightclub heyday came to a close. Comics were, once again, left asking themselves where to perform and how to evolve.

When the comedy boom went bust, stand-ups started to perform alongside poets and beatniks at the cultural center for such artists, the coffee shops. And it was in these coffee shops that another great shift took place: For the first time, comics began to talk about themselves.

Which is wild to think about. For fifty years, comedians watched one another deliver canned jokes in tuxedos, and no one ever thought "Holy shit is this corny." No one thought to turn the spotlight within. Sure, people spoke in first person, but they never spoke personally. It was all jokes told from a thousand yards away. Joke book comedy. It was comedy as the crow flies. They were master performers, blisteringly funny kill machines who didn't care about the material as long as it got laughs. This is why comedy at that time was so riddled with joke theft; it's easy to steal a joke from someone who didn't even write the joke themselves and about which there was nothing personal.

But if a comic writes material from their gut, material that is really about them and the way they see the world, it becomes nearly impossible to steal.

Comedy slowly went from: "I saw a guy walking down the street" to "I was walking down the street" to "I hate walking down the street. I hate streets. I hate walking."

That's a monumental shift. The comic went from performer to personality. From thespian to thinker. From clown to critic. Mort Sahl ditched the tuxedo and folded a newspaper under his arm, content to talk about his feelings on politics. Jonathan Winters stopped telling jokes altogether and allowed his brain to flow in a stream of consciousness onto the stage, discovering what the show was about at the same time the audience did. And Lenny Bruce shot heroin. It's from these three comics that modern stand-up really proceeds. Stand-up, now sixty years old, had grown up and discovered what it was really about in the first place: A person standing onstage, opening up their brain and showing you what's inside.

I've often wondered how stand-up is enjoyable at all. It's just some person onstage with a mic talking about their thoughts. It's the ultimate narcissist's art form (other than memoir). Imagine thinking, "You know what would make a good night out for you? ME!"

And yet it kills. Nothing else even comes close in terms of how much and how hard an audience will laugh. A comedic play? If you're lucky you get five big laughs before the main character deliv-

ers their "clawing at the sky, reaching for God himself" final dramatic monologue that reveals what the play is really all about. A
clown performance? Has *anyone* over four (age or IQ points) ever
found a clown funny? A funny movie? Not even close to the number
of laughs a good comic can get (the art house films of the *Jackass*
franchise being an exception).

Stand-up, if successful, has the entire audience laughing (or at
least being pressured to laugh by group suggestion and a two-drink
minimum) the entire time. Every punch line. Every joke. If they
aren't laughing, you are failing. You. Must. Kill.

Killing like this is what ushered in the golden age of stand-up: the
1980s. The boom. Or, at least, the last boom before I started. Each
of these eras was its own boom, but when I started comedy in 2002,
it was in one of those post-boom eras, like the space between vaudeville and nightclubs, or between nightclubs and coffee houses. I
started comedy at a time when no one really liked stand-up and no
one really cared. Don't get me wrong; there were big, famous comics
when I began. But by and large, it was a dead form.

The eighties started out exciting with Johnny Carson showcasing
comedian after comedian and comedy clubs opening in every small
town in America. This is the era of the Dr. Grins and the Chuckle
Hut, of Coconuts and Yuk Yuks and the worst-named club of all
time, according to *Shecky* magazine (which, let's be honest, doesn't
really have a lot of room to talk name wise): the now defunct, actual
comedy club named "P. Yopantz."

This is the era of the rolled-up jacket sleeved, coked out, waitress-
fucking, airplane-food-noticing eighties comic. It's what personified
the term *hack* and has inspired tons of current comics, too frightened to do actual comedy, to do meta-impersonations of the '80s
comics. These anti-comedy acts started to turn ouroboros and actually became hacky themselves, there were so many of them.

Comedy blew up so hard, so fast, riding the wave of Carson
Fever, that there were not enough good comics to fill all the clubs.
Demand was up, supply was rotten. After a few years of sitting
through awful shows, audiences stopped coming to P. Yopantz (and
its ilk), which dried up and never P'd again.

The eighties boom was the stuff of legend when I started comedy. At its great height, comedy had been ruined. Chewed up and destroyed by hackiness. This was what to avoid, and the road to avoidance was forked: alternative comedy* and offensive comedy. Sometimes both. Alternative comedy won.

Until it didn't.

I grew up in Oakland, as I am wont to scream when I lose control in an argument. Whenever I mention Oakland in a screaming match, I know I've lost and it's time to walk away. In the public schools, as a poor white kid with a deaf mom who couldn't afford to buy me cool shoes, every day was a chance for my peers to roast me. It was relentless, sad, and, sadly, often funny. I figured out early that if I wanted to survive I had to go up to the biggest, toughest kid on the yard, rip his throat out, and scream to the other kids, "I drink blood, if anybody's serving!"

But I was too frightened to do that, so I didn't. I learned how to be funny instead.

I'd make my classmates laugh by turning the roast around on them. Did this get me slapped from time to time? Yes it did. But it also delighted my classmates. I'd write elaborate fantasy stories, turning kids in the class into characters. I'd read them aloud to the howls of the students. I'd make a performance of measuring how wide the ass of my third-grade teacher was, sneaking up behind her with a ruler like a foreman on a job.

My grades were always lousy. I was diagnosed with learning dis-

---

* Alternative comedy was a response to the corniness of eighties comedians. It was created by a group of cool-kid comics in the late nineties who decided to eschew all the tropes of what comedy was supposed to look and sound like. So many great comics came out of this school (Patton Oswalt, Maria Bamford, Kumail Nanjiani, David Cross, Janeane Garofalo, Hannibal Buress, John Mulaney, and so many more), and so many bad ones, too. (Are you kidding? I'm not gonna name names. No fucking way.) It's not an exaggeration to say that for the first ten years I did comedy, this school was the only place anyone was looking for new talent.

abilities and ADHD, and I was always in trouble. And yet, in fourth grade, my teacher Mr. Wong pulled me aside and told me he wanted me to write the school play. He'd noticed how much I made the kids laugh and thought I'd make a great playwright. Boy, was he ever right. He also asked some talentless hack who got straight As to co-write it with me to ensure that, unlike my homework, I would actually complete the job. We were like a young Rodgers and Hammerstein sitting down to write a musical about the pioneers moving to San Francisco from the dust bowl in search of the "gold in them thar hills." We named it *Westward Ho!*

Jokes I could do, but I'd never written a song, so we just pilfered U2's catalog in a rousing allegorical rendition of "I still haven't found what I'm looking for." (It was gold.)

Not only was this my first commission as a playwright, but I was also cast as the lead pioneer in the play, becoming the first Jew in history to ride a stagecoach.

I had arrived.

But I was also obnoxious and constantly getting in trouble. One day, after repeatedly asking me to behave, Mr. Wong had had enough. I was standing out of line some morning, performing for the assembled students, when Mr. Wong grabbed me and yelled that I was hereby uncast as the lead and demoted to Indian Number Two.

This was a humiliating fall from grace, and by the time opening night arrived I was shaking with disappointment as I delivered my only line: "We are friends; we are here to help you. Here, take these berries." Of course there are no small parts, only small children, and I delivered this chewy, Sorkin-esque dialogue with aplomb. I'd had my start in showbiz. I'd tasted glory and disappointment.

I was hooked.

Around the same time, my brother, who is handsome, somehow got noticed by a child modeling agency in San Francisco called Stars. They wanted him to start modeling. So, of course, I thought, I should start modeling, too. After all, if it was stars they wanted, I'd *almost* starred in *Westward Ho!* I submitted my headshots and waited as my brother got audition after audition. Stars was playing hard to get, so I started accompanying my brother on trips to the agency whenever they'd invite him in. I'd sit in the lobby trying to look extremely fuckable, but I was nine years old and chubby. Finally, they lowered the boom: I was not wanted by the Stars Agency. I was simply a child of six and they worked with nines and above like my dumbass brother (who has never, to this day, written a musical).

But I didn't give up on my dream. I adjusted it. I attempted to do theater throughout high school, which was difficult to maintain between dropouts, drug addiction flare-ups, straight Fs, and getting in physical fights with the theater teacher.

Many years later I went back to college and took acting and screenwriting classes. I played a Vietnam vet in a student production of *Tracers* and won a one-act-play contest with an over-the-top abstract piece about school shootings told through a reimagining of "The Boy Who Cried Wolf" fable. I'm ashamed to admit I named it *The Wolf Who Cried Boy.*

I had a monologue published in a book called *Monologues for Men by Men, Volume Two,* which was an unfathomably dramatic piece about a young man getting AIDS that would probably destroy my career if it was ever discovered (it's available on Amazon right now through the subsidiary "Thriftbooks-Phoenix" in Used: Very Good condition).

I was wrestling between writing and acting (unaware of my true destiny as a multi-hyphenate) and believed I was close to becoming the next great American monologist like Spalding Gray or Eric Bogosian, when I took a fateful trip to New York in the summer of 2000.

My friend and a great comedian, Chelsea Peretti, was living in New York at the time. She and I had grown up together and had studied improv in her basement one summer, poring over Dario Fo and the book *Impro* by Keith Johnstone and acting out absurdly long-form improvs. Just the two of us.

When I came to New York, I looked her up and she told me she'd started doing stand-up. I kind of had no idea what she was talking about. I wasn't much of a stand-up aficionado growing up. I thought it was cool to listen to Andrew Dice Clay's filthy album *Dice* in the car with my deaf mom driving: "Hickory dickory dock, if my mom could hear she'd be in shock."

I loved early Eddie Murphy albums and Adam Sandler's first album was required listening for any Jewish boy in the 1990s looking to get Bar Mitzvahed. But other than that, and my frustratingly handsome brother playing me Janeane Garofalo's *HBO Comedy Half Hour,* where she seemed like the coolest, funniest person alive, stand-up comedy had had very little impact on my life. I hadn't seen much; it didn't mean much to me.

But on that trip to New York, I had a one-two punch of experiences that changed everything.

The first was *seeing* live comedy for the first time. Chelsea took me to the hottest comedy show in New York at the time, "Eating It" at the Luna Lounge. There, I saw Sarah Silverman followed by Patrice O'Neal. I had no idea who they were and no idea what I was watching. This was *so much worse* than Dice. His offensiveness seemed quaint in comparison. They were vicious, transgressive, and *fucking hilarious.* I don't really remember what they said but I know Patrice made fun of Michael J. Fox's Parkinson's disease tremors and I was totally shocked but also alight with mental possibilities.

This was the trend in comedy in the early aughts, which I would deem the "funny over everything" days. It was the sweet spot of history right between the finger-wagging church-centered morality of the past and the finger-wagging social-justice-centered morality of the future. It was also one of the times in history when people were paying attention to comedy the least, so you could say anything, do anything, get away with anything, as long as it was funny. It was a great time to start out.

Here were performers who had stripped away all of the pompousness of the theater and were just bleeding battery acid all over the stage. It had never occurred to me until that show that just being funny for its own sake was and could be a performative goal and a skill to hone.

In AA, the main place in my life at that point where I attempted to "get laughs," it was always in service of a broader rhetorical goal. To carry the message and get people sober. That night I had a profound alteration. Being funny, as funny as you could be, was a goal in itself and not an insufficient one. Besides being transgressive and edgy, I'd never seen anything close to as funny as Sarah and Patrice. Not anywhere. They seemed superhuman.

The next night I had an experience nearly as profound at a much smaller, much lower-key show. Chelsea was performing at a small bar show she cohosted with Bobby Tisdale, and I went to watch. Now, here was a very different show and a very different energy. Bobby played the piano and worked the room. It was much more playful and fun than the night before. It was loungy. The comedy was kinder. Then Chelsea did a set and again I was walloped. She was funny. *Really* funny. This was a person I *knew*. A woman I'd grown up with, went to Oakland public schools with. A friend. Not a superhuman, a human.

And she was *killing*.

I suddenly realized that stand-up was the amalgamation of everything I'd been doing. It was writing *and* performing. Not only that, it was something I could do. Or at least something I could try. I told Chelsea I would. This was in June. She was coming to San Francisco in August. I vowed to her that by the time she came, I'd have written five minutes and asked her if she'd take me to an open mic.

And with that, my fate was sealed.

My first open mic was in an art gallery called the Luggage Store Gallery on Market Street in San Francisco. It was hosted by a kind of impresario of the San Francisco open mic scene, the mayor of mics, Tony Sparks. Tony is a man whose destiny is clearly tied up in encouraging people. He's bright and supportive and positive, and when you perform at one of Tony's shows for the first time, he'll bring you up by setting you up for as much success as possible.

"Okay, we have a brand-new performer here tonight at the Luggage Store, and you know what that means, what are we gonna give him?!" he yelled at the crowd, who answered back, "A lot of love!"

"That's right!" screamed Tony. "A lot of love! Give it up real big for Moshe Kasher!!!!"

I walked up, took the stage, and started in. I'd worked hard those three months to come up with something to fill the five minutes I'd promised Chelsea. The first joke I ever wrote was actually somewhat sophisticated, a longer bit about how being gay used to be considered a psychological disorder, how it no longer is, and so how much fun would it be if, in the future, the trend continued and cities everywhere had a schizophrenic pride parade. I still remember the punch lines: "We schizophrenics are everywhere today! We are doctors! We are lawyers! We are dark servants of the evil lord Agamemnon!" Then I described the schizophrenic pride parade: 'Look, all the prominent schizophrenics are here! Look, it's Bill, and Susan and Tracy and Tom and . . ."

Then in another voice I answered myself, "No it's just you!"

Voice One answered back, "It's just me? Then who are you?!"

Voice Two responded calmly, "I'm also you. Kill your parents."

I was proud of the bit. And rightfully so. It killed! I then spent years writing nothing remotely close to as good. It was like a little gift of inspiration that got me past the threshold.

I started doing what comics do. Going onstage over and over and over again until I figured out who I was up there.

Open mics are brutal. As they should be. If you can't tough it through those opening stanzas of brutality, then you are sure not going to be able to stick it out through the much more soul-crushing moments that are to follow.

When you start, you don't have any idea you are fortifying yourself for a profession. You hardly know what you are doing there. You just want a set. Everyone's first years in comedy are characterized by waiting around for hours, watching the shittiest comedy you can imagine in order that you might eventually get onstage and do four minutes of material in front of the very performers you just rolled your eyes at.

You just want to get onstage. All the time. The more you get onstage the better you get. There is no other way to improve. Your tongue and your mind are the blade, and you have to put them to the whetstone of the stage and smell the chemical-burn smoke rise off as you sharpen yourself into the comic you are supposed to be.

Earlier in this book I told the story of Michelangelo's *David*, how he "chipped away all the parts that weren't David" until he found his masterpiece, and that's how stage time works, too. Personas aren't generally crafted; they are discovered. You perform every night, inching closer and closer to who you will settle into as a performer, all the while getting funnier and funnier (hopefully).

Those early years were fun as hell. And in the Bay Area, they were diverse as hell. In the early 2000s if you wanted to get onstage every day, you had to work a variety of rooms. Monday was Coach's, a Black bar in Richmond, California, which is like Oakland, only even more Oakland than Oakland. Tuesday was the Luggage Store where you got "A LOT of love" from "A LITTLE audience"; Wednesdays we went to Kimball's, a Caribbean nightclub that sold tickets to see nonprofessional white comics bomb in front of Black audiences, which is incredible entertainment in its own right. Thursdays was the marquee open mic in San Francisco, the Brainwash, where there was an actual attentive audience, seeing as the Brainwash was a laundromat and thus you were guaranteed the attention of people for at least as long as it took their underwear to dry.

By going back and forth between white rooms and Black rooms, alternative and regular rooms, all comics in the Bay Area learned how to adjust their acts and attempt to kill in different rooms with different tastes. What the grown and sexy crowd who'd been conned into buying a ticket to Kimball's wanted was different from what the people at the Brainwash wanted, which was fabric softener. On the weekends we did whatever booked shows we could. Some in bars, some in clubs, and sometimes, if we were lucky, we worked the road.

The first real road gig I ever got was at a place called the Fat Cat in Modesto, California. It was one of these comedy venues where they'd lure a crowd to the show by promising them free admission to the dance club that would be starting up as soon as the comedy was done. These people didn't give a single fuck about the show; they just wanted to get their groove on to "I Want It That Way" while drinking the coffee martini they'd be vomiting up later after getting into a fistfight with their sister-in-law.

This was the real road, the depressing road. Not the "I'm going to New York to perform for my fans" road, but the "I'm going to an agricultural community in the middle of California to perform for people antagonistic to my very existence" road. But I was *so* excited. It was my first out-of-town gig, my first comped hotel room, my first everything. A huge moment for me.

Then the show started. At some point early in my set I said, "So, I'm Jewish—"

Someone booed. Not at the joke. At the identification of a Jew in their midst. Apparently the shock of seeing a stand-up comedian from the Jewish faith was too much for this person to handle. Which, fair enough, I am one of the first of my people to ever try the form. Him being a Nazi, I attacked, and then something odd but familiar to any comedian happened: The audience turned on *me*! When he booed (I know I didn't identify him as a guy, but c'mon, you already knew it was) the audience was shocked and appalled by it. Of course they were. But the moment I went after him, called him out for what he'd done, I was the one that was making things weird. Me! In those moments of heckling that goes beyond drunk and good-natured and into "final solution" territory or similar, the audience expects you to perform a magic trick. Accept the cruelty, shut it down, but do it in a fun, entertaining way. If you can't do that? They will only remember the weird night you made them have, just like a typical Jew.

That show was *brutal*. But the road is like that. Some shows can be unexpected delights and some feel like actual perilous danger. The Fat Cat was my first out-of-town gig and also the first time I ever told a booker I didn't think I would return. When I told him that, I thought my career might be over. The booker of the Fat Cat would blacklist me, and I'd be done in that town.

The anti-Semitic Fat Cat incident did not end my career. We would work *anywhere*. Anywhere there was stage time, I'd claw my way in. It was the only way to do it. It requires almost everything of you to really learn how. I've performed at frat parties and pleasure cruises, dive bars, synagogues, senior citizen centers, public schools, Burning Man, AA conventions, dance parties, even Montana.

I hit the road again, this time to the Pacific Northwest, with the comic Alex Koll and me opening for the brilliant and odd comedian Brent Weinbach. We crawled up the coast, performing at black box theaters and rock clubs in Portland, Seattle, and Vancouver. These shows were stage-time manna from the heavens, audiences of cool kids with tattoos who got *Star Trek* references. But not every show could be like that. To pay the bills, we had to supplement the tour by driving long distances to small colleges throughout the Northwest. Colleges can be amazing, and they can be insanely awful. Attendance is at the mercy of whether or not a Bible study group on campus is giving away free pizza that night. Some nights there will be a huge enthusiastic crowd; some nights you'll be performing to six students in a cafeteria that can seat two thousand as you try to yell your jokes over the din of an industrial dishwasher. My wife once did a college where she was double booked against Jell-O wrestling. I mean, c'mon, Jell-O wrestling or comedy? What would *you* choose?

We closed these shows with a sketch, an audience participation bit where we'd extend a hand to an audience member and bring them onstage as the reader to "Help Brent with an Audition."

At one show, I tried a newer bit about how important it was to warn a friend when you bring a guest over who is an amputee or has some sort of a mangled hand, a brilliant and searing Carlin-esque deconstruction of the panic one feels when reaching out to shake a hand that is not there. Is it the best bit I have ever written? Well, it did set up one of the biggest karmic callbacks in my career. Brent began the audition sketch that would end the show, and when he reached down to help the audience member who would serve as the reader that night onto the stage, as luck would have it, the student he selected raised her arm, and her hand was just a thumb and two fingers. She looked right at me as if to say "Fuck you." The crowd oohed as if to say "Fuck you." I looked to the heavens as if to say "Oh, fuck me!" Not only was this humiliating to me, my ableist masterpiece was completely sabotaged when Brent, a perfect gentleman, grabbed her hand with ease and comfort. He could have at least pretended to recoil in shock to protect me! In the end, the show went fine, the girl was a good sport about it, all was well. It was just comedy grist for the mill. The mill that had crushed her index and ring fingers. I never told that joke again, except right now, where I'm putting it in permanent print for some reason. We jumped into the car, on to the next show.

We crossed the border into Montana. The speed limit became an infinity sign. I was cooking, doing about ninety. We laughed as the moment we crossed the state line, grim anti-meth billboards began dotting the landscape every few miles. BEFORE METH I HAD A DAUGHTER . . . NOW I HAVE A PROSTITUTE! FIFTEEN BUCKS FOR SEX ISN'T NORMAL . . . BUT ON METH IT IS! On one there was a photo of a filthy bathroom stall and the text: NOBODY THINKS THEY WILL LOSE THEIR VIRGINITY HERE . . . METH WILL CHANGE THAT! Montana seemed like it might be really fun!

The entire tour Brent had been complaining about my then-vegan diet and the "garbage farts" it produced. As we hit the 90 mph zone and perhaps to get my revenge for the hand bit, I clicked the window lock and unleashed a torrent of vegan garbage nerve gas. Brent clawed desperately at the window, trying to let some fresh Montana air in, but he was trapped. Doing the only thing he felt he could in that moment, he ripped the door open at nearly one hundred miles per hour. I screamed at him to close the door, that death was certain; he screamed back that he could not, that he preferred death to one more breath. There we were, screaming through Montana, our lives in our well-formed hands. It was like an episode of *Yellowstone*. That's how I'll always remember that tour, or as I call it, "My last trip before I got addicted to meth."

In the Bay Area on Sunday nights, every comedian gathered at the best show in town for up-and-coming comics, the showcase held at the legendary San Francisco Punch Line. My first night there I saw an old friend from community college, the comic Jacob Sirof, and we caught up. I told him I had just finished dinner with some non-comedy friends and his jaw dropped. He was appalled. "You still hang out with your old friends? You can't do that anymore. You'll never make it." This seemed insane to me, and still does, but it shows you exactly the length to which comics are willing to go to make it. Give it your entire life and, maybe 25 percent of the time, you will get a career in return.

The barrier to entry at the Punch Line was insanely high. You were expected to attend the Sunday night showcase sitting at the back bar for at least a year, often up to two years, in order to finally be asked to do one five-minute set. The booker, Molly, a striking redhead like the human half of a mermaid, covered in tattoos, filled with confidence and totally in charge of your fate, was the most intimidating person I had ever seen or interacted with in my life.

She held the key, so we all fell over ourselves to come up with things to talk to her about. When someone mentioned she was obsessed with the Dave Matthews Band, we'd come in humming "Crash into Me," just hoping she'd talk to us about it.

Molly had this torturous way of telling comics their time had come to perform. She'd walk up to a sitting comic, during the show, while another comic was onstage, point, and say, "You're next." I've never gotten her to admit it, but she also did this thing where, on approach, she'd kind of look at two or three comics at once, never quite focusing on anyone specifically, so that all three comics would sit up eagerly, preening and looking stage-ready, thinking this was their moment. Then, just at the peak of expectation, she'd crush you, pointing dramatically at the comic sitting next to you. "*You're* next." You'd shrink, defeated, in your chair and think, "Maybe next time."

I waited the full two years, smoldering, resentful at what I deemed to be the awful acts of some of the regulars on the show. I couldn't believe it. Come on. I was certainly better than them.

"Fuck it," I decided. "I'll do my own shows."

My years in the rave scene taught me that all you need to have a good time is a space, some flyers, and a will to produce. My farter partner Brent Weinbach and I started putting on small theater shows with the best young alternative comics in the Bay Area. Show by show, we began to sell out every time. We did shows at punk bars and abandoned factories, at art galleries and small theaters. We gave stage time to weird acts and, because it was the Bay Area, to more traditional stand-ups as well. We started getting notice for the shows and won a couple of "Best of" contests in the local free papers. People in our little scene started to get attention. We also started to lap the comics who'd come up before us, pissing them off, making them jealous. I was jealous, too. Everyone was jealous of everyone.

It was the time of my life. We lived for the next set. It was life in the trenches of comedy. We would try anything onstage. We would bomb, kill, bomb again, and then go make fun of each other for it at an all-night diner. We began to realize this was the beginning of a life, a career, a friendship circle, a scene.

It finally came. My time to shine. I did the Punch Line and proved to myself what I believed already: I was funny. Then I waited for my next spot. It took months. I was getting frustrated.

At the periphery of the group of comics I started with, the most driven and most quickly in touch with their comedic gifts started to get whisked off to Hollywood to be fawned over and offered things. They got selected for coveted spots at comedy festivals like the Montreal Just for Laughs festival and the HBO Comedy Arts Festival in Aspen. They started to get agents and managers, and some of them even got the elusive holy grail for young comics: a TV spot.

Meanwhile, I was still waiting for another five-minute spot at the Punch Line. People started to move away to go begin their careers. I felt like quitting.

I began to feel insane. One by one, all of my peers who I'd started with had gotten the gifts I imagined would make me whole.

I became obsessed with getting on TV. I'd lie in bed with a woman, and rather than my thoughts drifting to the naked lady in my bed, I'd imagine making my TV debut to the adoration of millions. Not even a naked lover was as attention grabbing as that.

I distinctly remember asking myself if I'd suck Jay Leno's dick for a spot on *The Tonight Show*. What was my answer? Let's just say I'd have needed a denim rag to wipe up. I wanted to move to L.A., but

I couldn't see how that would be a good idea without an agent, a manager, a spot on TV, or a festival.

I auditioned for Montreal's New Faces of Comedy showcase again and again and again. I got close but never got there. The conventional wisdom was that you needed a manager to get a spot on New Faces, but you needed New Faces to meet managers, so that wisdom didn't seem so wise.

Then it, finally, sorta happened.

They announced that Jamie Foxx was holding open auditions for a different New Faces show at an urban comedy festival called Laffapalooza in Atlanta. My years of performing in Black clubs made this feel less like an intimidating experience and more like a chance.

Plus, I'd already run the gauntlet of one of the most intimidating experiences the Black comedy scene had to offer. The comic Bruce Bruce had specifically requested a white opener for his sold-out weekend at the club Pepperbelly's (which no longer exists because it burned down after someone got literally murdered there), and I was thrilled when I got the call. It was six shows. Bruce Bruce and his crew barely acknowledged my existence when I said hi in the green room, but I was undeterred. I'd prove myself onstage. Then I saw the crowd, older, slightly conservative. Just before the first show, Bruce Bruce's middle act introduced himself and told me how to bring him up. "Say I've been on BET's *ComicView* and I write for Bruce. Oh, and the name's Black Boy."

"Hmm," I thought. "Interesting stage name." My shows ranged from kind of good to kind of bad, maybe because my whole set I knew what was coming: the introduction of the next comic. Six times I said, before an older, conservative, entirely Black audience, "Okay, that's my time. Now give it up for your next performer . . . Black Boy!"

You could hear the audience gasp, "What the fuck did he just say?!" They had no idea that was the guy's real name. They just thought I'd thrown caution to the wind and ended my set with a huge racist fuck-you to the next comic. I'd just stare at the floor and beeline to the back of the room and wait for Black Boy to clarify.

Luckily, he identified himself pretty early on in his set, so I could breathe a little easier. Each set, if I'd done well, Black Boy would compliment me and tell the crowd to give it up. If it had not gone well, he'd pretend we'd never met, and ask the crowd, "Who the fuck let him onstage?" Toggling back and forth for six sets like I was a stranger. I can still remember his opening joke, which still makes me laugh: "It's 2003, I better not hear another woman talking about how she has a big pussy. Bitch, that is not cute!" These days, in 2023, it has become very cute, but you know, times change.

So, yeah, auditioning for Laffapalooza didn't feel intimidating.

I'll never forget the call: "Moshe Kasher, this is Jon Johnson from Laffapalooza. You've been selected for the New Faces of Laffapalooza." I started leaping up and down in the elevator lobby of the Sorenson Video Relay Services center. I wouldn't be working there for long! This was it. My moment.

It was 2005. The appropriateness of me, a white guy, taking a spot at a Black comedy festival never occurred to me. I'd just attempted to enter the NBC diversity showcase by saying I had deaf parents. I was desperate. Which was why I didn't think about how weird it was that I had to buy my own flight to Laffapalooza.

By the way, I didn't need to be worried about taking the place of a comic of color. The moment I arrived, I realized I was there as the diversity hire, the white comic who rounded out the lineup. I was one of two white comics, the other was a guy named, I think, Weedman. He had an act where he just talked about getting high and closed by sticking his face in a huge prop hundred dollar bill and doing a stoned Benjamin Franklin character. I didn't think he posed much of a threat.

All the other new faces were as excited as I was. Until we arrived at the first show. For all the fanfare and the nationwide talent searches they'd done for this festival, they'd neglected to do literally any promotion for the shows themselves. At show after show, the audiences ranged from "literally no one" to "whoever we could convince at the bar next door to come watch a comedy show."

It was brutal, soul crushing, awful. Back at home these kinds of shows would have been just another unattended open mic, but since

I and the other comics there had thought this could be our big break, it hurt bad. Sure, there was no audience, but the festival *had* managed to get talent bookers from the Just for Laughs festival and Comedy Central to come to the "shows," watch us bomb in these impossible-to-succeed situations, and, therefore, form lasting and career-altering opinions of us. And maybe you think I'm being overly dramatic, that the bookers must have seen the circumstances we were in and not allowed these shows to cloud their opinions of us. Well, many years later, I straight-up asked the lady from Comedy Central about it after she'd finally started booking me on things, and she said, "Oh, yeah, I just always assumed you weren't funny after that. Sorry!"

There were actually a few good shows happening at the festival. The main-stage shows (which you can watch if you order the *Laffapalooza* DVD set on eBay) were produced in a hilariously duplicitous way. The festival advertised them as Cedric the Entertainer shows, but Cedric just came out and did five minutes, and then the audience was treated to a two-and-a-half-hour TV taping of comics they didn't know.

During these main-stage shows, which the New Faces were allowed to watch, perhaps as an aspirational exercise, observing what performing on a show with actual attendees would feel like, I saw one of the best TV tapings ever.

A somewhat short comic named Scruncho, who was a former Crip and looked so much like the rapper 50 Cent that we took to calling him 25 Cent, was onstage absolutely killing. So much so that he failed to see the sign that the line producer was furiously waving that read PLEASE WRAP UP!

Scruncho was twelve minutes into a seven-minute taping when he finally caught eyes with the panicked producer, who was flapping his arms back and forth trying to get Scruncho to stop. Scruncho now absolutely knew he needed to get offstage. But a look of mischief flashed in his eyes, he looked out at the audience, and said "Okay, y'all wanna take it to the *next level*?!" The producer started to panic, "NO! NO SCRUNCHO! PLEASE DON'T TAKE IT TO THE NEXT LEVEL!" It was too late, the next level was already in process of being tooken. Scruncho disappeared offstage and slipped on a pair of roller skates, and skated back onstage, skate moon-walking, skate C-walking, and doing the skate-splits. The crowd went absolutely insane with joy and the producer threw his head-phones off and walked straight out into traffic. That shit really was next level.

I, too, was ready to take shit to the next level. The festival was so comically disorganized that there was a "Best of New Faces" show that night at the comedy club in town, which assured it would have (GASP!) an audience, and none of the New Faces knew if they were on the show or not. Inspired by the confidence of Scruncho, I de-cided to not let this opportunity pass me by. I walked up to the booker and confidently said, "I need to be on that best-of show to-night." He smiled and said, "Okay." Fuck yes. I was going to rip that show so hard, I'd leave Weedman in the ashes of his bong.

When I arrived at the comedy club, oddly also named the Punch Line, oddly also booked by an intimidating beautiful hippie named Molly, I told her my name and she checked the list, shaking her head. "I don't have you down." This was a serious setback, but I was not going to be deterred. This trip had been a disaster, and I was determined that I'd at least get an inroad at this club out of it. In my back pocket was a VHS tape of my demo. I was gonna get up there, kill, and leave her with the tape to remember me by.

I insisted: "I'm supposed to be on the list. They told me I was. Please. Let me perform." Molly2 saw the look in my eye, the seri-ousness and desperation, the real comic in me. "Okay," she said. "I'll put you on last."

The show started at eleven, and after the "Best of New Faces" performed, it was approaching one-thirty in the morning. Weedman got on and absolutely fucking demolished. I started sweating. It was near two A.M. when I finally got onstage. Trying to hype them up, I asked the crowd, "You guys aren't tired, are you?!" As one voice, the entire audience chanted back, "Yes. We are."

I bombed so hard that I determined it wasn't worth the cost of a VHS tape to bother leaving my demo behind.

I flew home vibrating with grief and shame. What was I even

doing? All my friends had comedy credits, and all I had was a maxed-out credit card with a last-minute ticket to Atlanta on the statement. I thought this would be the high point of my career, but now I just felt like quitting. Again.

I arrived home on the Sunday before Halloween. The rule at the San Francisco Punch Line was that only performers in costume could get sets on the Sunday night before Halloween. The *last thing* I wanted to do was put a fucking costume on and go try again. I sat, head in hand, deciding what to do. I looked at my closet. "Fuck it," I thought. "I'll keep going." With incredible dignity, I pulled on a spandex iridescent astronaut jumpsuit and a plush, stuffed astronaut helmet, got in my car, and drove to the club. Molly walked right up to me, "You're next."

I got onstage at the second club called Punch Line in twenty-four hours.

And I fucking obliterated. I didn't have any roller skates, but I was dressed as an astronaut so in a way, I moonwalked. That set, on that night, in that place, broke something open in me. I clicked into myself as a comic in a way I knew felt tectonic. Maybe it was that one set, or everything that had led up to it, but I had leveled up. Comedy is not about whether you can succeed. It's about whether you can fail and keep going.

I decided I would.

With my funniest friends out of the picture in the Bay Area, and my skills at an all-time high, I started to spread my wings as a performer more and more. When I first started comedy, I was extremely loose onstage, going with whatever whim occurred to me, talking to the audiences, riffing on the space. My friend, and one of the best joke writers I know, Louis Katz, had scolded me years earlier for being too extemporaneous. "You're *too* loose for someone who's been doing it as long as you have," he told me. "Go learn to write jokes before you fuck around onstage." I took a few years and that's all I did.

After my breakthrough I decided that from now on, I would use the writing I had to allow me to go wherever I wanted onstage. On Sundays, where I was getting up more and more now, I would attempt to do my full set and never perform a single written joke, confident that I would find something up there that would make people laugh. I usually did. More and more this became my style and to this day the way I like to perform. The better the show, the more fun I'm having, the less written jokes I will end up telling.

Through talent, sheer will, and the process of elimination, I became the strongest comic left in the Bay Area from my generation. I was now at the peak of my powers, really in touch with exactly what it was that made *me* funny. But I was still no closer to having a manager, and no closer to an excuse to leave the Bay.

I'd been trying to present myself like a bright red baboon ass to managers for a while at that point, and no one had come over and mounted me. One day, an amiable and powerful older comedy manager reached out to me at the same time that a famous headliner, doing me a kindness, dropped my name to another, newer management company. I suddenly had two management companies flirting with me at once!

The older guy was my dream manager, a comedy powerhouse who had snagged most of my friends back in San Francisco. He was who I wanted to want me. The only problem was, he loved to dance around the idea of signing me, never quite pulling the trigger. One day, I asked him if his flirtations were leading to an official offer of representation.

Mistake number one.

I didn't know it then, but you *never* try to convince a manager to represent you. They should be falling all over themselves trying to convince *you* why you ought to pick *them*. At the time, though, I was so wide-eyed with desire for success that I couldn't see it.

"No," he said. "We aren't quite at the stage where we need to make things official, but I'm happy to help you out as you need it and I'd definitely want to know if anyone else was interested in representing you."

Ha! I had him.

"Well, that's why I'm asking actually. So-and-So over at What's-It-Called Management has been talking to me about just that."

I held my breath.

"Okay, let's make it official then!"

I was thrilled. I had a manager! I could move to L.A. now! Do you see the problem, though? Thirty seconds earlier he'd been unwilling to sign me. But now that someone else maybe wanted me, he'd said yes. How invested in my career did I think he would be?

Anyway, I ignored all that and began packing my bags and planning a move to Los Angeles. I had a manager! Hollywood, here I come.

Six months later I was close to finalizing my move to L.A.

Comics in San Francisco are afraid of leaving their nest, and I was no exception. Many who show great promise in the Bay Area stay until they wither on the vine. By the time they make the move, it's too late to care.

But not me! I had a manager!

The only problem was he never seemed to call me back. Or call me at all. Or return my emails. Or anything. But I *could* tell my peers I had a manager and watch their faces scrunch up in jealousy, so that was something. I called and called, trying to get him to get me stuff . . . stuff like a TV spot!

I called him so much that, one week before I was to move to L.A., he finally had to call back.

"Hey, buddy!" He always greeted me like that. It made me feel like . . . well, like we were buddies.

"I know you must be frustrated by me not calling you back," he said.

"You don't call me at all," I whimpered.

He cleared his throat. "You probably think I have too many clients, and to be honest, you're right! Sorry, buddy, but I think we need to go our separate ways."

Had we ever even gone the same way?

"Oh, okay then. I was just going to say that same thing." I was going to do no such thing.

Gutshot.

Even though absolutely nothing had changed, and nothing had happened, I was now "no one" again. A far cry from my former position of "no one but says he has a manager."

I had a move to make but no reason to make it anymore. I called the manager at the other company that had been looking into me. "I'm sorry," she said. "I'm pretty maxed out on clients right now." This was essentially manager-speak for "You hurt my feelings when you didn't decide to sign with me."

I was screwed. And I was pissed.

Why the hell had he offered to represent me if he wasn't going to represent me?

The answer now is obvious to me. It costs nothing to "represent" someone and wait around doing nothing in the hopes that your "client" might have some success while you ignore them and, if they do, you can swoop back in, thumbs up, grinning: "I knew you had it in you the whole time, buddy!"

The problem is, with no one on your side in Hollywood, it's very difficult to get that success at all. I was faced with a choice. Languish on the vine, a big withering fish in San Francisco, or leap into the abyss of not knowing in the biggest pond possible.

"Fuck it," I thought. "I'd rather go to L.A. and fail than stay here and wonder what might have happened."

So I leapt.

I arrived in L.A. having essentially started over.

In Los Angeles I was faced with the need to hit the very sort of open mics I had grown beyond back in San Francisco. I had moved to Los Angeles and, in so doing, suddenly become a very very little fish. A minnow. I did not like being a minnow. Glug, glug.

Speaking of little fish, after a few months of doing these open mics, yet another manager approached me, handing me a business card after a sad little show where I'd done well. I called him and we went back and forth on the phone trying to make a plan to meet. I was horny for him. I wanted him to want me so bad. He invited me to his office one day. I drove all the way to Beverly Hills and took the elevator to the fourteenth floor and walked to his office, a space so comedically small, it looked like Tinkerbell's Workshop. I ducked my head way down to fit through the door and sat on an American Girl doll office chair as he peered over his desk, which was really a toadstool. He took a sip of coffee out of a thimble and sighed. "Sorry to drag you all the way out here for bad news but my partners feel that we can't take on another client right now."

Rejected again and this time in miniature. I couldn't fucking believe it. I called my brother on the way out of the parking lot: "I think I maybe made a mistake moving here." He told me to breathe and to give it a few more months.

Toward the end of those few months, I was given an opportunity to audition for the Comedy Central stand-up show *Live at Gotham*. A huge chance. A big shot. My time to shine.

Sadly, though, when I arrived at the showcase, the audience hadn't taken into consideration how important this night was to me.

I'm not sure what makes a bad crowd. I've thought a lot about the randomness that goes into making a group of strangers who have come to a comedy club into a united non-laughing front and what makes another crowd "hot." It's a mystery of groupthink and demographics that no one really understands. At any rate, that night's crowd was a dud.

Comic after comic grabbed the mic on the biggest night of their career only to look down and see that it had transformed into a big fat shit sandwich that they would have to take a bite of. Comics were committing seppuku in the back of the room rather than performing. I watched my peers get shot down, one by one, like brigade mates in a pointless World War I trench battle.

I steeled myself, thinking, "You *have* to do well." I had to. Then, just as the comic before me was gasping her death knell in front of the worst crowd of all time, he walked in. My old manager. He who had turned his back on me. He didn't know that the crowd sucked; he'd just gotten there. He would see me eat that communal shit sandwich and think I'd prepared it myself. All of his doubts about me would be confirmed.

I took a breath.

"I fucking *have* to kill now," I thought.

My name was called. The crowd clapped apathetically. I took the stage. I grabbed the mic.

I dug deep into my guts and pulled all the lessons I'd learned in comedy, in every scene I had ever been part of, to will both myself and the audience into a changed state of being. For some reason, it all came together right there.

Seven minutes later, I was walking off the stage in triumph. I'd killed.

I went outside to catch my breath. The first person to follow me out was my old manager.

"That was just great, Moshe. Just great. Brilliant."

I could see the regret and desire in his eyes. I loved it.

"Thank you so much, man. Thanks."

I walked away grinning.

After the show, I was mobbed with agents and managers telling me how much they loved me. The people from Comedy Central fawned over me. It was exactly like being the new hot chick in a high school. I felt pretty.

After seven years of comedy, seven *minutes* had changed my life. That night, I met my current manager, got an agent, sealed my first TV spot, *and* got a booking on the Just for Laughs festival. I had arrived.

I quit my day job toiling away interpreting at the Burbank Sorenson Video Relay Services a few months later. I was a full-time comic. This was exactly what I'd been working toward the entire time I'd been doing comedy. This was my dream come true.

And I didn't even have to suck Jay Leno off.

Things changed quickly.

I performed at a comedy festival in Aspen, Colorado, and ended up winning an award and named "Best of the Fest." A few months later, my agent called and told me the legendary Comedy Works club in Denver wanted me to come perform there. "That's great!" I replied, thrilled. "Who am I opening for?"

My agent was confused. "No one. They want you to headline. You can do forty-five minutes, right?"

This is one of those questions that there's only one right answer to, so I lied, "Yeah! For sure I can! I assumed it was to headline, just working on performative humility these days!"

I flew off to Denver and was so grateful to see the club had a clock onstage where you could request it count *down* from forty-five minutes. I went through every single joke I'd ever written and *DING!* it was forty-five minutes exactly.

I was a headliner now. I lived lean, and if I got one $1,500 headlining gig a month, I could pay my rent. When I was a DJ I used to fantasize about being flown around the country and the world to play records. It seemed like the ultimate life. See cool things, investigate cities you'd never have discovered otherwise, drop into town, make people happy, and fly home. I got that with comedy. I spent the next ten years on the road, traveling city to city, gig to gig.

I once got an offer to play a comedy festival in Kilkenny, Ireland, at the Cat Laughs festival. It seemed like it would be a great time. A trip to a foreign land and a chance to do comedy? Nothing better. I even planned an extension of the trip, after the festival, to see the famed Ring of Kerry, as I figured there was a chance this would be the only time I'd make the trip to Ireland.

I arrived in Dublin and performed a pre-show at a super-hip bar. The show went great, and I took a shuttle into Kilkenny confident from the night before. I did my first show and things seemed okay; I had a fun performance with a crowd I would call very sympathetic to the Irish comics and very skeptical of the American ones. That seemed fair. I did well, got a good review in a comedy blog, and was feeling like I knew what I was doing.

That night I checked out a British comic named Tim Key who was so compelling and artful, I left the show impressed and jealous of him. That was night one.

The next night began my Irish Tragedy, a slog of slogs. Every show was worse than the last. Night after night I bombed harder than the IRA. There seemed to be some disconnect between the words I was saying and what I actually meant. We spoke the same language but were singing a different tune. I'll explain.

I used to be a strange-looking comedian. I had an extreme haircut that I used to call "the Gitler" (the Gay Hitler). Shaved on the sides, Proud Boy on top. It was hip at the time. It was a tough cut to live with as a Jew, due to the fact that, if ever a barber didn't quite understand what I wanted, I would have to use the word *Hitler* to describe it. "I'd like a kind of old-timey cut? Sort of a military cut from the 1930s?"

Confusion from the barber.

I'd try again: "You know! Kind of an angular . . . sort of a World War II style . . . *Hitler! Adolf Hitler! The destroyer of my people! Make me look like him!*" as my ancestors rolled over in their shallow, unmarked graves. This haircut was . . . my struggle.

So I had a weird haircut. And weird glasses. Large Coke-bottle hipster glasses that took up half my face. I'd round out the look with skintight jeans and a dress shirt and tie, which I thought looked cool but which definitely looked strange to more traditional crowds.

As a result, I found that sometimes certain audience members would start to laugh at me the moment I got onstage. Before I even opened my mouth. At first this made me feel self-conscious and insecure, but, like all comics, I found a way to turn that insecurity into a comic asset. I forged the weakness into a weapon. I'd actually rely on that opening laugh. I'd walk onstage and wait in the pocket for the laugh to come before I uttered my opening line. If no one laughed when I took the stage, I'd scrunch myself into a more gargoyle-like form and force a laugh. Finally, always, someone would laugh at me. Then I'd pounce with my opening joke, setting the stage for my character.

"Thank you," I'd say, "for the preliminary laugh at my physical appearance. That's how I know the show is going to go well, when you start by laughing not at the jokes I wrote but at the body I was cursed with. Go fuck yourselves!" A classic combo of intertwined self-deprecation and aggressive bravado. Crowds would laugh at

this admonition, understanding, "Okay, he said, 'Go fuck yourselves' but what he really meant was go fuck *him*self, not being sure
he fits in that haircut in the first place, ha-ha ha-ha, let's laugh at the
Jew!'"

They got it.

But not in Kilkenny.

You could actually feel the crowd react as one every time I said
"Go fuck yourselves!" *Why would he say, 'Go fuck yourselves'? We
just met the guy!* It was a bad way to start a show. Unfortunately, I
was much newer in comedy and didn't have a different way to open
the show at that time, so I kept making the same mistake, over and
over again, hoping it would work somewhere, but the result was
many consecutive bad shows.

I can deal with a bad show. I'd been doing comedy long enough
to know some shows just aren't going to work. Some markets won't
like what you have to offer. I was a big boy. But then I would leave
the show, and on the five-block walk back to my hotel room, I would
get made fun of for the way I looked. Open mockery from the good
people of Kilkenny. And these were not members of the audience
who were streaming out, encountering me after already having established a relationship of disdain toward me. That, I could have
understood. I'd told them to fuck themselves, and they were here to
get their revenge. But no. These were random people, drinking and
partying in the streets, who simply could not look at someone like
me without pointing and laughing. It was depressing. Mostly because of how excited I'd been about my visit. I have some Irish an-
cestry, so I was super-excited by the prospect of seeing the country
and the people. I'd had this super-romantic notion of the people I
would encounter there, Samuel Beckett types, cable-knit-sweater-
wearing guys with corncob pipes, puffing away and muttering, "Let
me tell you about fighting against the English!"

But the people I ran into were more like, "Let me tell you about
picking on the gay kid in high school!"

By the end of the week, the stack of bad shows and the harrowing
walks home started to weigh on me. I wanted to get out of there. I
heard that the brilliant comic Tim Key had performed the same act

I'd been so impressed with at another venue and had had things thrown at him in protest of his artsy version of stand-up. That made me feel better. If someone I was impressed with was being tortured by the Kilkenny masses, I might be doing something right.

The night of the last show began, and about three minutes into my act, which was already not going well, a man yelled from the audience, "NEXT!" That is a *brutal* heckle. If you ever want to wreck someone onstage, scream *Next!* as loud as you can. But also, don't, you rude reader! I was shocked. I just thought "NEXT?! Next?! I want this guy to *die* next! Tonight. I want him to drive home, crash into a brick wall, and burn to death in front of his family." And when I say I thought that, I mean I screamed that into the microphone in front of a crowd of three hundred shocked Irish people. So, yeah, not a great way to end a festival. When I finally got out of the show, it was about one-thirty in the morning and I still had that crucible of a walk home.

I was river-dancing my way around piles of Guinness vomit, almost to my hotel without incident, when an old man stopped me in the street. This man was the oldest, Irish-est person I had ever seen in my life. He was clad in plaid, a different kind on each limb. He looked to be leaning against a strong wind. The soles of his feet were made of bog peat. He approached me with a hearty "Hello!"

I winced. "Hello, sir."

My new Irish grandpappy asked me "And what's your name?"

"Moshe," I replied.

"And what are you doing in Ireland, Moshe?"

I gulped, "Comedy? Theoretically, I guess?" He smiled. "Well, let me tell ya somethin', Moshe! I want to say thank you. Thank you for comin' all this way. We know how far ya come just to entertain us, and I want to say thank you. Thank you, lad."

I could've cried. "No, thank *you*. Thank you, sir! With this small piece of human connection and kindness, you've totally changed my perspective on this whole trip. Here I was thinking I'd come to a bad place and encountered bad people. Thanks to you I realize I just had some bad luck! All I needed was another human being to see me and reach out to me in brotherhood, so thank you. Thank you! Thank you!"

I started to walk and got about twenty feet away when the old man stopped me again. *"HEY, MOSHE!"* I turned around and when I did, he started screaming, grabbed his crotch, and tugged on it like Roseanne singing the national anthem, and then growled at me like an angry dog, sticking his tongue out like Gene Simmons while flipping me off. It was such a strange, psychedelic form of cruelty, I couldn't even learn a life lesson from it. I just had to stuff it into my backpack of human experiences that weigh you down over the course of a life. I didn't have time for existential angst. I went back to my hotel room and packed because I was leaving the next day. To make matters worse, I wasn't heading home; I was going on vacation to the fucking Ring of Kerry.

The last thing I wanted to see was "more Ireland," but I'd already purchased the ticket and, at the time, the cost of a flight on Ryanair was more than I could afford to lose. I'd made a reservation at a rental car place and planned to take a drive around the ring, see some pretty Irish landscapes, and fly back to the States. I boarded the flight in Dublin, landed in Kerry on a sunny day, walked straight to the rental car spot, and presented my ID. They didn't have a rental car reservation for me.

"Oh, okay, no problem, how much to rent a car then?" I asked.

"A million euros."

I don't remember how much they actually said, but it was so astronomically high that I literally could not afford it. I didn't know what to do. I walked outside the rental car agency to collect my thoughts, and a fucking deluge from the Celtic gods unleashed on my head. A tsunami of rain. A torrent with the wet anger of occupied Ireland. Soaked through and near tears, I ran right back into the airport, blasting past security to the gate I'd landed at twenty minutes earlier, begging them to please just let me fly back to Dublin, as though I'd never heard of air flight rules or how twenty-first-century travel worked. This was not a stagecoach that had just taken me into town. They looked at me like I was insane and said no. I walked back outside, pulling my hair out, drenched, lost in Kerry. A bus drove by so I ran after it begging it to stop, which it did. I got into town and checked in to a hostel for the night. Dry bed, warm water.

The next day I took a lovers' bus tour of the Ring of Kerry. I sat in front as fifteen couples cuddled and cooed at each other. I took sad selfies at the Ring. I cut such a pathetic swath that one of the men in one of the couples offered to let me borrow his girl to pose with.

I counted the hours until my return flight. But my nightmare was not over, because the moment I landed in the United States I was headed right back out to a road date. More comedy. The last thing on Earth I wanted to do. All I wanted to do was fly home, crawl into bed, hide under the covers, and contemplate quitting comedy forever from underneath the supportive embrace of synthetic down. But I didn't have that option. This is what I do for a living. The show must go on.

And I wasn't even going to some cool comedy club in some cool town. I was headed to a place called Crackers Comedy Club in Indianapolis. Crackers. CRACKERS. CRACK-ERS. I'm not anti-cracker. I'm not. But think about my psychological state in Ireland when I opened the email and read "You're headed to Crackers!" Does Crackers sound to your ear like the right place for me to get my comedic legs back under me? Does Crackers sound like a fertile ground for a little Jewish phoenix to resurrect and fly again? Does Crackers sound like where Moshe got her groove back? No. But I had to do it.

So I did it.

I flew into Indianapolis, stepped onstage, grabbed the mic, and . . . someone started laughing at me before I even began to speak. Here we go again.

"Thank you . . ."

Dread. Shiver.

"For the preliminary laugh at my physical appearance . . ."

Wince. Terror.

"That's how I know the show is going to go well, when you start by laughing not at the jokes I wrote but the body I was cursed with."

Panic. Horror.

"Go fuck yourselves!"

. . .

Everybody laughed.

I'm not a particularly patriotic man. I never really have been. But in that moment, I just thought, "God bless America! And God bless these crackers!"

It worked. I got my groove back. I kept going.

As my career progressed, the satisfaction I imagined I'd feel once I got the things I wanted quickly attached itself to a new set of things I wanted. The moment I grabbed the ladder rung I'd been staring at for years, I was confronted with another rung, just above it, even shinier and prettier. The ladder goes forever, obviously. Somewhere, way high up the ladder, is Brad Pitt grabbing a rung, looking above him at the soles of Timothée Chalamet's shoes, wondering how he got lapped, wondering how far down the ladder goes, wondering if he could survive a fall.

Climbing the ladder outside of a corporation feels awful because the whole reason you didn't get a corporate job was because you hate the very idea of a corporate ladder, and yet here you are, sincerely trying to climb this alternative ladder. To compensate for this conflict, comics convince themselves that they are rare truth tellers, philosophers who are the only people capable of discovering and telling said truths. That to be a comedian is to be a deconstructor. To view the world and examine it to find the absurd core of everything. To strip away sincerity and pomp and get to the meat of the thing.

The comic thinks he or she grabs the bones of life, sucks the marrow out, and, rather than drinking this richness down, spits it back onto the face of the world, of the audience, so that the juice can drip down onto their tongues. Now having tasted it, they can lean into their neighbor and say, "That's so true! We *are* just like that!" All this while the comic stands onstage, wasting away, the pounds falling from him even as he feeds the world.

This process, that of deconstructing the world and reducing it to its absurd molecular level, is one that can be destructive to your own experience of the world. You examine the world looking for the awful, the ridiculous, the laughable. You take this information and turn it into a joke that you tell people. They laugh, you cry, that's the agreement. Seeing the world this way affects you over time. Slowly, you become a slightly worse person.

I'll give you an example from my own life.

When I first started comedy, I found Holocaust jokes distasteful and offensive. I didn't tell them; I didn't laugh at them. Fast-forward a few years and I made my television debut *performing* a Holocaust joke on TV. I'd become a worse person. Fast-forward a few *more* years and I systematically exterminated my entire family. See? I never talked like that pre-comedy.

But I've slowly come to realize that the vision of the comic as the brave truth-telling martyr is something comics work to convince ourselves of. We do this out of an insecurity about the value of our work, to justify those first years of bombing at open mics and the later years of shilling ourselves on absolutely any podcast or TV show that will have us on. It's hard to reconcile fearless truth teller with podcaster reading ads for erectile dysfunction wholesalers.

As I aged in comedy, I got more and more comfortable with the idea of myself as a person whose job it was to make people laugh, with no more or less responsibility than that. I actually wasn't a truth teller or a philosopher. I was just a laugh getter. That's all. And so were all other comics.

Take George Carlin, often cited as people's philosophical comedic hero. People didn't go to a Carlin show to be introduced to the concept of anti-censorship. They went to laugh at Carlin's take on the absurdity of censorship. Seven dirty words didn't introduce the world to the concept of vulgarity rules stepping on the toes of free expression. It sharpened the focus of the argument by putting it into terms people understood. In this way comics aren't philosophers at all; we are dumb downers. Comedy, even when it's trying to make a point, has always made those points in a dialogue with its greater goal: entertainment.

I reject any notion that "idea comedy" is the ultimate comedy. Steve Martin is no less or more of an artist than Bill Hicks. There is room for absurdity, philosophy, vulgarity, anodyne observation, and more in comedy. Comics are not *supposed* to provoke, but sometimes they do. Stand-up is not *supposed* to reveal ugly truth, but sometimes it can. Comedy is not *supposed* to speak truth to power, but sometimes it does. Comedy is only *supposed* to be funny. Funny is, of course, subjective, but the goal itself is objective.

None of this is bad, by the way. There's a reason I didn't major in philosophy, and that reason is it's fucking boring. And full of itself. And not fun. And I'm not smart enough to understand it.

So why is it not enough that we just make people laugh? Why do comics and comedy fans need to feel like comedy represents some foundational pylon in the undergirding of society? Why do we need to pretend that laughter is a Trojan horse, smuggling in revolutionary ideas that are saving free speech and civil society, or poisonous ideas that corrode the social contract and promote violence?

Comedy is a joke.

All this hand-wringing about comedy reached an inflection point ten years ago on one balmy Friday night at the Laugh Factory in Hollywood. Daniel Tosh was onstage and was heckled after making a joke about sexual assault. A woman was upset and let him know. He shot back a defensive comeback that was, let's say, harsher than the joke she was upset about.

This interaction was no different from a million such back-and-forths in comedy clubs throughout history. Most comics I know had a rape joke or two in their acts back then, men and women alike, some were funny, some less so. Also, every comic I know had been trained in heckling situations to come back hard, quick, shut down the heckler with the fiercest retort that occurred to them in the moment, regain control of the show, and move on.

There was nothing different about that night. Nothing Daniel did or said was more or less offensive than countless other comics before him. What was different was the internet and the shift society was going through.

The story was uploaded onto Tumblr, a kind of pioneer site for getting angry online, and the modern dialogue about what's funny began. Comics, like the rest of the world soon thereafter, were about to get a crash course on online outrage and the speed of information transmission in a digital age.

Within a week, the story had been picked up by every news outlet in America. Articles printing which comics came to his defense were juxtaposed with serious feminist thinkers explaining why rape jokes are never funny in any context, which were re-juxtaposed with other serious feminist thinkers disagreeing with that assessment and explaining that jokes must punch up, and that within that context, jokes about anything, including sexual assault, can be funny. Debates about the topic were hosted on TV shows where comics and pundits debated what should and should not be said onstage.

Comics were taken aback by this. It wasn't the first time in history a comic got in trouble for a joke, not by a long shot. As early as vaudeville there were articles written about the tasteless jokes for which comedians got in trouble. Lenny Bruce got arrested for saying *cocksucker.* Andrew Dice Clay was the subject of many a pearl-clutching mom in the nineties.

But the scale of this conversation was different. It was dizzying. Comics in the "funny-over-everything" generation reacted with a circling of the wagons, defending Tosh's right to make whatever joke he wanted. No one realized this conversation would be going for the next decade and that the very comics who were defending Tosh would themselves have to grapple with what to say or not say onstage from that point forward.

All of this coincided with two major shifts in the national dialogue. First, across the country, young people were owning language and the cultural conversation in ways they hadn't before.

I grew up in the nineties and didn't have a serious political thought until I was thirty. These days you have twelve-year-olds with RBG neck tattoos arguing about the Senate parliamentarian's role in enforcing stare decisis. People wanted change in society and they wanted it now.

The other big change was in the way people spoke to one another. The internet, with its two-pronged spear of anonymity and ability to convince every person that what they said held value, created a kind of dialogue that was nastier and more public than ever. Comics were provocative speakers, but at least they were professionals. Even when they were ignorant, they'd at least practiced. They'd at least tried to make things funny. The internet made dialogue hit rock bottom quickly. Everyone was a fucking idiot, a rape apologist, a cuck, a libtard, a racist, a communist, a Nazi, and, because it was the internet, a dirty Jew.

The social media mentions of comics (and everyone else) quickly became so nasty they were hard to deal with. You'd get attacked from both sides of a joke with such ferocity it made your brain seize. Getting used to public abuse became part of what it meant to be in the public eye. To make matters worse, as a comic, you had pretty thin ice from which to lodge complaints about people talking shit, since it was literally your entire job. Dish it out and take it, bitch.

The comments about what was funny quickly became trench warfare between comics and free-speech absolutists and those who wanted speech to change and change now. Little of the dialogue was actual dialogue. Most of it was choir preaching, most of it was grandstanding.

This changed a lot of things about comedy. Alternative comedy was the only game in town for so long. When I started comedy, looking like a bespectacled hipster (if you have to reduce me to my disability and impeccable fashion sense), people would scrunch their faces in confusion when I told them I did comedy. It did not compute. To them, in the Bay Area at that time, a comic was a cornball, an old guy; it was Jay Leno with his cock freshly sucked. Everyone young was a DJ; no one did comedy.

I and the other young comics of my generation ignored these confused looks and chased after the stars of our generation for long enough to watch stand-up comedy become the thing that everyone did. It's actually currently illegal to have a social media bio that does not include the word *comedian:*

Anti-Racist Activist / Cultural Attaché to the
UN Security Council / Comedian

For a time, the one place where the cultural divide did not seem to exist was in comedy circles. Since the only rooms with any real industry buzz were the alternative rooms, club comics would perform there so often there that there slowly became zero real distinction between club comedy and alternative comedy. Some comics had legitimately alternative acts—Emo Philips, Maria Bamford, Reggie Watts, for example—styles that were consequentially different from traditional comedy. But for the most part, especially toward the later years, an alternative comic was basically just a club comic who referenced the Marvel Cinematic Universe.

I always did every room. I loved clubs, I loved alternative rooms, I made adjustments based on both. I like to think I did well and got along with everyone. But of course I did—these freaks are my people.

The thing I always loved about comedy was how much everyone (kind of) got along. How we were a community. A comic from a more conservative background like Nate Bargatze had no trouble getting along with a more liberal comic like Marc Maron. What mattered was funny. All that mattered was funny. And in that, I always felt like the comedy community had a lesson to teach the world. If you focus on the things that connect you, you can stay unbothered by the things that society says should tear you apart.

Sadly, the things that tear us apart began to expand at an exponential rate. They began to lap what comedy could take. Comics started taking refuge in comedic echo chambers, rejecting one another as unfunny or insufferable if they came to jokes from different political standpoints.

As this was happening, the fever with which the media reported on the "comedy problem" was relentless. It never seemed to die down. It took on an outsize position in the cultural conversation. All of the problems in comedy exist in every other subculture, but with comedy it always seemed like a national emergency.

Some comics, as comics tend to do, rallied round their kin and began to defend one another regardless of what the accused was said to have done. Suddenly accused rapists were getting the same voracious defense as people who told rape jokes.

We were all told that comedy was in dire trouble, never mind that it had a larger audience than ever before. Alternative comedy stopped being the only game in town. Club comics, podcasters, and comics-turned–TikTok stars carved massive audiences out of the digital landscape. These comics started to have breakout superstars selling out gigantic theaters and arenas while most people in America had little idea of who they were. The Hollywood machine ignored them (and largely still does) and they couldn't care less. These comics didn't need gatekeepers to come see them and give them opportunity. They'd used the internet to make opportunity come to them. They'd built their own gates. They were millionaires of their own making. If you don't read the comments or the news, it's a good time to be a comic.

But it's also a profoundly annoying time to be a comic. Comics have reacted to this constant barrage of media onslaught in two ways, both stupid:

One faction of comics seems to be locked into defending comedy at *any* cost, as if it's one of the core sacred forces in the universe, beyond critique, metaphysically important. These people are dedicated to the "never apologize for a joke" principle, even if the joke was something you regret. Even if the joke was actually a mistake. No matter what, never apologize. In fact, even if it was not a joke, if you accidentally hurt someone's feelings or did something rude, never *ever* apologize ever. Some of these folks are more known for starting fights with other comics in the name of defending comedy's honor than for their actual jokes. They remind me of those weird, overly protective boyfriends, screaming at anyone who looks in the direction of their lover: "DON'T LOOK AT HER, DON'T TALK

TO HER, SHE'S MINE!" These same people went atomically apoplectic when *Nanette* dropped on Netflix, their veins bulging, pushing their neck tattoo of that old-timey rockabilly mic to its breaking
point, seething "IT'S NOT FUNNY ENOUGH!" Like, dude, who
cares? Literally every other special for the past fifty years was an
hour of jokes. Why does one woman getting praise for a special you
didn't like matter to you at all?

The other faction seems to have become obsessed in the other
direction, with turning comedy into a venue for social justice plat-
forming. Impassioned, sometimes punch-line-less speeches that blur
the boundary between TED Talk and sixth-grade civics class video.
These people finally reached orgasm when they watched *Nanette*,
moaning that finally someone had cracked the code of punching up
so hard, they touched the G-spot.

I have had to figure out how to navigate these two streams, both
of which simultaneously aggravate me and elicit my sympathy, depending on my mood. I *do* think being able to think and speak freely
is incredibly important, but I also think it's not the only important
thing in the world. I *do* care about my comedy not being hurtful to
someone, but I also think people should be less sensitive about jokes.
I *do* think cancel culture describes something real and that it can be
a pernicious problem, but I don't think that means people should be
automatically excused for actions or, yes, even words, that are hurtful, just because they're a comic. I, like most people who haven't
decided to throw their lots in with a group of ideologues, have had
to figure out how to navigate my old beliefs with the changing culture.

I came to realize that comedy will always end up offending someone. You can't avoid it. The most progressive comic in the world
will eventually end up pissing someone off. It's the nature of making
fun of stuff. Since you can't avoid that, the only litmus test for your
comedy should be yourself. Can *you* stand behind a joke? Can *you*
justify telling it? This is not a license to be cruel— it's a license to be
an artist. I have to appeal to my own moral core to find if what I'm
saying or doing is justifiable. At the same time, I never want that
moral core to become calcified by a fear of change. I never want to

refuse to learn because I'm afraid of how that learning will affect my persona or my career. I want to evolve, but not past being funny.

I once had a five-minute fat joke, and it was good. It killed. A real banger about seeing someone eating a king-size ice cream Snickers bar by scooping out the ice cream with a bunch of Fritos Scoops. But then I heard an episode of *This American Life* where author Lindy West (herself often a critic of comedy, and not one I always agree with) talked about what her life was like navigating the world as a fat person, and I had a shift. It stopped feeling worth it for me to do fat jokes onstage. So I stopped.

Does this mean I think fat jokes are immoral and that no one else should tell them? No. I don't have any feeling on that. Because I still believe that funny is funny.

My first Netflix special has jokes I wouldn't tell today. But I'm not ashamed of them. I'm proud of those jokes but understand what they are: a time capsule of my journey as a comic and an artist and a person. I find the strip-mining of people's old tweets and material to find problematic sentiments to be sorely lacking in understanding that people change with time.

I still love offensive jokes. I still tell them.

All of these impulses, sometimes contradictory, are part of being a person, comedian or not, in the world today.

Despite how annoying comedy has become, I still love comics. Give me a party with comedians over anyone else on Earth. Will they bully me? Yes. Will I laugh? Yes. Will I be bored? No. Comics are my people.

One in particular.

I got my first TV writing job in 2012. I was completely elated. After a decade of stand-up, I was ready to stay in town for a little bit. In 2009, I recorded my first hour special, and it was one of the first specials ever acquired by Netflix. It was so long ago that I was actually *embarrassed* to be on Netflix. "Who has a special on Netflix?!"

I toured and toured and started to feel like, for the first time, people were coming out to see me, and not just to cash in their "free admission" coupon for the comedy club they'd gotten because they upgraded to the rainbow wax at the carwash.

After that I published my first memoir and I toured relentlessly to support it. I had fans now and that was exciting, but I was tired of the endless road. Of waking up at three A.M. for a flight in the morning to Grand Rapids, where I'd spend eight hours in my hotel room, alone and bored, and one hour onstage alive and connected. Then I'd fly home to wait for the gig the next weekend. I wouldn't have to unpack. Just remove the dirty underwear from last weekend's suitcase and replace with clean underwear. Grab suitcase, start again. I relished life on the road, no boss, no alarm clock, but I also wanted to try different stuff.

So the TV writing job was exciting.

In the writers room, I learned how to craft a script from the older writers, and they learned what meaningless sex was like nowadays from me.

That was my role in the room: young guy who still had fun. I regaled my co-workers with tawdry tales of single debauchery, but I was tired of that, too. I mean, I wasn't actually, but I did want something different. I'd been in therapy for years at that point to work on my utter inability to forge a meaningful and lasting relationship with a woman. I'd been working on it internally, but externally it was getting a little grim. I was barely even trying anymore.

I'd go to the Comedy Store, which, at the time, was like a haunted house with the ghosts of dead careers floating through drafty hallways. The Comedy Store is where Sam Kinison and Richard Pryor cut their teeth and their lines of cocaine. It has since become one of the hottest rooms in Los Angeles, but for years it was limping along, a club on life support. It sat about twenty minutes down Sunset Boulevard from my house.

At that time, the odds of having a fun set at the store were about 70/30. If I had a bad set, I'd start texting girls from the parking lot, hoping a booty call would reach in and pick me up out of the void. If, by the time I hit the Winchell's Donut House on Western and Sunset, no one had texted me back, I'd pull in, grab a buttermilk old-fashioned doughnut and house that thing by the time I made it home.

That's what sex was like for me. More drugs than decadence.

I'd play videogames on the nights I wasn't gigging and would distractedly text girls while I played. One would come over, I'd press pause on the game, we'd retire to the bedroom for exactly one fuck's worth of time. When she left, I'd sit down, press play, and pick up where I left off.

I'd started to abandon hope of any real connection when someone I'd been friends with, had done sets with, and admired from afar for years invited me to a dinner party. Her name was Natasha.

I'd never really considered Natasha romantically because she was always dating someone else, usually a comic. But she was single now, and I was invited to her house. At that party I watched as she flirted with a twenty-two-year-old intern from *The Pete Holmes Show* and decided it still wasn't time to try.

I had a dream about her that night. She was absolutely laid up on a bed of roses as the intern ravished her body in every way possible. I'm kidding, it was PG. I also had a dream about Whoopi Goldberg that night.

I decided that I would tell Natasha I had a dream about her, but add in the presence of Whoopi, as it felt like it defused the creep factor. I texted her, *"Had a dream about you and Whoopi Goldberg last night."* She texted back, *"Come over tonight and let's smoke some cigarettes."* She didn't even mention my nocturnal vision of Whoopi. Anyway, it looked like the intern hadn't made it past the second interview.

That was ten years ago.

In the writers room they applauded when I said I had a girlfriend. They were definitely happy to see me change. I was scared at first, but every time my familiar intimacy panic kicked in, I told myself, using the tools I'd acquired in therapy, "This isn't real. There is no crisis. All is well."

Natasha was elegant, she was beautiful, she had an Oakland bootie, she never annoyed me (this would change), but most of all, she was funny. She made me laugh. And she laughed at my jokes. That allowed me to stay when my panic told me to run.

We got married after three years together.

We struggled for a long time trying to get pregnant in the traditional style (doggy). People would ask if we were "trying," which always made me uncomfortable. It felt like my mother asking if we were having raw-dog, condom-free sex. Which actually wouldn't be that weird for my particular mom to ask, but imagine your mom asking. And yeah, Mom, we were. We struck out, though the process was fun. It was disheartening, but remember the great lesson of comedy? It's not about if you can succeed; it's about if you can fail and keep going.

We kept going.

We started trying IVF and hormone therapy. Each night I'd jab a syringe into Natasha's ass and inject her with egg-producing chemicals. Watching bruises form on what was the single most important thing in the world to me was tough, but we thought it would be worth it. That didn't work either.

Natasha, who was a famously anti-parenting comedian with quotes like, "Having a baby is like a DUI from the universe" and "I'll never be pregnant . . . for long," had nonetheless frozen eight eggs when she was thirty-seven on the off chance that she'd someday encounter a Jew captivating enough to change her mind.

Having failed every other way, we finally thawed them eggs for me to blast on. Only four survived the thaw-blast. We tested the rest, and only two survived the testing. We implanted one and it resulted in an ectopic pregnancy which is only viable in the state of Missouri.

We had one chance left.

It was starting to seem like we would be cursed to have to spend our child-raising years suffering through multiple extravagant trips to Europe. But we kept going. One last egg. One last shot.

It took.

Nine months later, wide-eyed and terrified in an operating room, I was holding my baby. Natasha was sick and groggy, so I was charged with watching this tiny thing. Just the two of us, sleeping together on a hospital couch. Finally, a few hours later, a nurse came in and told me she'd take the baby for a bath and to conduct some tests. I could have a break. I ran across the street and bought a buttermilk old-fashioned doughnut, which I housed like I'd just had a bad set.

I have discovered, through writing this book, that doughnuts are my coping mechanism.

Our baby grew and is now our roommate. She's given me a revolution in perspective and optimism. She's given me a context in which to place the importance of my career, which is that it isn't important anymore. But how important is she? I would suck Jay Leno's dick to protect her.

If I'd never gone to New York that summer with Chelsea? If I hadn't sat through all those Sundays at the Punch Line? If I hadn't put on that astronaut suit? If I hadn't failed and failed and kept going and kept going and going, I never would have met her, never would have made her. And that would have been the only way I'd have really failed.

She's funny, too. Kind of. She knows that's what Mom and Dad like, she knows that's where the juice is, so she tries all the time to make us laugh. "Knock-knock?" she'll ask.

"Who's there?" I answer, knowing where this is going.

"Tree."

"Tree who?"

"Tree . . ." she'll answer, waiting just a second to let the tension build up. "Tree . . . pee! Poo! Is that a funny joke?!"

"No," I answer. "No, it is not."

I can't lie to her!

But I love that she's trying to get laughs.

Just like her dad. And her mom, but this book is about her dad.

Epilogue

In 2006, the DJ named Girl Talk released his mixtape *Night Ripper* and ripped open the seams of American youth culture. It was an exciting and unexpected form of music that, rather than being a self-generated creation, combined elements of existing hits to create a new semi-genre: the mashup.

He mashed up the Waitresses' "I Know What Boys Like" with Juelz Santana's hook "I Know What Girls Want" from "Run It!" by Chris Brown. This hook was an homage to Jay-Z's "I Know What Girls Like," which was itself an homage to the Waitresses' hit.

It was a layered and Escher-esque amalgamation. The mashups came a mile a minute, relentless and pounding, building and building. This wasn't mixing two songs together, this was grinding them into a paste, reconstituting them and creating what sounded like a soundtrack of the future, which was odd, since the entire mixtape reached back and regurgitated the past.

In her book *Collage Culture,* the poet Mandy Kahn argued that this mix was a pivot point in American culture. It represented a new era, the end of the self-generated creation of culture, the beginning of the smushing of everything that had come before into one big, exciting lump. It wasn't just music that was being mashed up.

It was everything.

In the eighties and nineties, subculture was king. Your destiny was shaped by the people you fell in with. If your dad bought you a skateboard and you took to it, odds were you'd be smoking blunts under an overpass and writing graffiti someday relatively soon. If you liked Tolkien and *Beetlejuice* a lot, odds were you'd be wearing thick rubber platform boots and doing bloodletting ceremonies to Skinny Puppy in a few years.

Subcultures, at the time, represented hidden paths, obscured from view but promised to unfurl for you; all you had to do was look hard enough. Every book I ever loved when I was young was about a weak kid who one day discovered they actually had great power that had been concealed from them. Their hero's journey was to discover that, while they'd felt they were boring and alone, in fact, they were mighty and had a great community waiting for the moment they seized their destiny.

This journey, the same one Harry Potter and Luke Skywalker and the Narnia kids and countless other white fantasy children went through was the same journey teens in the nineties went through. Only for me, the tools were drugs and dancing, not magic and swords. The things I found on my journey felt like superpowers. If only for a while.

Subculture was a discovery of your people. It was everything.

I have always been attracted to people who stood out, the agitators against the dominant culture, those who didn't accept the rules society set out for them. The weirdos. I have chased those kinds of people and those kinds of experiences my whole life.

Maybe my destiny was always set in this direction, as the groups I wrote about that don't *exactly* fit the classic mold of true subcultures—specifically the Jewish and deaf communities—were a part of my life long before I got high with my friends, before I went to rehab, before I went to my first meeting, my first rave, my first burn, did my first stand-up set. These were foundational elements in my identity from my earliest memories and set in motion my affinity for the people outside the margins of society.

I was troubled as a kid. As I mentioned before, I really *felt* my difference and my imagined ugliness acutely. There was something thirsty about my identity, and the groups I found when I was young quenched that thirst. It was less that I felt comfortable once I found them but more that they allowed me to feel like comfort in my own skin could be redefined within the new framework I'd discovered.

Subculture, finding your people, was the whole journey of youth for me. It created my life. And as rough as parts of my life were back then, at least I grew up in a big city, and for me, finding my people was an easy process. They were everywhere; they were all around me.

But if you were the lone goth in your small agricultural community, pulling on black fishnets as the rooster crowed, climbing on the tractor to thresh corn into pentagram shapes, it could be a lonely existence.

Then came the internet.

The early internet was like a portal for isolated freaks, out there floating in middle America, looking for their people. YouTube and message boards allowed you to be exposed to a subculture, connect with people from it, order the garb, and become an affiliate member of the hippie, punk, rave, goth, or underground hip hop scene without leaving your house. For many this was a huge expansion of their lives. For some, queer kids especially, it was a potential *saving* of their lives.

But then the internet changed. It grew, it metastasized. I'm not an anti-tech guy by any means; the personal advantages my deaf mom received from the internet are too consequential to ever condemn it altogether. I am aware that a forty-three-year-old writing about how things have changed has a kind of "old man shakes fist at clouds" feel to it. But this is what I think happened to American subculture: As the internet grew and pop culture simultaneously collapsed on itself, what took the place of those twisting paths of destiny became a mega mall of monoculture.

The internet *is* culture. The internet is music, fashion, politics, people. It's everything.

Culture itself has reflected the mashing. Music now can feel genreless. Hip hop can be driven by a techno beat or have a guitar riff by Ed Sheeran. Hip hop fashion looks like rock fashion looks like goth. Kanye looks like he's going skiing. Art is made for Instagram. The revolution is contained in a hashtag.

The internet consumed desire, aesthetics, music, art, identity, everything. Everything is one now. Teens don't look for their people anymore; their people are TikTok. Everything is a meme. All dance is a #challenge. The hero's path is now a thoroughfare, it's a highway.

Maybe I'm overstating it. I know young people still have distinct interests. I know outliers still find one another online. But I feel sad that what was a chance adventure is slowly becoming more of a set path.

When I look at my daughter, who is now five, I can't even imagine how homogenized and prepackaged culture will be by the time she is old enough to go looking for her own identity. So in some ways I wrote this book for her. So that she could see what I loved about the various spaces in which I spent my life. Each of them so distinct from one another. Each of them their own ecosystem, each set in motion by disparate elements, each scene an entire world.

From AA, I hope she knows that no matter how badly things go, redemption is always possible and that from pain often comes growth. And that no matter how badly things go, you are not alone.

From Judaism and the Hasidim, I hope she remembers who she is, that history is important, that fighting for survival and identity is the antidote to hatred.

From the rave scene, I hope she remembers to dance. It's *way* more important than it seems.

From Burning Man, I hope she finds the moments in life that are worth living simply for their own enjoyment, that immediacy and experience isn't incidental; it's medicinal. You need presence in spontaneity.

From the deaf community, I hope she learns that communication is the basis of all knowledge and that you can never allow another to define what makes you you. Self-determination is not a goal; it's an imperative.

From comedy I hope she remembers to laugh, to think, to push the envelope, and to never take herself too seriously.

And when, in 2080, she is strapping on her cybernetic eyeball and plugging the external hard drive into her brain stem, stepping out into the 180-degree summer heat of the plantless wasteland that is Earth, I hope more than anything that she's found the way to a world of her own. I hope she's leading the life *she* discovered, the one that's uniquely hers. I hope she's found her path. I hope she's found her secret superpowers.

I hope she's found her people.

Sources

I can't believe I wrote this book. I spend my life making shit up for comedic effect and thought that granted me the ability to never again have to pull all-nighters with stacks of academic books in front of me, but I realized very quickly upon biting off this project that I'd need help from people smarter than me.

But I'm not doing a bullshit-ass bibliography like this is my dissertation. If anything, making a living in comedy allows me to not care if I get called before an academic tribunal for insufficiently cited sources. Come and get me, academic cancel culture! I will tell you the books I read and people I pestered repeatedly about this book. If I got any details wrong, it's their fault and not mine at all. I truly did try to get everything right here historically, but I am *positive* I failed repeatedly, so please forgive me if there are any historical inaccuracies.

I read a shit-ton of books for this and so many were amazing. For the section on AA and recovery I attempted to read William White's intimidating tome *Slaying the Dragon: The History of Addiction Treatment and Recovery in America*. I looked up AA literature like the shockingly well written *Dr. Bob and the Good Oldtimers*. AA World Services were very helpful in sending me a recording of one of my old AA talks. Of course I also reread the Big Book, AA's central text, *Alcoholics Anonymous*.

In the rave section I was helped along by great documentaries like *Pump Up the Volume: A History of House Music* from British broadcaster Channel 4, *What We Started* on Netflix, and a super helpful email back from a legend, Mr. Marshall Jefferson. How giddy I was when he responded. (I've now cited two movies and an email, so I know the PhD isn't coming through.)

Let's get more serious:

I could not have written the Burning Man chapter without the help and support of my friend Brian Doherty and his incredible book *This Is Burning Man,* which in my mind is the seminal work on the subject. Alexi Borshart, Buck Down, and others helped me fact-check.

For the Judaism section, I just used Wikipedia. JK. But actually not JK; I did use it. My brother, the Rabbi David Kasher, was unfairly tasked with being my go-to source for every single question I had. When his wisdom failed me, I turned to Professor David Henkin from UC Berkeley's history department. For my family history I owe a huge debt to my amazing tante, the poet Breindie Kasher, I love you. Also my cousin Mendel Horowitz was supremely helpful in untangling the family knot.

Deafness and interpreting were a deep dive into a history I knew but didn't know as well as I thought. Shoshannah Stern helped so much, as did Professor Douglas Baynton, who fact-checked this section and was so kind, as I was a stranger to him. My mother was invaluable as she always is, and she dumped a stack of books on deafness so tall I thought I'd never get through any of them. I read A LOT. Katie Booth's *The Invention of Miracles* shed light into the twisted mind of Alexander Graham Bell and his world. Oliver Sacks's classic *Seeing Voices* was a delight to revisit and led me to the definitive book on the subject, Harlan Lane's *When the Mind Hears,* which I loved and learned so much from. The history of the deaf community in Martha's Vineyard was brought back in full color by the delightful book *Everyone Here Spoke Sign Language* by Nora Ellen Groce.

Comedy, the world I currently inhabit and make a living from, was so much fun to research thanks to Kliph Nesteroff, who is the absolute authority on the subject and who called me back whenever I had a question. His book *The Comedians* is required reading. Wayne Federman's *The History of Stand-Up* is also a fun read and made so many things clear to me that I hadn't understood before. He also pitched me titles for this book! What a guy! And he's hilarious. Louis Katz let me run ideas by him even though he didn't always agree with my conclusions. Joe Mande, Brent Weinbach, Andrew Michaan, and Nick Thune helped me figure out when things were too corny. I owe every comedian for inspiring me and making our history come alive in real time. It's a great and awful time to make a living in comedy.

Other people I owe a thanks to are Ahamed Weinberg, who told me a joke I'd written in this text wasn't offensive. It was later removed from the book by my editor, so I guess he was wrong. Guy Branum was generous with me when I needed a last-minute joke and I was stumped. John Rose and Truck Torrence offered feedback and friendship.

I am realizing that this section about sources is turning into an acknowledgments, so let's just do that.

Acknowledgments

Thank you so much to the people who helped me along as I wrote this book. I needed help and got it! First and foremost, to my wife, Natasha, who suffered bravely through late-night poetry slam–style readings of the latest paragraph I was proud of. She just wanted to go to bed, and I'm grateful she didn't. I am also so grateful to my editor, Ben Greenberg, for doing this book that we made a decade after the last one. It's a joy to work with someone as talented as you. Thanks to my manager, Josh Lieberman, at 3 Arts for always being someone I can trust. To Richard Abate also at 3 Arts for helping me craft and sell this book just like the last one. To Zach Drucker, Andrew Russell, Kathleen Lewis, and everyone at WME. Thank you to Jacob Daneman, my boardgame publicist. Thank you to Alicia Zelandonii, Sabin MacPhee, Kristine Sag, Lily, Juanster, Entropy, Low Rent the Clown, Crybaby, Demetrius Semien, Jeremy Bispo, and everyone else who made even a small contribution to this work. I couldn't have done it without you.

About the Author

MOSHE KASHER is a stand-up comedian, writer, and actor. He is the author of *Kasher in the Rye*. He has written for various TV shows and movies, including HBO's *Betty,* Comedy Central's roasts and *Another Period, Zoolander 2, Wet Hot American Summer,* and many more. His Netflix specials include *Moshe Kasher: Live in Oakland* and *The Honeymoon Stand Up Special*. He's appeared in *Curb Your Enthusiasm, Shameless, The Good Place,* and other fun things. He co-hosts *The Endless Honeymoon* podcast with his wife, Natasha Leggero. Kasher lives in Los Angeles with Leggero and their daughter.

moshekasher.com
Twitter: @moshekasher
Instagram: @moshekasher

About the Type

This book was set in Sabon, a typeface designed by the well-known German typographer Jan Tschichold (1902–74). Sabon's design is based upon the original letterforms of sixteenth-century French type designer Claude Garamond and was created specifically to be used for three sources: foundry type for hand composition, Linotype, and Monotype. Tschichold named his typeface for the famous Frankfurt typefounder Jacques Sabon (c. 1520–80).